The Wilding of America

Money, Mayhem, and the
New American Dream

Contemporary Social Issues

George Ritzer, *Series Editor*

Contemporary Social Issues

Series Editor: George Ritzer, *University of Maryland*

The Wilding of America

Money, Mayhem, and the New American Dream

Fourth Edition

Charles Derber

Boston College

Worth Publishers

Acquisitions Editor: Erik Gilg
Executive Marketing Manager: John Britch
Associate Managing Editor: Tracey Kuehn
Project Editor: Stephanie Roulias, Scribe
Art Director: Babs Reingold
Text Designer: Lissi Sigillo
Cover Designer: Lyndall Culbertson
Photo Editor: Cecilia Varas
Production Manager: Barbara Seixas
Composition: Matrix Publishing Services
Printing and Binding: RR Donnelley
Cover photo: Terry Husebye/Getty/Image Bank

ISBN-13: 978-0-7167-8257-5
ISBN-10: 0-7167-8257-X

Kind permission from the author has been given to reprint excerpts from Phillipe Bourgois in a *New York Times* article, discussed herein.

Printed in the United States of America

Second printing

Worth Publishers
41 Madison Avenue
New York, NY 10010
www.worthpublishers.com

To my students, past and present, who give me hope for our future.

About the Author

Charles Derber is professor of sociology at Boston College and former director of its graduate program on social economy and social justice. He is a prolific scholar in the field of politics, economy, international relations, and U.S. culture, with 10 internationally acclaimed books and several major research grants. Derber's most recent book is *Hidden Power: What You Need to Know to Save Our Democracy* (Berrett-Koehler, 2005). Other recent books include *People Before Profit: The New Globalization in an Age of Terror, Big Money, and Economic Crisis* (Picador, 2003), which has been translated into Chinese, German, Arabic, and British English, as well as *Corporation Nation* (St. Martin's, 2000), a widely discussed analysis of the growing power and responsibilities of corporations in the U.S., recently translated and published in China. Three others of note are *The Pursuit of Attention* (Oxford, 2000), *The Nuclear Seduction* (with William Schwartz, University of California Press, 1989), and *Power in the Highest Degree* (with William Schwartz and Yale Magrass, Oxford, 1990).

Derber espouses a public sociology that brings sociological perspectives to a general audience. Derber lectures widely at universities, companies, and community groups, and appears on numerous media outlets. His op-eds and essays appear in *Newsday*, the *Boston Globe*, and other newspapers, and he has been interviewed by *Newsweek*, *Business Week*, *Time*, and other news magazines. He speaks frequently on National Public Radio, on talk radio, and on television. His work has been reviewed by the *New York Times*, the *Washington Post*, the *Boston Globe*, the *Boston Herald*, the *Washington Monthly*, and numerous other magazines and newspapers.

Contents

Foreword

As we move on in the twenty-first century, we confront a seemingly endless array of pressing social issues: urban decay, inequality, ecological threats, rampant consumerism, war, AIDS, inadequate health care, national and personal debt, and many more. Although these problems are regularly dealt with in newspapers, magazines, and trade books, and on radio and television, popular treatment has severe limitations. By examining these issues systematically through the lens of sociology, we can gain greater insight into them and be better able to deal with them. It was to this end that St. Martin's Press created this series on contemporary social issues and that Worth Publishers has chosen to continue it.

Each book in the series casts a new and distinctive light on a familiar social issue, while challenging the conventional view, which may obscure as much as it clarifies. Phenomena that seem disparate and unrelated are shown to have many commonalities and to reflect a major, but often unrecognized, trend within the larger society. Or a systematic comparative investigation demonstrates the existence of social causes or consequences that are overlooked by other types of analysis. In uncovering such realities the books in this series are much more than intellectual exercises; they have powerful, practical implications for our lives and for the structure of society.

At another level, this series fills a void in book publishing. There is certainly no shortage of academic titles, but they tend to be introductory texts for undergraduates or advanced monographs for professional scholars. Missing are broadly accessible, issue-oriented books appropriate for all students and for general readers. The books in this series occupy that niche somewhere between popular trade books and scholarly monographs. Like trade books, they deal with important and interesting social issues, are well written, and are as jargon free as possible. However, they are more rigorous than trade books in meeting academic standards for writing and research. Although they are not textbooks, they often explore topics covered in basic textbooks and, therefore, are easily integrated into the curriculum of sociology and other disciplines.

Each of the books in the "Contemporary Social Issues" series is a new and distinctive piece of work. I believe that students, serious general readers, and professors will all find the books to be informative, interesting, thought provoking, and exciting. Among the topics to be covered in forthcoming editions in the series are the declining wealth and increasing indebtedness of the middle class and the risk-taking nature of contemporary Americans.

—*George Ritzer*

Preface

More than 10 years ago, I went to New York City to talk about "wilding" on WABC, the flagship radio station of ABC. The station invited me shortly after the brutal Central Park rape of a jogger—the event that led the media to coin the term *wilding*. While I hoped to educate New Yorkers, it turned out that the Big Apple still had a few things to teach me about my subject.

As I was waiting in the studio for my turn, I heard my talk-show host, Bob Grant, talk about the city's grafitti problem and his own solution, cutting off the hands of the young offenders. I sensed I had some differences with this tough hombre, but I realized why he had invited me down. He and his callers were obsessed with the disintegration of the city and with young wilders running loose on the streets.

I soon learned why, in a very personal way. The day after my conversation with Grant, I drove down to a conference on the lower west side of Manhattan. After about an hour, I had a premonition that I had better check my car, this feeling probably a residue of my conversation with Grant. I walked quickly back to the street and could hardly believe my eyes. My new Honda Accord was sitting only on its naked brake drums—tires, rims, and lug nuts all stripped. In the wink of an eye, my car had been transformed into one of those abandoned vehicles one sees in deserted areas of the South Bronx, except that the windows were not broken nor the inside looted.

It was an early Saturday afternoon with a lot of people around. In a state of disbelief, I ran up to two policemen who had just arrived at the corner to write up an unrelated accident. They told me to wait, and in the next 15 minutes, I watched a parade of people drive up to my car, stop, get out, and survey my vehicle. I quickly recognized that they were interested in finishing the job: the radio, the carburetor, anything to sell.

When I pleaded with the police to help me tow the car to a garage before it was picked clean, they shrugged their shoulders and told me they could not tow it unless I had committed a crime in it. I was lucky enough to find a garage, a tow truck, and a tire shop. The shop proprietor, who told me his own car had disappeared from in front of his house in the Bronx, sounded just like Bob Grant and his callers. He wanted to know if Massachusetts, where I am from, had a death penalty. When I mentioned I was a teacher, he said he figured kids today were becoming a generation of criminals and needed a moral education more than technical skills. As I drove off, he waved and yelled out, "Please help us raise a better generation."

His plea helped to define the mission of this book. As we move into the new century, the crises of greed and violence that motivated my desire to write this book have deepened. The most sensational news stories of the 1990s were about individual wilding by O. J. Simpson and Tonya Harding. But the most dramatic stories in the first few years of the twenty-first century have been about Enron, the Catholic Church scandal, the political "culture of corruption," terrorism and torture, and America's war in Iraq. Greed and violence remain epidemic among individuals, but it is wilding by giant institutions in the economy, the government, and civil society that is now making headlines.

This has led me to publish a new edition. When wilding becomes entrenched in our most powerful institutions, it changes and debases the American Dream. Wilding becomes normalized, and the new generation is socialized to an ethos that accepts greed and violence as the path to success. Elites at the pinnacle of corporation, church, and state redefine success itself as simply money and power.

But Americans, though deluged with stories of crime and corruption, are not making the connections that would help explain the real nature of the wilding problem or what might solve it. The media continues to publicize sensational street violence and personal crimes, such as the Lacey Peterson murder and the Elizabeth Smart abduction, which sell tabloids and TV advertising. But wilding, as viewed by a sociologist, involves multiple forms of immorality perpetrated in the corporate suites as well as on the streets. Few media analysts suggest that the criminals in the corporate boardrooms and street wilders share elements of the same greed and the same dream.

Individual wilding and institutional wilding are racing out of control at the same time, reflecting new contradictions between today's American Dream and American prospects for success in an age of economic crisis and decline. Americans pursue divisive and increasingly unattainable goals, which cannot meet our deepest needs for respect, love, and justice. As the Dream beckons and recedes, the price of failure is frustration and rage; the price of success, too often, is inner emptiness and debilitating fear of those left behind. Deepening inequalities, rising tides of social frustration, and corrosive moral decay threaten the bonds of community and the very survival of the social fabric.

For the citizen, this is frightening, but for the sociologist the fear is tied to a burning intellectual mission. The impending sense of social breakdown raises the question of what makes community—and society itself—

possible at all. This is the core problem of sociology, one with special urgency for our highly individualistic and competitive capitalist societies, but it is not a problem for sociologists alone.

The metaphor of societal illness that the wilding epidemic evokes points to the need for all of us to become practitioners of the art of social healing. This book offers one diagnosis of our weakened but still resilient collective condition. My hope is that the illness cannot long resist an awakened community brave enough to look deeply at its shared pathologies and empowered with the insights of the sociological imagination.

Acknowledgments

I am grateful to many friends and colleagues whose excitement about this book helped it come to fruition. The enthusiasm of David Karp and John Williamson nourished my own belief in the project, and their close reading of the manuscript helped me improve the book at every stage and in every edition. Morrie Schwartz spurred me on in the original edition with his insights and always generous emotional support. I thank Michael Burwawoy, Noam Chomsky, Jonathan Kozol, Howard Zinn, Robert Reich, Robert Coles, Philip Slater, and Alvin Poussaint for reading the manuscript and responding to it. I am also grateful to my colleagues Mike Malec, Paul Gray, Eve Spangler, S. M. Miller, Ritchie Lowry, and Severyn Bruyn for helpful suggestions. I thank also many former and present students, including Deb Piatelli, Colleen Nugent, Michelle Gawerc, Alexandra Singer, Jonathan White, Ted Sasson, Bill Hoynes, David Croteau, and Bill Schwartz, as well as all the other teachers, students, and readers who have let me know how valuable this book has been to them.

George Ritzer encouraged me to publish this book in the current series. Erik Gilg, my editor in this edition, brought vision, generous support, and enthusiasm to the work, and I am very grateful to him and to all of those at Worth Publishing who have supported this book.

I owe much to my parents, who nurtured the concern for society that animates this book. And also to Elena Kolesnikova, who heroically endured the obsessions of an author about his work. She contributed ideas, helped me overcome my doubts, and nourished me all along the way.

The Good Man Fills His Own Stomach

All-American Crimes and Misdemeanors

The readings of history and anthropology . . . give us no reason to believe that societies have built-in self-preservative systems.

—Margaret Mead

Wilding in Black and White

"All day I got grabbed," said Yaneira Davis, 20, a Rutgers student. She was describing her bad Sunday, Puerto Rican Day, on June 11, 2000, in New York City's Central Park. "The attitude was," Yaneira continued, " 'I'm going to touch you, and I don't care what you say.' " Ashanna Cover and Josina Lawrence, both 21, who were also in Central Park that day, said that they were sprayed, groped, and had their tops pulled off. Stephanie, who did not want her last name used, said that 20 guys "were coming at me from all directions, and they were grabbing my butt, groping my butt, and I was screaming and I was trying to get through, trying to get away." At least 46 other women reported that groups of young men stripped them, groped their breasts and genitals, and robbed them of jewelry and purses.[1]

Videotapes captured the scene, which was then beamed around the world by satellite TV. While onlookers, including police, watched passively or with some amusement, the young victims ran in terror, trying to keep their clothes from being torn off and often screaming hysterically. The young men, many drunk or stoned, seemed to be greatly enjoying themselves, going from one woman to another and yelping with pleasure as they ogled, chased, stripped, and groped their prey.[2]

The violence began during prefestivities the night before as the young men, according to one of their lawyers, "were there chillin', smokin' a couple cigarettes and watchin' the babes go by." They escalated the violence in broad daylight and inflicted mayhem throughout the day and into the evening. Twenty men were eventually arrested. Some of the victims filed suit against police at the time for doing nothing to protect them.[3]

The graphic videotapes catapulted the event into the headlines and provoked debate everywhere about violence in America. Media pundits called the gangs of young men a "wolfpack" who felt free to commit unusually savage behavior in full public view. Journalists agreed that this was another outbreak of "wilding," reminding readers of a terrifying crime that had gripped the nation 10 years earlier. We have to return to that event if we want to understand how the term *wilding* entered our culture and became a symbol of one of America's deepest social crises.

On April 19, 1989, a group of six teenagers, ages 14 to 16, went into Central Park, the very same site as the Puerto Rican Day assaults. According to police at the time, the youths came upon a young woman jogging alone past a grove of sycamore trees. Allegedly using rocks, knives, and a metal pipe, they attacked her. Some pinned her down while others beat and raped her. Police reported that one defendant, 17-year-old Kharey Wise, held the jogger's legs while a friend repeatedly cut her with a knife. They then smashed her with a rock and punched her face.[4]

What most captured public attention about the story were the spirits of the assaulters during and after their crime. According to 15-year-old Kevin Richardson, one of the boys arrested, "Everyone laughed and was leaping around." One youth was quoted by police as saying, "It was fun . . . something to do." Asked if they felt pretty good about what they had done, Richardson said, "Yes." Police reported a sense of "smugness" and "no remorse" among the youths.[5]

From this event, a new word was born: _wilding._ According to press reports, it was the term the youths themselves used to describe their behavior—and it seemed appropriate. The savagery of the crime, which left the victim brain-damaged and in a coma for weeks, evoked the image of a predatory lion in the bush mangling its helpless prey. Equally shocking was the blasé attitude of the attackers. It had been no big deal, a source of temporary gratification and amusement. They were "mindless marauders seeking a thrill," said Judge Thomas B. Galligan of Manhattan, who sentenced three of the teenagers to a maximum term of five to ten years, charging them with turning Central Park into a "torture chamber." These were youths who seemed stripped of the emotional veneer of civilized humans, creatures of a wilderness where anything goes.[6]

The story of wilding quickly became tied to the race and class of the predators and their prey. The convicted youths were black and from the inner city, although from stable working families. The victim was white, with degrees from Wellesley and Yale, and a wealthy 28-year-old investment banker at Salomon Brothers, one of the great houses of Wall Street.

To white, middle-class Americans, wilding symbolized something real and terrifying about life in the United States. Things were falling apart, at least in the hearts of America's major cities. Most suburbanites did not feel their own neighborhoods had become wild, but they could not imagine walking into Central Park at night.

The fear of wilding became fear of the Other: those locked outside of the American Dream. They had not yet invaded the world most Americans felt part of, but they menaced it. The Central Park attack made the threat real, and it unleashed fear among the general population and a backlash of rage among politicians and other public figures. Mayor Ed Koch called for the death penalty. Donald Trump took out ads in four newspapers, writing, "I want to hate these murderers. . . . I want them to be afraid." Trump told *Newsweek* that he "had gotten hundreds and hundreds of letters of support."[7]

On December 19, 2002, in a sensational turn of events, Justice Charles J. Tejada of Manhattan's State Supreme Court took only five minutes to reverse the convictions of the five "wilders," who had already served their multiyear sentences. The judge acted after another man, Matias Reyes, in jail for murder and rape, confessed to committing the Central Park rape himself, and DNA evidence conclusively linked Reyes to the crime. It appears that the earlier confessions may have been forced in a circus trial potentially involving police misconduct and racism. Patricia Williams, a law professor who attended the 1991 trial, remembers a hysterical atmosphere in the courtroom, with tourists and celebrities "lined up around the block for admission, as though it were a Broadway show." Williams noted that the confessions were full of inconsistencies elicited by "unorthodox" police tactics. These included 18 to 30 hours "of nonstop questioning," sometimes taking place "in the back of a police car" and "in the middle of the night."[8] Twelve years later, it seemed as if the public and the police had needed to confirm their views of African-American and Latino youth—and all the "Others" in America at the time—as wilders.[9]

But while the term *wilding* may have come into the media based on a false conviction and racism, it is a surprisingly useful way to characterize an evolving and deeply disturbing feature not of African-Americans or the Other but of American society as a whole. Instead of focusing mainly on the "black wilding" that did not occur in the park, suppose we think of "white wilding" as a way to characterize morally unsettling and often violent behavior that is rampant throughout our culture. As an extreme example, consider a second remarkably vicious crime that grabbed people's attention all over the country just a few months after the Central Park rape. On October 23, 1989, Charles and Carol Stuart left a birthing class at Boston's Brigham and Women's Hospital, walked to their car parked in the adjoining Mission Hill neighborhood, and got in. Within minutes, Carol Stuart—eight months pregnant—was dead, shot point-blank in the head. Her husband, a stunned nation would learn from police accounts two months later, had been her assassin. He had allegedly killed her to collect hundreds of thousands of dollars in life insurance money in order to open a restaurant. Opening a restaurant, Americans everywhere learned, had long been Charles Stuart's American Dream.

Many white, middle-class Americans seemed to believe Stuart's story when he told police that a black gunman had shot him and his wife, leaving Carol Stuart dead and Charles Stuart himself with a severe bullet wound in the abdomen. When Stuart's brother, Matthew, went to the police to tell them of Charles's involvement, and when Charles Stuart subsequently apparently committed suicide by jumping off the Tobin Bridge into the Mystic River, some of the threads connecting his crime to the horrible rape in Central Park began to emerge. Stuart had duped a whole nation by playing on the fear of the wild Other. Aware of the vivid images of gangs of black youths rampaging through dark city streets, Stuart brilliantly had concocted a story that would resonate with white Americans' deepest anxieties. Dr. Alvin Poussaint, Harvard professor and adviser to Bill Cosby, said, "Stuart had all the ingredients. . . . [H]e gave blacks a killer image and put himself in the role of a model, an ideal Camelot type that white people could identify with."[10]

Charles Stuart's crime became a national obsession. A 21-year-old Oklahoman visiting Boston told a *Boston Globe* reporter, "You wouldn't believe the attention this is getting back home. It's all anyone can talk about. I've taken more pictures of this fur shop and Stuart's house than any of the stuff you're supposed to take pictures of in Boston."[11] The quiet block the Stuarts lived on in Reading, a Boston suburb, became what the *Globe* called a "macabre mecca," with hundreds of cars, full of the curious and the perplexed, parked or passing by. One reason may have been that white, middle-class Americans everywhere had an uncomfortable sense that, as the 1990s emerged, the Stuart case was telling them something about themselves. Stuart, after all, was living the American Dream and reaping its benefits—he was a tall, dark, athletic man with working-class roots, making more than $100,000 a year selling fur coats, and married to a lovely, adoring wife, living the good life in suburban Reading, complete with a swimming pool. Had the American Dream itself become the progenitor of a kind of wilding? Was it possible that not only the inner cities of America but also its comfortable suburbs were becoming wild places? Could "white wilding" be a more serious problem than the "black wilding" publicized in the mass media and so readily embraced by the public at large? Was America at the turn of the decade becoming a wilding society?

To answer these questions, we have to look far beyond such exceptional events as the Central Park rape and the Stuart murder. We shall see that there are many less extreme forms of wilding, including a wide range of antisocial acts that are neither criminal nor physically violent. Wilding includes the ordinary as well as the extraordinary, may be profit oriented or pleasure seeking, and can infect corporations and governments as well as individuals of each race, class, and gender.

The Mountain People: A Wilding Culture

Between 1964 and 1967, anthropologist Colin Turnbull lived among the people of Uganda known as the Ik, who were unfortunately expelled by an uncaring government from their traditional hunting lands to extremely barren mountainous areas. In 1972, Turnbull published a haunting book about his experiences that left no doubt that a whole society can embrace wilding as a way of life.[12]

When Turnbull first came to the Ik, he met Atum, a sprightly, barefoot old man with a sweet smile, who helped guide Turnbull to remote Ik villages. Atum warned Turnbull right away that everyone would ask for food. Although many would indeed be hungry, he said, most could fend for themselves, and their pleas should not be trusted. Turnbull, Atum stressed, should on no account give them anything. But before he left that day, Atum mentioned that his own wife was severely ill and desperately needed food and medicine. On reaching his village, Atum told Turnbull his wife was too sick to come out. Later, Turnbull heard exchanges between Atum and his sick wife, and her moans of suffering. The moans were wrenching, and when Atum pleaded for help, Turnbull gave him food and some aspirin.

Some weeks later, Atum had stepped up his requests for food and medicine, saying his wife was getting sicker. Turnbull was now seriously concerned, urging Atum to get her to a hospital. Atum refused, saying that "she wasn't that sick." Shortly thereafter, Atum's brother-in-law came to Turnbull and told him that Atum was selling the medicine that Turnbull had been giving him for his wife. Turnbull, not terribly surprised, said that "that was too bad for his wife." The brother-in-law, enjoying the joke enormously, finally explained that Atum's wife "had been dead for weeks" and that Atum had "buried her inside the compound so you wouldn't know." No wonder Atum had not wanted his wife to go to the hospital. Turnbull thought, "She was worth far more to him dead than alive."[13]

Startling to Turnbull was not only the immense glee the brother-in-law seemed to take in the "joke" that had been inflicted upon his dying sister, but the utter lack of embarrassment that Atum showed when confronted with his lie. Atum shrugged it off, showing no remorse whatsoever, saying he had simply forgotten to tell Turnbull. This was one of the first of many events that made Turnbull wonder whether there was any limit to what an Ik would do to get food and money.

Some time later, Turnbull came across Lomeja, an Ik man he had met much earlier. Lomeja had been shot during an attack by neighboring tribesmen and was lying in a pool of his own blood, apparently dying from two bullet wounds in the stomach. Still alive and conscious, Lomeja looked up at Turnbull and asked for some tea. Shaken, Turnbull returned to his Land Rover and filled a big, new, yellow enamel mug. When he returned, Lomeja's wife was bending over her husband. She was trying to "fold him up" in the dead position although he was not yet dead, and she started shrieking at Turnbull to leave Lomeja alone, saying Lomeja was already dead. Lomeja found the strength to resist his wife's premature efforts to bury him and tried to push her aside. Turnbull managed to get the cup of tea to Lomeja, who was still strong enough to reach out for it and sip it. Suddenly, Turnbull heard a loud giggle and saw Lomeja's sister, Kimat. Attracted by all the yelling, she had "seen that lovely new, bright yellow enamel mug of hot, sweet tea, had snatched it from her brother's face and made off with it, proud and joyful. She not only had the tea, she also had the mug. She drank as she ran, laughing and delighted at herself."[14]

Turnbull came to describe the Ik as "the loveless people." Each Ik valued only his or her own survival and regarded everyone else as a competitor for food. Ik life had become a grim process of trying to find enough food to stay alive each day. The hunt consumed all of their resources, leaving virtually no reserve for feelings of any kind or for any moral scruples that might interfere with filling their stomachs. As Margaret Mead wrote, the Ik were "a people who have become monstrous beyond belief." Scientist Ashley Montagu wrote that the Ik are "a people who are dying because they have abandoned their own humanity."[15]

Ik families elevated wilding to a high art. Turnbull met Adupa, a young girl of perhaps six, who was so malnourished that her stomach was grossly distended and her legs and arms spindly. Her parents had decided she had become a liability and threw her out of their hut. Because she was too weak now to go out on long scavenging ventures, as did the other children, she would wander as far as her strength would allow, pick up scraps of bone or half-eaten berries, and then come back to her parents' place, waiting to be brought back in. Days later, her parents, tiring of her crying, finally brought her in and promised to feed her. Adupa was happy and stopped crying. The parents went out and "closed the asak behind them, so tight that weak little Adupa could never have moved it if she had tried."[16] Adupa waited for them to come back with the food they had promised, but they did not return until a whole week had passed, when they knew Adupa would be dead. Adupa's parents took her rotting remains, Turnbull writes, and threw them out "as one does the riper garbage, a good distance away." There was no burial—and no tears.[17]

Both morality and personality among the Ik were dedicated to the single all-consuming passion for self-preservation. There was simply "not room in the life of these people," Turnbull observes dryly, "for such luxuries as family and sentiment and love." Nor for any morality beyond "marangik," the Ik concept of goodness, which means filling one's own stomach.

The Ik in Us

Long before the rape in Central Park or the Stuart murder, Ashley Montagu, commenting on Turnbull's work, wrote that "the parallel with our own society is deadly." In 1972, when Turnbull published his book, wilding had not yet become part of the American vocabulary, nor did most Americans face declining living standards, let alone the kind of starvation experienced by the Iks. Americans were obviously not killing their parents or children for money, but they dedicated themselves to self-interested pursuits with a passion not unlike that of the Ik.

In America, a land of plenty, there was the luxury of a rhetoric of morality and feelings of empathy and love. But was not the American Dream a paean to individualistic enterprise, and could not such an enterprise be conceived in some of the same unsentimental metaphors used by Turnbull about the Ik? The Ik community, he writes, "reveals itself for what it is, a conglomeration of individuals of all ages, each going his own way in search of food and water, like a plague of locusts spread over the land."[18]

America now faces a wilding epidemic that is eating at the country's social foundation and could rot it. The American case is much less advanced than that of the Ik's, but the disease is deeply rooted and is spreading through the political leadership, the business community, and the general population. Strong medicine can turn the situation around, but if we fail to act now, the epidemic could prove irreversible.

Only a handful of Americans are "ultimate wilders" like Charles Stuart. Such killers are noteworthy mainly because they may help wake us up to the wilding plague spreading among thousands of less extreme wilders who are not killers. Wilding includes a vast spectrum of self-centered and self-aggrandizing behavior that harms others. A wilding epidemic tears at the social fabric and threatens to unravel society itself, ultimately reflecting the erosion of the moral order and the withdrawal of feelings and commitments from others to "number one."

The wilding virus comes in radically different strains. There is *expressive wilding*: wilding for the sheer satisfaction of indulging one's own destructive impulses, the kind found among the American youth who heave rocks off highway bridges in the hope of smashing the windshields of unknown drivers passing innocently below. The hockey and soccer fathers who attack coaches and other parents are expressive wilders, as are drivers engaging in road rage. Road rage has reached such epidemic proportions—as has workplace rage, school rage, and air rage—that leading pundits now talk of "dies irae," or America's day of rage. The country's most famous perpetrators in recent years include O. J. Simpson, who acted out the domestic violence that is one of the most common and Ik-like forms of expressive wilding. His alleged repeated abuse of his wife to sate his jealousy, maintain his control, or simply gratify his emotions of the moment evokes serious questions about the nightmarish spread of family violence among rich and poor alike. The national obsession with Simpson during his trial reflects the fear that when a country's icon beats his wife black and blue, smashes her windshield with a baseball bat, stalks her, and is finally charged with her murder and acquitted in a controversial verdict, we all participate in the crime, for heroes act out the passions and values of the cultures that create them.

Although mainly an example of expressive wilding (in 2001 he was arrested for road rage violence), Simpson also modeled *instrumental wilding*. Not simply for fun or purely emotional gratification, instrumental wilding is wilding for money, career advancement, or other calculable personal gain. Simpson began as a youngster, running with gangs and stealing food. Fantastically ambitious and opportunistic, he later naturally took to a life of single-minded corporate salesmanship, obsessively remaking his voice, wardrobe, and demeanor according to the image lessons of the Hertz ad executives who greased his career. He wheeled and dealed to sign movie deals and buy companies, such as the Pioneer Chicken franchise (destroyed in the LA riots), and eventually succumbing to the greed-soaked financial dealings that led him, along with other entrepreneurial high rollers of his era, to bad loans and collapsed business deals.

Most instrumental wilding involves garden varieties of ambition, competitiveness, careerism, and greed that advance the self at the cost of others. Expressive and instrumental wilding have in common an antisocial self-centeredness made possible by a stunning collapse of moral restraint and a chilling lack of empathy. I am mainly concerned in this book with instrumental wilding because it is the form most intimately connected with the American Dream and least understood in its poisonous effects on society.[19]

Although much wilding is criminal, there is a vast spectrum of perfectly legal wilding, exemplified by the careerist who indifferently betrays or steps on colleagues to advance up the ladder. Some forms of wilding, such as lying and cheating, are officially discouraged, but others, like the frantic and single-minded pursuit of wealth, are cultivated by some of the country's leading corporations and financial institutions. Likewise, there are important differences in the severity of wilding behaviors; killing a spouse for money is obviously far more brutal than stealing a wallet or cheating on an exam. But there are distinct types and degrees of infection in any affliction, ranging from terminal cases such as that of Stuart, to intermediate cases such as the savings-and-loan crooks of the 1980s, to those who either are petty wilders or who rarely exhibit symptoms at all. The latter categories include large numbers of Americans who may struggle internally with their wilding impulses but remain healthy enough to restrain them. The variation is similar to that in heart disease: Those with only partial clogging of their arteries and no symptoms are different from those with full-blown, advanced arteriosclerosis, and those least afflicted may never develop the terminal stage of the illness. But these differences are normally of degree rather than of kind; the same underlying pathology is at work among people with both mild and severe cases.

There are, nonetheless, real differences between white lies or misdemeanors (forms of petty wilding) and serious wilding of the Central Park or Charles Stuart variety. Petty wilding occurs in all cultures, will persist as long as most people are not saints, and, in limited doses, does not necessarily threaten civil order. When wilding is so limited that it does not constitute a grave social danger, it might better be described as "incipient wilding" and is not of concern here.

10

However, certain types of petty wilding are growing at an alarming rate in America, as I document in Chapter 3 in my discussion of minor lying, cheating, and ordinary competitiveness with and indifference to others. Such transgressions on an epidemic scale can reach a critical mass and become as serious a threat to society as violent crime or huge investment scams on Wall Street. Lying is an important example of petty wilding that now not only infects many friendships and marriages but also has become a pervasive problem in our political system, with leaders charged with lying to the nation about their reasons for going to war, about authorizing torture, and about misrepresenting scientific findings, such as whether such problems as global climate change are caused by human activity. It is not the degree of brutality or violence, but the consequences for society that ultimately matter, and I thus consider the full spectrum of wilding acts—from petty to outrageous—that together constitute a clear and present danger to America's social fabric.

Economic, Political, and Social Wilding

Wilding, in sociological terms, extends far beyond random violence by youth gangs (the current definition in *Webster's Dictionary*) to include three types of assault on society. *Economic wilding* is the morally uninhibited pursuit of money by individuals or businesses at the expense of others. *Political wilding* is the abuse of political office to benefit oneself or one's own social class, or the wielding of political authority to inflict morally unacceptable suffering on citizens at home or abroad. *Social wilding* ranges from personal or family acts of violence, such as child or spousal abuse, to collective forms of selfishness that weaken society, such as affluent suburbs turning their backs on bleeding inner cities.

Economic wilders include convicted billionaire executives Bernie Ebbers, former CEO of WorldCom, and Dennis Kozlowski, former CEO of Tyco. Ebbers was convicted of masterminding an $11 billion fraud that brought down WorldCom in the biggest corporate bankruptcy in history. Kozlowski was also a big-league economic wilder, convicted of stealing $600 million from Tyco. Economic wilders are a different species from the kids in Central Park, since they wild for money rather than fun or sex. Partly because of differing opportunities and incentives, people wild in different ways and for exceedingly varied reasons and motives, ranging from greed and lust to the gaining of attention or respect.

The different forms of wilding, however, are all manifestations of degraded American individualism.

Wilding is individualism run amok, and the wilding epidemic is the face of America's individualistic culture in an advanced state of disrepair. An individualistic culture promotes the freedom of the individual and in its healthy form nurtures human development and individual rights. In its degraded form, it encourages unrestrained and sociopathic self-interest.

Wilding and Not Wilding: Varieties of Individualism

Wilding—a degenerate form of individualism—encompasses a huge variety of antisocial behavior. It includes so many seemingly unrelated acts that it might appear to stand for everything—or nothing. But wilding includes only a small subset of the entire range of behaviors that sociologists describe as *individualistic*, a term that arguably can be applied to any self-interested behavior. In a society such as that of the United States, which is dominated by individualistic values and a market system that rewards self-interest, some might argue that virtually all socially prescribed behavior has an individualistic dimension.

I propose a far more restrictive definition of *wilding*. Not all individualistic behavior is wilding, nor is *wilding* an umbrella term for any form of self-interested or "bad" behavior. As noted earlier, *wilding* refers to self-oriented behavior that hurts others and damages the social fabric, which excludes many types of individualistic action. The Jewish sage Hillel wrote, "If I am not for others, what am I?" Yet he also said, "If I am not for myself, who will be for me?" His maxims suggest that many forms of self-interest are necessary and contribute to the well-being of others.

A doctor who works hard to perfect her medical skills may advance her own career, but she also saves lives. A superbly conditioned professional athlete may enrich himself by his competitiveness or ambition, but he also entertains and gives pleasure to his fans. If I strive to be the best writer I can be—an individualistic aspiration—I am educating others while fulfilling myself. In none of these cases is individualistic behavior itself necessarily wilding. Actions that advance one's own interests and either help or do not harm others are not forms of wilding, even when motivated by competitiveness or acquisitiveness.

12

Wilding includes only individualistic behavior that advances or indulges the self by hurting others. If the doctor advances her skills and career by cheating on tests, trampling on her colleagues, or using her patients as guinea pigs, her self-interest has degraded into wilding. The athlete who illicitly uses steroids to win competitions is wilding by cheating against his rivals and deceiving his fans.

Whereas all wilding behavior hurts others, not all hurtful behavior is wilding. If I get angry at a friend, I may hurt him, but that reaction does not necessarily make it wilding. Such anger may be justified because it was motivated by a wrong done to me, and it may ultimately serve to repair the relation even if I am mistaken. Interpersonal relations inevitably involve misunderstanding, aggression, and hurt, which degrade into expressive wilding only when the hurt is intentional and purely self-indulgent, and when the perpetrator is indifferent to the pain inflicted on the other. Motivation, empathy, and level of harm inflicted are key criteria in deciding whether wilding has occurred. Deliberate physical or emotional abuse is clearly wilding, whereas impulsive acts that cause less harm and lead to remorse and remediation are more ambiguous cases and may not constitute wilding at all.

Similarly complex considerations apply to institutional wilding enacted by corporations or governments. Instrumental wilding takes place whenever institutions pursue goals and strategies that inflict serious harm on individuals, communities, or entire societies. Some of the most important forms of economic wilding, both legal and criminal, involve routine profiteering by rapacious businesses exploiting employees, consumers, and communities. As discussed in Chapter 4, the line between corporate self-interest and economic wilding is blurred in today's global economy, but not all profits arise out of exploitation, and many profitable businesses are not engaged in economic wilding. Socially responsible or employee-owned businesses that add to social well-being by creating jobs, raising the standard of living of employees, improving the environment, and enhancing the quality of life of their customers may be highly profitable but are hardly examples of wilding. Systemic connections exist between American capitalism and wilding, but not all forms of capitalism breed wilding.

Finally, not all crime, violence, or evil behavior is individualistic wilding. The horrific ethnic cleansing in Bosnia and the genocidal warfare in Rwanda and the Sudan constitute wilding by almost any definition, but such wilding is rooted in fierce and pathological tribal or communal loyalties and is hardly an expression of rampant individualism. Individualism and communitarianism can each generate their own forms of wilding; I focus on the individualistic variant in this book because it is the type endemic in the United States. My indictment of individualistic wilding should not be viewed as a preference for the communitarian form, because wilding in many of the world's cruelest societies has its roots in the excesses of community. Wilding can be avoided only by respecting the rights of individuals and the needs for community, a balancing act too many societies have failed dismally to achieve.

The Two Americas: Are We All Wilders?

Although the wilding epidemic now infects almost every major American institution, cooperative behavior survives, and in every community one finds idealists, altruists, and a majority of citizens seeking to live lives guided by moral principles. About two-thirds of Americans give money to charity, and about half roll up their sleeves and do volunteer work or become social activists; these are among the many hopeful indications, discussed later in Chapter 10, that America can still purge itself of this epidemic.

For an analyst of wilding, there are two Americas: the America already seriously infected, which is the main subject of this book, and the America that has not yet succumbed and remains a civil society. The majority of ordinary Americans, it should be stressed, are part of the second America, and they retain a moral compass and emotional sensibilities that inhibit severe wilding behavior. But as the epidemic continues to spread, individual interests will increasingly override common purposes, and the self—rather than family or community—increasingly will grab center stage in both Americas. Not everyone will become a wilder, but nobody will be untouched by wilding culture.[20]

Wilders who catch the fever and play by the new rules profoundly infect their own vulnerable communities, families, and workplaces. One dangerous criminal on a block can make a community wild, inducing aggression, violence, and a fortress mentality among normally peaceable neighbors. A particularly competitive salesperson or account executive can transform an entire office into a jungle, because those who do not follow suit may be left behind. The new ethos rewards the wilder and penalizes those who cling to civil behavior. One defense against wilding in modern America is to embrace it, spreading wilding behavior among people less disposed to be wilders and still struggling against wilding as a way of life.

Many Americans misread the epidemic of AIDS as a problem of deviant and disadvantaged groups. They are at risk of making the same miscalculation about the wilding epidemic, to which no sector of the society has any immunity. Its ravages may be most noticeable among the poor and downtrodden, but the virus afflicts the respected and the comfortable just as much; it exists in the genteel suburbs as well as in the inner cities. Indeed, American wilding is, to a surprising degree, an affliction of the successful, in that the rich and powerful have written the wilding rules. It is ever more difficult to climb the ladder without internalizing those rules.

The progress of the wilding epidemic is shaped less by the percentage of sociopaths than by the sociopathy of society's elites and the rules of the success game they have helped define. A wilding society is one in which wilding is a route to the top, and in which legitimate success becomes difficult to distinguish from the art of wilding within—or even outside—the law.

The wilding epidemic is now seeping into America, mainly from the top. Although the majority of business and political leaders remain honest, a large and influential minority not only are serving as egregious role models but also are rewriting the rules of the American success game in their own interests. CEOs who build their corporate fortunes on the backs of downsized workers at home and sweatshop workers abroad are recreating the rules of last century's greed-soaked, robber baron capitalism. Similarly, Presidents Reagan, Bush I, Clinton, and Bush II have all helped fuel the wilding crisis, partly by virtue of the corruption and scandals in their administrations but, more important, through radical new policy directions.

Our current wilding crisis is rooted politically in the "free market" revolution that began with President Ronald Reagan. The "Reagan Revolution" advanced the most ambitious class agenda of the rich in over a century, creating an innovative brew of market deregulation and individualistic ideology that helped fan the flames of wilding across the land. In the 1990s, a new Republican congressional majority led by Speaker Newt Gingrich, and the "new Democrats" led by President Bill Clinton, launched their own wilding initiatives and raced against each other to dismantle the social programs that symbolize our historic commitment to the poor, the needy, and to each other. President George W. Bush, despite his rhetoric of compassionate conservatism, has tried to complete the revolution of greed that Reagan began, while also taking the country to war on false pretenses (see Chapter 8), one of the worst forms of political wilding.

Wilding and the New American Dream: Individualism Today and Yesterday

Many signs point to a corruption of the American Dream in our time.[21] Most Americans do not become killers to make it up the ladder or to hold on to what they have, but the traditional restraints on naked self-aggrandizement seem weaker—and the insatiability greater. Donald Trump is only one of the multimillionaire cultural heroes who define life as "The Art of the Deal" (the title of Trump's best-selling autobiography). Trump seems to feel no moral contradiction about building the most luxurious condominiums in history in New York, a city teeming with homeless people. He writes triumphantly about the Trump Tower: "We positioned ourselves as the only place for a certain kind of very wealthy person to live—the hottest ticket in town. We were selling fantasy."[22]

The fantasy mushroomed in the late 1990s with young dot-com entrepreneurs dreaming of becoming millionaires before turning 30. The "new economy" brought the age of "me.com" in which everyone looked for a fast fortune, whether by creating a new tech start-up or scoring big in day trading. Jonathan Lebed, a 15-year-old New Jersey suburban high school kid, made over $800,000 day trading and recommending stocks on the Internet. In 2000, the Securities and Exchange Commission accused him of violating laws regulating stock promotions and made him return over $200,000. This didn't stop many of his fellow students and even many of his teachers from rushing to join him on a new Internet venture that might make them all rich.[23]

In 2001, journalist David Callahan bemoaned the new ethos of greed: "The economy of the late 1990s offered the promise of such extraordinary wealth that it brought out the worst in people. . . . The ideal of working hard over many years to achieve wealth lost traction. The pressure to pursue wealth instead of other goals grew enormously as the media focused on those winning big in the new economy. It became easy to feel that missing the gold rush was plain stupid." A young person himself, Callahan continues, "I've seen the resulting distortion of values everywhere in Generation X—my generation and in those coming after it. It's hard to stick to a goal related to something other than money. . . . Who wants to be a school teacher when you can be a millionaire."[24]

A new version of the American Dream has now emerged, more individualistic, expansive, and morally perverted than most of its predecessors. America has entered a new Gilded Age, where, as journalist John Taylor writes, the celebration and "lure of wealth has overpowered conventional restraints."[25] Journalist Laurence Shames suggests that the name of the American game has become simply "more."[26] Unrestrained greed has certainly been the name of the game for America's richest people. In 2005, presenting its annual list of America's 400 wealthiest individuals, *Forbes* reported that, for the first time, virtually all 400—to be precise, 374—are billionaires, with Bill Gates leading with a net worth of $51 billion and Warren Buffet second with a worth of $40 billion.[27] The collective wealth of just these 400 individuals shot up to $1.13 trillion, an astonishing amount about equal to the annual income of half the world's population, or 3 billion people.[28] Gates himself had as much net wealth as that owned by 45 percent of the U.S. population.[29]

For less privileged and especially poor Americans, the new gilded Dream became a recipe for wilding based on collapsed possibilities. A dream of having more had been sustainable when real income for ordinary Americans kept growing, as it had through most of American history. But when real income begins to decline for millions in the bottom half of America, an unprecedented development in the last decades of the twentieth century, an outsized Dream becomes an illusion, inconsistent with the reality of most Americans' lives. In 2002, the IRS reported that, for the first time in history, the real incomes of Americans had declined for two consecutive years, a trend continuing in 2003 and 2004, as wages stagnated.[30] The ratio between the average CEO's pay and the average worker's wage went from 41 to 1 in 1975 to 419 to 1 in 2001.[31] As wages declined, millions more Americans went into debt in order to try to achieve an American Dream receding out of their reach: outsized Dream, downsized lives. To weave grandiose materialist dreams in an era of restricted opportunities is the ultimate recipe for social wilding.

A new age of limits and polarization in the early twenty-first century sets the stage for an advanced wilding crisis. In an America deeply divided by class, the American Dream, and especially the new gilded Dream, cannot be a common enterprise and is transformed into multiple wilding agendas, unleashing wilding among people at every station, but in different ways. Among those at the bottom, the Dream becomes pure illusion; wilding, whether dealing drugs or robbing banks, beckons as a fast track out of the ghetto and into the high life. Among the insecure and slipping great American middle class, wilding becomes a growth area for those who are endowed with classic American initiative and ingenuity and are unwilling to go down with their closing factories and downsized offices. For the professional and business classes at the top, wilding passes as professional ambition and proliferates as one or another variant of dedicated and untrammeled careerism. Ensconced inside heavily fortified suburban or gentrified enclaves, these elites also pioneer new forms of social wilding in what former labor secretary Robert Reich calls "a politics of secession," abandoning society itself as part of a panicky defense against the threat from the huge, covetous majority left behind.[32] The wilding crisis, as we see later, arises partly out of a virulent new class politics.

The seeds of America's wilding plague were planted long before the current era. A century ago, Alexis de Tocqueville observed that conditions in America led every "member of the community to be wrapped up in himself" and worried that "personal interest will become more than ever the principal, if not the sole spring" of American behavior.[33] Selfish and mean-spirited people can be found in every culture and every phase of history, and wilding, as I show in the next chapter, is certainly not a new phenomenon in American life. As one of the world's most individualistic societies, America has long struggled to cope with high levels of violence, greed, political corruption, and other outcroppings of wilding.

Over the last 100 years, American history can be read as a succession of wilding periods alternating with eras of civility. The robber baron era of the 1880s and 1890s, an age of spectacular economic and political wilding, was followed by the Progressive Era of the early twentieth century, in which moral forces reasserted themselves. The individualistic license of the 1920s, another era of economic and political wilding, this time epitomized by the Teapot Dome scandal, yielded to the New Deal era of the 1930s and 1940s, when America responded to the Great Depression with remarkable moral and community spirit. The moral idealism of a new generation of youth in the 1960s was followed by the explosion of political, economic, and social wilding in the current era.

American wilding is a timeless and enduring threat, linked to our national heritage and most basic values and institutions. Although this book focuses on wilding today, the wilding problem riddles our history, for it is embedded in the origins of free-market capitalism and the individualistic culture that has helped shape the American Dream and our own national character. What distinguishes the current epidemic is the subtle legitimation of wilding as it breeds a new culture of corruption in Washington; the severity of the wilding crisis in the current U.S. imperial and militarist foreign policy that is undermining our most precious civil liberties; the wilding epidemic, symbolized by the Enron debacle, in banking and commerce; the spread of wilding into universities, films, TV, popular music, and other vital cultural centers; and the subsequent penetration of wilding culture so deeply into the lives of the general population that society itself is now at risk.

18

Roots of Wilding: Durkheim, Marx, and the Sociolgoical Eye

More than a century ago, the founders of sociology had their own intimations of a wilding crisis that could consume society. The great French thinker, Émile Durkheim, recognized that individualism was the rising culture of the modern age. While Durkheim believed that individualism could ultimately be a healing force, he also feared that it could poison the bonds that make social life possible. Karl Marx, who gave birth to a different school of sociology, believed that the economic individualism of capitalism might erode all forms of community and reduce human relations to a new lowest common denominator: the "cash nexus."

Sociology arose as an inquiry into the dangers of modern individualism, which could potentially destroy society itself. The prospect of the death of society gave birth to the question epitomized by the Ik: What makes society possible and prevents it from disintegrating into a mass of sociopathic and self-interested isolates? This core question of sociology has become the vital issue of our times.

Although sociology does not provide all the answers, it does offer a compelling framework for understanding and potentially solving the wilding epidemic. Durkheim never heard of wilding or the Ik, but he focused like a laser on the coming crisis of community. He saw that the great transformation of the modern age was the breakdown of traditional social solidarity and the rise of an individual less enmeshed in community. In Durkheim's view, egoism posed a grave danger, arising where "the individual is isolated because the bonds uniting him to other beings are slackened or broken" and the "bond which attaches him to society is itself slack." Such an individual, who finds no "meaning in genuinely collective activity," is primed for wilding, the pursuit of gain or pleasure at the expense of others with whom there is no sense of shared destiny.[34]

The other great danger is _anomie,_ which Durkheim defined as a condition of societal normlessness that breeds crime and suicide. Anomie arises when social rules are absent or confusing and individuals are insufficiently integrated into families, neighborhoods, or churches to be regulated by their moral codes. Durkheim believed that modern individualistic societies were especially vulnerable to this kind of failure of socialization. As community declines, it leaves the individual without a moral compass, buffeted by disturbing and increasingly limitless "passions, without a curb to regulate them."[35] Anomie fuels instrumental wilding, making the individual more vulnerable to fantasies of limitless money and power. It also feeds expressive wilding of the O. J. Simpson variety, weakening the personal and community controls that sustain civilized values.[36]

Although Durkheim captured the kind of breakdown of community that is currently contributing to the American wilding epidemic, he lacked the economic and political analysis that would help explain why wilding is startlingly pervasive among America's ruling elites and trickling down to the population at large. As I will argue in chapters to come, American wilding is a form of socially prescribed, antisocial behavior, modeled by leaders and reinforced by the rules of our "free-market" game. As such, it reflects less the insufficient presence of society in individuals than overconformity to a society whose norms and values are socially dangerous.

Marx wrote that the market system "drowns the most heavenly ecstasies of religious fervor, of chivalrous enthusiasm, of philistine sentimentalism, in the icy water of egotistical calculation." In capitalism, from a Marxist perspective, wilding is less a failure of socialization than an expression of society's central norms. To turn a profit, even the most humane capitalist employer commodifies and exploits employees, playing by the market rules of competition and profit maximization to buy and sell their labor power as cheaply as possible.[37]

The champions of Western capitalism—from Adam Smith to Milton Friedman—agree that self-interest is the engine of the system and individualism, its official religion; but they reject Marx's equation of a regime built around economic self-interest with exploitation and wilding. Marx was wrong, in fact, to assume that capitalism inevitably destroyed community and social values. In some national contexts, including Confucian Japan and social-democratic Sweden, the individualizing forces of the market are cushioned by cultures and governments that limit exploitation and help sustain community.

In the United States, however, rugged individualism has merged with raw capitalism, creating a fertile brew for wilding. A Marxist view of institutionalized wilding—and of political and business elites as carriers of the virus—helps correct the Durkheimian hint of wilding as deviance. Durkheim, in a major oversight, never recognized that egoism and anomie can themselves be seen as norms, culturally prescribed and accepted.[38]

This point is a theoretical key to understanding wilding in America. Wilding partly reflects a weakened community less able to regulate its increasingly individualistic members. In this sense, the American wilder is the product of a declining society that is losing its authority to instill respect for social values and obligations.

But Marx's view of institutionalized wilding suggests that wilders can simultaneously be oversocialized, imbibing too deeply the core values of competition and profit seeking in American capitalism. The idea of oversocialization, which I elaborate on in the next chapter, suggests not the failure of social authority but the wholesale indoctrination of societal values that can ultimately poison both the individual and also the society itself. As local communities weaken, giant corporations, including the media, advertising, and communications industries, shape the appetites, morality, and behavior of Americans ever more powerfully. For the rich and powerful, the dream of unlimited wealth and glamour, combined with the Reagan revolution of corporate deregulation and corporate welfare, opens up endless fantasies and opportunities. As Durkheim himself noted, when the ceiling on ordinary expectations is removed, the conventional restraints on pursuing them will also rapidly disappear. This situation produces socially prescribed anomie and wilding among elites that is based on unlimited possibilities.

A different version of socially prescribed wilding trickles down to everyone else. For those exposed to the same inflated dream of wealth, glamour, and power, but denied the means of achieving it, illegitimate means provide the only strategy to achieve socially approved goals. Whether involving petty or serious wilding, such behavior gradually permeates the population. Sociologist Robert Merton wrote that crime is a product of a disparity between goals and means. If that disparity becomes institutionalized, crime and other forms of deviance are normalized, and antisocial behavior becomes common practice. Wilding itself becomes a societal way of life.

New economic realities, including the fact that the coming generation faces the prospect of living less well than its parents, could trigger a healthy national reexamination of our values, and the pursuit of a less materialistic and individualistic life. The polarization of wealth and opportunity could also prompt, before it is too late, a rethinking of our class divisions and economic system. But without such a rescripting of the American Dream and our ruthless corporate capitalism, the new circumstances could create the specter of an American nightmare reminiscent of the Ik.

The Ultimate Wilders

Prisoners of the American Dream

Why should we be in such desperate haste to succeed? And in such desperate enterprises?

—Henry David Thoreau

In December 2004, a jury convicted 31-year-old Scott Peterson of killing his pregnant wife. Prosecutors accused Peterson, from Modesto, California, of weighting Laci Peterson's body with concrete anchors and dumping her into the San Francisco Bay on Christmas Eve 2002. Prosecutor Rick Distaso argued that Peterson was unhappy in his marriage and that his motive was to free himself from the unwanted burden of paying child support and alimony if he were to divorce.[1]

Like Charles Stuart, Peterson, a business manager and salesman, blamed a robber for the murder. After the murder, also like Stuart, he lived a high lifestyle with his mistress, Amber Frey, an attractive masseuse. (Frey was not aware that Peterson was married.) He faced growing financial problems before murdering Laci, with 70 percent of the couple's take-home income going toward credit card debt and Peterson badly failing to meet his sales quotas at his company. Moreover, the couple had recently taken out $250,000 life insurance policies on each other. After his murder conviction, Peterson sued from jail to collect the money, apparently as eager as Stuart had been to reap the spoils of his wife's death.[2]

Peterson is just one of a long list of people who have been convicted or indicted in recent years for killing their spouses. On November 6, 2005, James Keown, 31, a popular Missouri radio talk show host, was arrested and charged with killing his wife, Julie, a nurse, by spiking her Gatorade with antifreeze. Prosecutors alleged that Keown had deceived his wife about their deteriorating financial situation and had taken out a $250,000 life insurance policy on her, the likely financial motive for the crime.[3] Keown allegedly told a friend that he was eager to get a BMW and a new house with the money.[4] As is the case in other "antifreeze" spouse murders, Julie died an agonizing death over months, suffering dizziness, nausea, vomiting, and kidney failure.

On October 16, 2000, a North Carolina state jury formally indicted Deidre Lane for killing her husband, NFL running back Fred Lane. Prosecutors contended that the motive was money. Deidre, who confessed to the murder but claimed it was in self-defense, stood to gain $5 million in life insurance from a policy on her husband's life that had been issued in 1999.[5]

Two years earlier, in 1998, east Texas pharmacist Frederic Welborn Lunsford pleaded guilty to killing his wife of 14 years, Janice Pamela, by poisoning her with prescription medicine. One night, he gave her a large dose of methadone to induce a coma-like sleep. He then shot her in the chest and slit her wrists to make it look as though she had committed suicide. Lunsford admitted to the murder after his secret lover came forward and told police that he had talked about hiring someone to kill his wife. Lunsford had told his mistress that he couldn't deal with the financial consequences of an impending divorce. He paid child support for two children from a prior divorce and desperately had feared being saddled with the costs of two more. It was easier to kill his wife than lose his kids and deal with the debt.[6]

A few years earlier, Pamela Smart, an ambitious, pretty New Hampshire high school media services director, seduced an adolescent student and persuaded him to help her kill Gregory Smart, her 24-year-old husband. After the murder, her teenage lover went to jail, and Smart got thousands in insurance money. But she wasn't able to enjoy it for long because the real story finally leaked out from the boy and his friends. Smart was convicted of first-degree murder and sent to jail in Bedford Hills, New York, where she is incarcerated to this day. Still, Smart realized one of her ambitions—to become famous. Hollywood made a movie *To Die For*, about her venomous crime, with Nicole Kidman playing the "black widow," as women who kill their husbands for money are called.

All these killers are "ultimate wilders," Charles Stuart "look-alikes" prepared to do anything for money. Smart is most reminiscent of Stuart because she was ambitious, competitive, successful, and an "all-American" cheerleader and honor roll student. She aspired to be the next Barbara Walters, and many believed she'd make it. Smart, like Stuart, seemed the embodiment of the American Dream.

In this chapter, I describe people who have murdered their own spouses or children. Crimes of this horrible nature have many causes and happen in many cultures. Personal psychopathology, idiosyncratic family dynamics, and other personal or temperamental factors help explain these crimes. But I discuss them here because there are also wilding themes in American culture and today's American Dream that help unleash these crimes. Some individuals are more vulnerable to these cultural influences than others, with the people described here being obviously a small minority of Americans, different from their neighbors because of personal and psychological factors. The role of culture does not exonerate these individuals from personal responsibility, but it does show that we are looking at sociological patterns rather than just individual cases of psychopathology. For example, the startling fact that the most common source of death among pregnant women in the United States is murder by their husbands suggests that social as well as psychological forces help explain the behavior of people such as Charles Stuart and Scott Peterson. As you read through these grim case studies, keep in mind also that one-third of all female murder victims are killed by their husbands or boyfriends. These trends make clear that we are dealing in this chapter not just with deviance or psychopathology but disturbing social and cultural patterns.

Sociologist C. Wright Mills argued that the sociological imagination connects personal biography to the social structure and culture of the times. In Chapter 1, I argued that our current wilding wave began around 1980, as a new American Dream and a new economy began to take form. Consider next three of the most infamous wilders who all committed their crimes during this latest epidemic.

Robert Oakley Marshall: "Speed Demon on the Boulevard of Dreams"

After the prosecutor had summed up the case against their father, and there could be no doubt in anyone's mind, not even their own, about the horrific fact that he really had killed their mother, Roby and Chris, aged 20 and 19, were thinking the same thing: Their lives were a lie. They had always been envied, admired, and privileged. They had had money and a perfect family. "How much in love with each other they'd all seemed. . . . The all-American family. The American Dream that came true."[7]

The sons now knew the truth—that their father, Rob, a spectacularly successful New Jersey life insurance salesman, had indeed arranged for professional assassins from Louisiana to come up on the night of September 7, 1984, to Atlantic City; that he had arranged the same night to drive his wife, Maria, to dinner at Harrah's in his Cadillac Eldorado. After dinner and wine and some late gambling in the casino, Rob had driven his sleepy wife back toward Toms River, pulled off the parkway at the Oyster Creek picnic area to check out what he told Maria seemed to be a problem in the tire. Going out to examine the tire, he had waited for the paid executioners to steal up to the car, shoot Maria point-blank in the back, and swat Rob on the head to draw a little blood and make it look like a genuine robbery. (The Louisiana men had wanted to inflict a gunshot wound, but Rob had gone white and almost fainted—saying, "I'm not the one getting shot"—and insisted on only being hit on the head.) Rob had returned home looking strangely buoyant after his trauma, striking one detective as behaving more like a man ready to go out sailing on his yacht than someone who had just lost his wife. Rob Marshall had reason to feel a large burden had been lifted from his shoulders: He now stood to collect approximately $1.5 million from the insurance policy he had taken out on Maria, more than enough to clear $200,000 in gambling debts that he owed in Atlantic City and to set himself up handsomely for his next steps on the ladder of the American Dream. He could pay off the mortgage, buy new cars for himself and each of his boys, and indulge in a whirlwind romance with his sexy mistress.

Rob Marshall had good cause to feel that the police would not come after him. Gene, his brother-in-law and a lawyer, pointed out that it did not look especially good that Rob was deep in debt and stood to gain such a huge insurance payment. Rob responded that the police could not possibly suspect him: "I'm much too high up the civic ladder. My reputation in the community, in fact, places me beyond reproach."[8]

He was right about one thing: The police themselves called Rob a "pillar" of the community. Back in the early 1970s, Rob had quickly proved himself a sensational salesman, selling more than $2 million in life insurance in his first year; in his second, he was again among the top 50 Provident Mutual Life salespeople in the country. Rob and his family had moved into a big house, and he had driven around town in a flashy red Cadillac. Rob had also scored big in his private life, capturing Maria, a Philadelphia Main Line doctor's daughter who was exquisitely beautiful and always kept herself and her sons impeccably groomed. Maria was Rob's proudest possession. He loved her beauty. When he was arranging to have her killed, Rob told the executioners they must not mar Maria's looks; he could not stand that idea.[9]

Rob and Maria, journalist Joe McGinniss writes, were like royalty in Toms River. One neighbor said they "seemed to have the ideal family and lifestyle. You know, like you'd see on TV."[10] Everyone admired how they looked. They also admired Rob's business success and the fact that the Marshalls "were always buying something new." They moved to a bigger house and joined the country club. Maria was invited to join Laurel Twigs, a prestigious charitable organization, and Rob became a mover and shaker in the Rotary Club, the United Way, and the country club.[11]

There was not much doubt about how Rob had gotten so far so fast. The man was driven, being the most aggressive salesperson Toms River had ever seen. Kevin Kelly, the prosecutor who had once bought insurance from Rob, said Rob pushed through the deal while half his hamburger was still on his plate and the engine was still hot in the parking lot. "The guy could fit in three or four lunches a day, the way he hustled." His drive—and his ego—seemed as big as Donald Trump's, who happened to own the Atlantic City casinos where Rob gambled and where he staged Maria's last supper.[12]

Over the course of his nationally publicized trial, later celebrated in the TV miniseries *Blind Faith*, Rob's shameless behavior confirmed the nefarious picture of a sociopathic, greed-soaked personality painted by the prosecutor. In the first few weeks after the murder, Rob could barely conceal his excitement about his new freedom, not only making quick moves to get his hands on the insurance money but also charming at least three different women into his wife's bed, even before he had figured out how to dispose of her remains. He staged a phony suicide attempt, giving himself the opportunity to leave "suicide tapes" by which he could publicly display his love of his children and Maria. The fact is, as prosecutor Kevin Kelly showed, nobody close to Rob ever heard him weep or saw him show any real grief or sense of loss over Maria. In fact, Rob had indifferently left her ashes in a brown cardboard box in a drawer in the funeral home, while at the same time he put back on and prominently wore at the trial the gold wedding ring Maria had given him. Rob would embarrass his sons by his public demonstrations of his love for them, wearing signs for the cameras saying "I love you" even as he was desperately urging them to perjure themselves and risk jail to save his neck.

Prosecutor Kevin Kelly summed up Rob's personality: He's "self-centered, he's greedy, he's desperate, he's materialistic, and he's a liar. . . . [H]e will use anybody, he will say anything, and he will do anything—including use his own family—to get out from under." Rob was single-mindedly out for number one; he "loves no one but himself."[13] Kelly was not greatly exaggerating, but what he knew and did not say was that many of the same epithets could be applied to many other Toms River residents. The fact is, as one native observed, Rob was in many ways not very different from his neighbors. Rob's case, one resident wrote, was compelling precisely because there was an intimate connection between "the town's collective values and the story of Rob and Maria Marshall." Indeed, the spotlight on Rob—and the community's obsession with the trial—stemmed from the fact that it helped to bring into sharp definition what the community was really about.[14]

Toms River in the 1970s was full of people in a hurry, many of them like the Marshalls, recent immigrants to the town who were scurrying to cash in on one of the biggest housing booms on the New Jersey shore. Ocean County was the second-fastest-growing county in the country, which caused real estate values to soar and triggered spectacular business opportunities. The mostly blue-collar and lower-middle-class migrants who flocked to Toms River caught the fantastic entrepreneurial fever. Everyone in Toms River was suddenly making deals, and limits on the money to be made evaporated. Since most people were new to the community, conspicuous consumption became the quickest way to become known and command respect. "I shop, therefore I am" became the Toms River credo long before it started showing up on bumper stickers around the country. Lots of Toms River folks were joining the country club and driving their Cadillacs up to Atlantic City at night, joining Rob for the big bets at the high-priced blackjack tables.

Rob was a hustler, but hustling was the name of the game in Toms River, just as it already was in Atlantic City and as it was increasingly becoming in Ronald Reagan's Washington, D.C., and on Wall Street. Rob, a number of commentators observed, was remarkably tuned in to the spirit of his times. The commercials about getting yours and getting it now were ringing in his ears. And as the 1980s progressed, Rob tuned in to bigger dreams than Toms River could offer. "See, all around Rob in the eighties," one old friend said, "everybody was scoring everything: sex, dope, big-money deals. At least, he thought so."[15] If those young kids out of business school could be making their first million on Wall Street before they were 30, Rob was missing something he deserved. As his success grew, so did his aspirations, his sense of deprivation, and his gambling debts. Like the country as a whole, Rob planned to leverage himself into a real fortune.

Yet if the resonance between Rob and the collective values of his time was electric, most people in Toms River and Atlantic City were not murdering their wives to cover their debts and advance one more step up the ladder. Rob was different, but mainly because he personified so purely and acted out so unrestrainedly the hungers driving his neighbors. Others were dreaming the same big American Dream. But Rob was completely engulfed by it, his personality a machine perfectly dedicated to "making it." Rob was abnormal because the American Dream that was becoming the new standard had penetrated every fiber of his being, purging all traces of the emotional or moral sensibilities that restrained his neighbors. Rob's aggressiveness was startling even in an age of hustlers, his narcissism more extreme than that of most of his fellow travelers in the "Me Generation," and in an age of moral decline, his conscience was exceptionally elastic.

Undoubtedly, Rob's "abnormality" had roots in his past—perhaps in the Depression, which had ruined his family and turned his father into an alcoholic; perhaps in his chronic sense of being an outsider, having moved at least 10 times before he was 16. But if Rob had not murdered his wife, he would never have come under the psychiatric microscope, because his extreme traits were exactly those that people on the way up were supposed to exhibit—to propel them to the top. For 15 years, Rob's "abnormality" had helped make him the biggest success in his community.

Rob got into trouble only because his dreams finally outstripped his own formidable capacities. He probably would not have killed Maria if he had not fallen so deeply into debt, and he might not have gotten into such debt if he had not been lured by the bigger dreams and looser moral sensibilities that his friends said had gotten under his skin and then possessed him. The reckless and grandiose entrepreneurial culture of Toms River that had swept across America released the extremes in Rob's personality, nurturing his sense of himself as a legend in his own time, free to make his own rules and look after number one first. When he got into deep financial trouble, values and a culture that might have restrained him were not in place, and his deep-seated potential for wilding was unleashed.

Them and Us: Violence and the Oversocialized American Character

Public reaction to ultimate wilders like Rob Marshall, Charles Stuart, and Pamela Smart has been schizophrenic. Utter shock that anyone could indifferently wipe out a wife, husband, mother, or child for money is linked with a sliver of recognition that there is something familiar about these killers. "The first thing people want to know," Alison Bass wrote in the *Boston Globe*, is "how could anyone so carefully and coolly plan the murder of a wife, a child, anyone?"[16] But the second, usually subliminal, question is, "Could my spouse do it?" or, even more subliminally, "Could I?"

Do ultimate wilders tell us something important about ourselves and our society, or are they just bizarre sideshows? Reassuring responses come from many commentators, such as psychiatrist Dr. Charles Ford, who believes that although people such as Rob Marshall, Charles Stuart, and Pamela Smart "on the surface look very normal," they are suffering from either mental illness or deep-seated "character disorders" such as narcissism or sociopathy, that radically differentiate "them" from "us."[17] Criminologists James Alan Fox and Jack Levin describe sociopaths such as

Charles Stuart as people who "blend in well and function appropriately" but are "far from normal." Criminologists explain that sociopaths "know the right thing to do" in order to emulate the rest of us; they are consummate actors: "Sociopaths lie, manipulate, and deceive. They are good at it. Like actors, they play a role on the stage of life."[18]

When they murder, ultimate wilders clearly act differently from the majority of the population, but the clinical accounts of their character disorders do not provide a persuasive argument for the difference between "them" and "us" and make reassurances by psychological professionals ring hollow. The Bible of psychiatry, the *Diagnostic and Statistical Manual of the American Psychiatric Association*, defines *narcissistic personality disorder* as "[t]he tendency to exploit others to achieve one's own ends, to exaggerate achievements and talents, to feel entitled to and to crave constant attention and adulation."[19] Criminologists Fox and Levin define sociopaths as "self-centered, manipulative, possessive, envious, reckless, and unreliable. They demand special treatment and inordinate attention, often exaggerating their own importance. . . . On their way to the top, sociopaths ruthlessly step over their competitors without shame or guilt." These are common human faults, and Fox and Levin acknowledge that they are widespread among Americans. In trying to predict when the difference between "them" and "us" emerges, Fox and Levin end up in another conundrum, for they acknowledge that most sociopaths rarely reach the point "at which they feel it necessary to kill. Most of them live ordinary lives." Distinguishing "them" from "us" then seems a bit like the dilemma American soldiers faced in Vietnam—trying to distinguish the enemy guerrillas from the rest of the population.[20]

It is time for sociologists to adopt the idea of sociopathy, a concept as useful for understanding a sick society as a sick psyche. A sociopathic society is one, like that of the Ik, marked by a collapse of moral order that is the result of the breakdown of community and the failure of institutions responsible for inspiring moral vision and creating and enforcing robust moral codes. In such a society, the national character-type tends toward sociopathy, and idealized behavior, although veiled in a rhetoric of morality, becomes blurred with antisocial egoism. The founders of modern sociology, especially Émile Durkheim, as noted in Chapter 1, worried that modernity threatened to turn the most developed industrial cultures into sociopathic cauldrons of raw egoism and anomie, and they conceived of the sociological enterprise as an effort to understand how societies could find their moral compass and preserve themselves in the face of the sociopathic threat.

In sociopathic societies, a clinical effort to dissect the sociopathic personality cannot be separated from an analysis of national character and ideology. Rob Marshall, Charles Stuart, and Pamela Smart may be deranged, but their derangement mirrors a national disorder. As the United States enters the twenty-first century, the official religion of the free market increasingly sanctifies sociopathy in the guise of individual initiative, entrepreneurship, and "making it." As the American Dream becomes a recipe for wilding, clinicians and criminologists need to deepen their sociological understanding, or they will continue to misread Marshall, Stuart, and Smart as a failure of socialization rather than a pathology of oversocialization. Marshall internalized too deeply the core American values of competitiveness and material success, discarding any other values that might interfere with personal ambitions. Marshall, Stuart, Smart, and other ultimate wilders are most interesting as prisoners of the same American Dream that compels the rest of us, but does not consume us with quite the same intensity.

Lyle and Erik Menendez: A Family of Competitors

On the evening of August 20, 1989, as José Menendez was watching TV in the spacious den of his $14-million Beverly Hills estate, he had reason to feel pretty good about his life. José was a perfectionist who, according to his older son, Lyle, felt he could never "do something well enough." But even José, with his high standards and consuming ambition, might have admitted that an impoverished immigrant who by age 45 had risen to become a millionaire in Hollywood's inner sanctum had not done too badly. He could count celebrities such as Barry Manilow, Kenny Rogers, and Sylvester Stallone as his friends. Founder and president of Live Entertainment, Inc., a successful national videocassette distributor, his was a Horatio Alger story come true. Journalist Pete Hamil wrote in *Esquire* magazine that José was a "glittering" testimony to the American Dream of the Reagan years.[21]

As he sat with his wife, Kitty, that evening, eating fresh berries and cream, José would certainly have gotten deep satisfaction from the comments of his fellow executive, Ralph King, who eulogized José in the *Wall Street Journal* after his death as "by far the brightest, toughest businessman I have ever worked with," or of former Hertz chairman, Robert Stone, who said he "had never known anyone who worked harder, worked toward more goals." José, according to Stone, probably "would have become president of the company" had he stayed at Hertz. Coming to the United States from Cuba at age 15, José had dedicated every ounce of his being to getting ahead, vowing to "develop strip malls" if that was what it took to "succeed by age thirty." He could not have been better psychologically equipped. He was an intensely aggressive and competitive man brimming with entrepreneurial energy. Straight out of accounting school, he had hustled from Coopers and Lybrand to a Chicago shipping firm to Hertz, and then to RCA, successfully signing performer José Feliciano. After being passed over for a promotion to executive vice president at RCA, Menendez achieved a brilliant coup by creating Live Entertainment, Inc., the video arm of Carolco Pictures, where he sat on the board, and which had gone big-time with its smash hit, *Rambo II*.[22]

Turning to his two handsome sons as they burst into the room, José could savor a different kind of pride. José had a burning desire to see his sons succeed as he had, and he had dedicated himself to that end with the same relentless passion with which he had pursued his business goals. He drilled Lyle and Erik for hours on the tennis courts and constantly exhorted them to outperform their peers on and off the court. "There is a lot of pressure," Erik said, "to be great." Lyle, aged 22, was to graduate soon from Princeton, and Erik, aged 19, had gotten into UCLA and was talking about wanting to realize his father's own ambition of becoming the first Cuban-American U.S. senator.

José was probably more puzzled than frightened when he saw that Lyle and Erik were both carrying shotguns. But he had no time to ask questions. Within seconds of barging into the den, as police reconstruct the scene, the two sons had fired eight shots point-blank at their father and five at their mother. Just to make sure he was dead, they thrust the barrel of one gun into their father's mouth and blew off the back of his head. Police would later say that the scene was so gruesome that it could not possibly have been a Mafia hit, as some had first speculated, because Mob kills are "clean." Erik later told reporters that his parents' ravaged, blood-spattered, lifeless bodies "looked like wax."[23]

Lyle and Erik claimed that they had gone out that evening to see the James Bond film *License to Kill* but had ended up seeing *Batman* instead. They came back late at night, they said, horrified to find the carnage at home. Neighbors reported that they heard the sons screaming and sobbing, presumably after discovering the bodies. But police suspected Lyle and Erik from the very beginning—and not only because, as District Attorney Ira Reiner put it, a $14-million estate provided "an ample motive." The boys were not able to produce ticket stubs for *Batman*, and police had found a shotgun shell casing in one of Lyle's jackets. Then investigators discovered that in high school two years earlier, Erik had cowritten a play about a wealthy teenager who murders his parents for money, a creation that made his mother, who helped type the manuscript, proud of her son's gifts. But it was about six months later that police found the smoking gun they were seeking when they confiscated tapes of psychotherapy sessions with both boys that apparently offered direct evidence of their involvement in the crime.[24]

The Menendez brothers eventually confessed to the killings, acknowledging that they had followed through on a calculated plan to shoot their parents. But Lyle and Erik presented themselves in court not as brutal murderers but as innocent victims. They said they killed in self-defense and because of years of emotional and sexual abuse. Erik claimed that his father had been sexually abusing him since he was 5 years old, forcing him repeatedly to have oral and anal sex.

The prosecution, however, as well as many followers of the trial, were skeptical about this "abuse excuse," noting accurately that it had been one of the more fashionable and disturbing trends in legal defenses at the time. It had cropped up in such infamous trials as the Bobbitt case, in which a sexually abused wife defended cutting off her husband's penis because he beat her. There were reasons to doubt the truth of the Menendez brothers' sexual abuse claims, among them the fact that in their time in psychotherapy the boys had never mentioned sexual abuse to their therapist, Dr. L. Jerome Oziel, who was the one to initially get (and tape) the boys' murder confession. Erik and Lyle had given Dr. Oziel written permission when they entered therapy to share their confidences with their parents, an unlikely act for young men who would presumably be using the therapy to discuss their parents' alleged mental, physical, and sexual abuse. In addition, the abuse defense was introduced late in the game, many months after the killings and shortly before the trial opened. Family members and others who had known the family well and were familiar with José's many mistresses and affairs, were reported to be incredulous, partly because none of them had ever heard any whisper of this other side of the macho José's sexual life.

Even if José had sexually abused his sons, such abuse would neither justify the killings nor constitute proof of the real motive of the shootings. There were other ways for these smart and wealthy young men to defend themselves and escape the family's oppressive yoke, including running away and assuming new identities, seeking shelter with friends, relatives, or protective social service agencies, or going off to boarding school and college, as Lyle, in fact, had done. But all of these strategies would probably have cost Lyle and Erik their inheritance and certainly would not have given them immediate access to their parents' huge estate.

The remarkable behavior of Lyle and Erik after the killings offers the most revealing clues about why the brothers committed them. Neither boy wasted any time. Lyle dropped out of Princeton and, after flirting with the idea of a professional tennis career (he had once ranked 36th in the U.S. juniors), decided "to build a business empire from the ground up." Taking his share of an initial $400,000 insurance payment, he bought Chuck's Spring Street Café, a popular student hangout near the Princeton campus specializing in fried chicken. Lyle immediately began drafting plans to open franchises in other states as part of a nationwide chain. His entrepreneurial ambitions extended far beyond restaurants. Lyle began traveling widely to help realize his dream of making a "fortune in, among other things, show business and real estate." He founded Investment Enterprises, a financing shell for channeling the millions of dollars he would inherit into quick, high-yield returns.[25]

Erik, however, was serious about professional tennis, immediately dropping out of UCLA and hiring a professional tennis coach for $50,000 a year. He moved into the exclusive Marina City Club Towers, a glamorous ocean-side setting south of Los Angeles. Erik worked as hard at his tennis career as Lyle did at his restaurant and real estate ventures, practicing for hours on the court and taking his coach along to boost his performance in tournaments. Erik, however, did not limit himself to a future in tennis. Still proud of his earlier murder script, he believed he had a spectacular future as a screenwriter. In his spare time, he worked on his plays and poetry. He told his roommate at Marina that he was confident he would "produce an unbelievable script."[26]

It took little imagination to view the killings, as the police did, as a grand entrepreneurial scheme, an ironic testimony to the grip of a father's deepest values on the minds of his sons. More than anything else, José had wanted Erik and Lyle to follow in his footsteps and live out the American Dream that had guided his own life. He had raised them to be aggressive competitors like himself who would seize every opportunity to get ahead and make something of themselves. "He wanted us," Erik said, "to be exactly like him." Lyle and Erik converted patricide into a carefully planned strategy for catapulting their careers into fast-forward. In a bizarre twist, they proved how fully they had imbibed their father's values and opened themselves to the entrepreneurial spirit of the decade that shaped them.[27]

Lyle and Erik were themselves fully aware of the power of their ties to the father they had killed. "We are prototypes of my father," Erik pronounced after the shootings. He added, "I'm not going to live my life for my father, but I think his dreams are what I want to achieve. I feel he's in me, pushing me." As for Lyle, he all but admitted that his whole life had been a preparation for the day when he could jump into his father's shoes. Two days after the killings, Lyle told his friend Glen Stevens, who had commented on how well Lyle seemed to be holding up, "I've been waiting so long to be in this position." Later, commenting on his ambitious business plans, Lyle said, "I just entered into my father's mode."[28]

The Menendez brothers had become prisoners of the American Dream, captives of their father's extravagant ambitions. Theirs may have been "ambition gone berserk," as a *Wall Street Journal* report put it, but it represented less a crazy break from reality than an excessive vulnerability to the culture around them.[29] The messages coming from their father, from Beverly Hills, from Princeton, and from Wall Street were telling them the same thing: Money is good, more money is better, and they had only themselves to blame if they did not seize every opportunity to strike it rich. The seductive power of these messages on the boys is apparent in their uncontrolled orgy of spending after getting the first cut of their inheritance. Lyle bought a new Porsche, which was not especially unusual, but his spending on clothes was extravagant, even for Princeton. Upscale clothier, Stuart Lindner, remembers Lyle coming into his store "dressed in an expensive black cashmere jacket and wearing a Rolex watch," which Lindner priced at about $15,000. On that occasion, Lyle bought some $600 worth of clothes, including five $90 silk shirts. "We've had bigger sales," Lindner said, "but not in four minutes."[30]

The sons worshiped the same god as their father, but they gave the family religion a new spin. They had grown up in the era of Donald Trump and Bill Gates, both of whom had made their father's career path seem slow and his fortune paltry. Lyle told Venanzia Momo, owner of a Princeton pizza parlor Lyle tried to buy, that he did not want to have to struggle like his father had to succeed. "He said he wanted to do it faster and quicker," Momo said. "He said he had a better way."[31]

The seeds of Lyle's and Erik's ultimate wilding can be seen in a trail of small wildings reflecting the casual morality of the quick-money culture that engulfed them. Even as an adolescent, Lyle frequently went on spending binges, once running up a huge hotel bill in Tucson that his father had to cover. He racked up so many traffic violations that his license was suspended twice, and several times he got into trouble with the police during his travels in Italy. At Princeton, he copied a fellow psychology student's lab report and was told he could leave voluntarily or be expelled. Meanwhile, Erik also had brushes with the law, ending up in juvenile court on a number of occasions. José, however, was always there to bail the boys out, perhaps a fatal source of support, for it may well have been that their success in getting out of small jams that helped persuade them they could also get away with murder.

The Menendez case "speaks to every parent," says television producer Steven White. "Matricide and patricide go back to Greek drama." But

Lyle and Erik are products of America. Their abnormality lies most of all in their uncritical receptivity to the "look after number one" message at the heart of contemporary American life. Lyle's and Erik's pathology was that they allowed themselves to be socialized so completely. They lacked the capacity to resist their father's dreams and the current era's mesmerizing obsession with money. What José had not realized was that it was not his children's ambition he had to cultivate—the larger culture would see to that—but the tender sentiments and moral sensibilities that might have prevented their ambition from metastasizing into a cancer of wilding.

Then and Now: An American Tragedy

In 1925, *An American Tragedy*, by Theodore Dreiser, was published. One of the country's great works of literature, it is about a young man, Clyde Griffiths, who plots to kill his pregnant girlfriend, Roberta, so that he can take up with a woman who is rich and well connected. The story is based on a real murder committed in 1906 by Chester Gillette, a New Yorker who drowned his pregnant girlfriend in order to be free to pursue a woman in high society. The striking resemblance of Dreiser's protagonist to both Lyle and Erik Menendez, and to other contemporary men in a hurry such as Charles Stuart and Rob Marshall, suggests that wilding, even ultimate wilding, is not new. But if the parallels tell us something important about the deep historical roots of American wilding, there are also noteworthy contrasts that hint at how the virus has mutated for the worse.

Like Erik and Lyle, Clyde was an authentic prisoner of the American Dream (as, presumably, was the real Chester Gillette, for as H. L. Mencken notes, Dreiser stayed "close to the facts and came close to a literal reporting"). When Dreiser described Clyde as "bewitched" by wealth, as a personification of desire for all the glitter and beauty that money can buy, he could also have been describing Erik and Lyle. Indeed, Dreiser saw young Clyde as so vulnerable to the seductive temptations that surrounded him, so helpless in the face of the material pleasures just beyond his reach, that Dreiser asked whether the real guilt for the crime lay not with Clyde but with the culture that had debased him. Perhaps future novelists or historians will instructively engage the same question about the Menendez brothers, whose vulnerability to modern capitalist seduction is one of the most poignant aspects of their story.

Dreiser selected the Gillette case, as critic Lawrence Hussman informs us, because he considered it "typical enough to warrant treatment as particularly American." Dreiser recognized that whatever psychological pathology was involved could be understood only in the context of a diagnosis of the health of American society and an inquiry into the moral ambiguity of the American Dream. *An American Tragedy* was compelling to millions of Americans in the 1920s because it held up a mirror in which they could see their collective reflection. The novel's success suggests that there was something of Clyde in many Americans of his era, which tells us how deeply the wilding virus had already insinuated itself into American life. Indeed, as early as the robber baron era of the late 1800s, the wilding streak in American culture had become too obvious to ignore, a matter of preoccupation for satirist Mark Twain, philosopher Henry David Thoreau, and critic Lincoln Steffens.[32]

Yet if Dreiser's work suggests that wilding defines a continuity, not a break, in American life, it also hints at how things have changed. Unlike Rob Marshall or Erik and Lyle Menendez, Clyde could not actually go through with his diabolical scheme. After becoming obsessed with plans to kill his girlfriend, he lures her into a canoe with the intent of drowning her, but, whether out of weakness or moral compunction, he cannot do it. His problem is solved only because she accidentally falls into the water, along with Clyde himself. Clyde does not try to save her, partly because he is afraid that her thrashing about will drown him, too, but that is quite different from deliberate murder. Perhaps in the America of 1925 it was still not credible to Dreiser or his audience that anyone could actually carry out such a crime, although the real Chester Gillette was only one of a number of such accused killers in the first quarter of the twentieth century. While such murders still shock the public, Americans today, according to pollsters, not only believe that such crimes can be committed but, as noted earlier, worry whether their spouses, or they themselves, could succumb to the impulse.

That the constraints on wilding may have weakened over the last 75 years is suggested further by the centrality of the theme of guilt and moral responsibility in Dreiser's work. Clyde is a morally weak character, but he is not entirely devoid of conscience. After Roberta's death, Clyde is not able to absolve himself of responsibility because he is plagued by the question of whether he was guilty of not trying to save her. In contrast, the most extraordinary aspect of Rob Marshall and the Menendez brothers is their apparent lack of remorse. Friends of Rob Marshall, Erik and Lyle Menendez, Pamela Smart, and Charles Stuart commented on how well they looked after the killings; it was widely reported that they all seemed happier and better adjusted after their violent deeds and never appeared to suffer even twinges of conscience.

Dreiser's *An America Tragedy* is ultimately an indictment of the American Dream. The "primary message of the book," Lawrence Hussman reminds us, concerns the "destructive materialistic goals" that obsess Clyde and drive him to his murderous plot. Dreiser refused to accept that the evil could be explained away by Clyde's moral weakness or some presumed individual psychopathology; it was only the inability to question "some of the basic assumptions on which American society is based" that could lead anyone to that line of thinking. Dreiser himself concluded that Clyde had to be held morally accountable but that society was the ultimate perpetrator of the crime. He implicitly instructed his readers that such American tragedies would recur until the country finally triumphed over its obsessions with materialism and ego and rediscovered its moral compass.

Dreiser's musings on the American Dream remain stunningly relevant today, and the book is an eerie prophecy of current cases of wilding. But if Dreiser saw how the American Dream of his era could beget extreme individual wilding, he could not have foreseen the historical developments that have made the dream a recipe for a wilding epidemic. In Dreiser's day, the "American Century" was dawning on a glorious future; the prosperity of the 1920s was a harbinger of a new era of plenty in which all Americans could reasonably look forward to their share of an apparently endlessly expanding pie. Despite the dark side of the materialistic preoccupation, which divided people as they competed for the biggest slices, the Dream also brought Americans together, for as long as the pie was growing, everybody could win.

It took a new age of limits and decline, during which growing numbers of Americans would see their share of the pie shrinking and others see it permanently removed from the table, to set the stage for a full-blown wilding epidemic. Dreiser saw a foreshadowing of this in the Great Depression, which turned him toward socialism. But America pulled together in the 1930s, and the wilding virus was kept largely in check, as I discuss in Chapter 10. It would take a very different set of economic and political reversals, half a century later, to fuel the kind of wilding epidemic that Dreiser vaguely anticipated but never experienced.

It is apt testimony to Dreiser, as well as to the ferocious spread of the epidemic he could only dimly envisage, to mention in conclusion the rapidly growing crowd of modern-day Chester Gillettes. In addition to the Menendez brothers, Charles Stuart is one of the most remarkable Gillette "look-alikes," not only because he killed his pregnant wife but because, like Chester, he was from a working-class background and had disposed of his wife because she had become an impediment to his upward mobility. Stuart, of course, trumped Gillette's achievement by collecting several hundred thousand dollars in insurance money.

Susan Smith: Infanticide and the Honor Student

Susan Smith, now serving a life sentence in prison, hauntingly evokes *An American Tragedy*'s main character and theme. Smith is the young mother from Union, South Carolina, who confessed to strapping her two young sons—Michael, age 3, and Alex, age 14 months—into their car seats in her Mazda and driving the car onto a boat ramp leading into John D. Long Lake. She watched as the vehicle rolled into the water, carrying her two trusting infants to a grave at the bottom of the lake. The car sank slowly, still floating as the infants cried plaintively for their mother, who had run off to give her alibi to police. Because Smith initially told police that the children had been kidnapped by a gun-toting black man, reporters compared her to Charles Stuart, who had concocted a similar racist story to throw off Boston police. Like Stuart, Smith triggered a national firestorm of self-examination. Americans everywhere wondered how a hardworking, church-going, honor society graduate in South Carolina's "City of Hospitality" could commit such a horrifying double murder.

Pundits and politicians offered their own explanations, including former Speaker of the U.S. House of Representatives Newt Gingrich, who at the time of the killings on October 25, 1994, was one of the most powerful politicians in America. Gingrich said the Smith murders showed "the sickness of our society" and was a "reason to vote Republican." But Gingrich, once a history professor, should have noticed the resemblance of Smith to Chester Gillette and realized that both Smith and Gillette had deeply imbibed the intensely individualistic version of the American Dream that Gingrich was selling.[33]

The relevance of Dreiser's novel and the American Dream to the Smith saga began with Smith's mother, Linda Sue, who in 1977 divorced her first husband, a blue-collar worker named Harry Ray Vaughan, to marry a stockbroker. Vaughan, Susan Smith's father, committed suicide a year after Linda Sue had left him to "marry up."

Susan Smith's romantic ambitions resembled her mother's and are intimately tied to the murders. Shortly before the killings, Smith had separated from her own blue-collar husband and had started to date Tom Findlay, the wealthy son of a corporate raider. Tom's father owned the textile factory where Susan worked as a secretary. Smith was struggling financially, living on $125 a week of child support and a $325 weekly salary; she found it hard to meet the $344 monthly payments on her red brick house. Susan dreamed of marrying Tom, who lived in a plush mansion called "the Castle." Tom, who was known to secretaries in the office as "the Catch," was feverishly pursued by many local women, and he complained to one friend not long before the killing, "Why can't I meet a nice single woman? Everyone at work wants to go out with me because of my money. But I don't want a woman with children—there are so many complications."[34]

Police regard the triggering event as the letter Tom sent to Susan on October 18, in which he broke off their relationship, explaining that he "did not want the responsibility of children." Susan got painful evidence of Tom's seriousness about leaving and enjoying a less encumbered life when, only hours before she killed the children who had become the obstruction to her dreams, she found Tom in a bar flirting with three pretty single women.

After her confession, speculation in Union was rife that she did it for the money. In her confession, she wrote that she had "never been so low" because of her financial problems and that Findlay's rejection meant the loss not only of love but also of the wealthiest man in the county. Police believed that Smith's desperation "to jump from the listing boat of the working class" appeared to be "a major motive" for her crime.[35]

There are haunting similarities with the Dreiser story, down to the detail of drowning as the way to free oneself for marrying up. Like Gillette, Susan and her mother both saw marriage as their path to the American Dream. Known in high school as the most "all-American," Susan found it too painful to see her dream slip away. Wealthy Tom Findlay was the ticket, and Susan saw no way to keep him other than killing her own children.

Susan Smith and the whole rogues' gallery of modern-day Dreiser characters are just the tip of the iceberg, not only of the larger wilding epidemic but also of the roster of ultimate wilders, male and female, rich and poor, who are now grabbing headlines. Experts conservatively estimate that hundreds of such calculated, cold-blooded family murders for money have taken place in the past decade. What is striking is not just the numbers but the percentage of those who were described by friends, associates, and the police as all-American types, defying the suspicion of many because they so purely embodied the qualities and the success that Americans idealize. Most Americans, of course, do not become killers, but as we see in the next chapter, an epidemic of lesser wilding has consumed much of popular culture and marks the lives of millions of ordinary Americans.

Cheaters, Cynics, Dot-Commers, and Survivors

Wilding Culture in the Media and Everyday Life

This whole world is wild at heart and weird on top.
—"Lula" in *Wild at Heart*, 1990

In September 2000, five teenagers in Queens, New York, were arrested for ordering take-out food from a Chinese restaurant and allegedly bludgeoning the owner to death when he personally delivered the order. They had no grudge against the owner; they had killed, police said, for a free meal of shrimp egg foo yung and chicken with broccoli. A few months later in Reading, Massachusetts, near Boston, one hockey dad assaulted and killed another, the latest in a string of attacks across the country by fathers against coaches, players, and other parents. On December 4, 2000, Shirley Henson, 41, from a suburb of Birmingham, Alabama, was sentenced to a 13-year jail sentence after shooting to death another driver, Gina Foster, a 34-year-old mother of three, in an infamous incident of road rage.[1] On June 24, 2003, Anna Gitlin, 25, who was angry about being held up in traffic after a fatal accident in Weymouth, Massachusetts, yelled at a police officer, "I don't care who [expletive] died. I'm more important." She was later charged with attempted murder of the officer when her car struck him, putting him in the hospital.[2]

But it is perhaps not such extreme acts of wilding but the small wildings that ripple through our daily experiences that are most revealing. *Boston Globe* columnist, Susan Trausch, satirizes her own propensity for wilding: "An extra 10 bucks dropped out of the automatic teller machine the other day and I didn't give it back." There were, after all, "no guards. No middleman. . . . The machine doesn't ask questions." Trausch "grabbed the bills" and stifled "the impulse to shout, 'I won!'" Later, she asks herself, "Is this why the world is a mess? People don't want to be chumps so they say, 'I'll get mine now,' and then they grab an illicit brownie from the pastry tray of life. And oh, the noise we make if we don't get what we consider ours! If, for instance, only forty dollars had come out of the slot instead of fifty dollars, my outrage would have echoed in the aisles from aerosols to zucchini." But beating the system "made me want to play again," Trausch admits. "Maybe there was a gear loose. Maybe hundreds of dollars would come out." Trausch concludes that although she'd "like to report that at least the illicit money went to charity, it didn't. I blew it on lottery tickets."[3]

Trausch's lingering moral pangs are quite unusual. One sociologist laughed after reading her story, speculating that he and most other Americans would have pocketed the illicit greenbacks without a second thought, with no flickering of the conscience whatsoever. According to Queens, New York school board member, Jimmy Sullivan, a streetwise, savvy observer of American life, "Everybody cheats." It "isn't just some people," Sullivan emphasizes pointedly. "It's 95 percent of the people. Some cheat a little. Some cheat a lot. You work in an office, you take home supplies. People work at a construction site, they take home two-by-fours. Unfortunately, we've become a nation of petty crooks." Admitting to a reporter that his main concern as a school board official was patronage jobs for his "people"—white political cronies in his clubhouse—Sullivan makes no apologies. Everybody is doing it, cheating to get theirs, especially now that times are getting tougher. Sullivan certainly knows what he's talking about: he himself was manipulating a multimillion-dollar budget to build his own corrupt school fiefdom. Sullivan explains, "We're a nation of [expletive] and gangsters because that's what we glorify in Americana." It's all part of the American Dream today.[4]

Sullivan pleaded guilty to using coercion to support institutionalized cronyism. He had not counted on the fact that there are still honest people, like his school superintendent, Coleman Genn, who switched from working with Sullivan to wearing a hidden microphone for an independent commission investigating school corruption. Genn is part of the "second America" discussed in Chapter 1, the majority of Americans who have been touched but not debased by the wilding epidemic and continue to struggle honorably to maintain their integrity. Sullivan, nonetheless, put his finger on a contradiction that was tearing America apart. The pushers of dreams, the creators of "Americana," are feverishly selling the high-roller version of the American Dream in movies, magazines, and videos. While Americans are being willingly seduced, swimming in exquisitely alluring images of the pleasures only money can buy, money itself is getting harder to come by for a large percentage of the population. As

Americans dream big, economic shadows are lengthening and darkening. This contradiction between the glamorous life on the screen and the contrasting opportunities of real life has the potential to spread the epidemic deeply into the "second America" that, until now, has kept it at bay.

Temptation and Survival: Reality TV and the Ik-ing of America

If the ratings are to be believed, millions of us are addicted to reality TV. *Survivor* was the biggest hit of recent years, and copy-cat shows like *The Mole*, *Temptation Island*, and Donald Trump's *The Apprentice* have also been very popular. *Survivor II: The Australian Outback*, drew 30 million viewers when it first aired in 2001.

Richard Hatch, the now rich and famous winner of the original *Survivor*, symbolizes what reality TV is all about. Hatch never concealed his intention to win the million-dollar prize by remaining completely emotionally detached from everyone else. While others might have found it difficult to repress real feelings for other players, Hatch was the consummate strategist and schemer. Drawing on his skills as a management consultant, he seemed to build alliances effortlessly with other participants while plotting how to dispense with each of them. Ironically, at the time of this writing, Hatch is on trial, charged with cheating on his income taxes; he is facing a 10-count indictment—including charges of tax evasion, wire fraud, and the filing of false returns—that could lead to a $1-million fine and 30 years in jail. Hatch claims that he thought the *Survivor* show had already paid some or all of the taxes on the million dollars he had won on the show, and that he actually had filed for a refund on his tax statement. But the show's producer, Mark Burnett, said that Hatch's contract made clear that Hatch was responsible for paying taxes on any money he won on the show. Hatch's alleged wilding in the real world seems like a criminal extension of his reality show wilding.[5]

The subtext of *Survivor* is that if you want to survive and make large amounts of money, you have to learn how to manipulate people even as you partner with them. The manipulation is ruthless, since it requires throwing people off of the island—a kind of mirroring on TV of the culture of downsizing that prevails in U.S. business. Robert Allen, the CEO of AT&T who laid off 70,000 workers while raising his own salary by millions, said that he "felt good about himself" because he was just looking after business—and succeeding.[6] All *Survivor* participants have to buy into a similar premise: that it is necessary to cultivate strategies for eliminating others on the team while plotting a path of success. Inflicting harm on your own teammates becomes not only essential but also virtuous. Perhaps only a business culture based on big money and disposable labor could create a TV concept quite like *Survivor*.

The original *Survivor* series seemed almost benign, however, compared with *Survivor II*. Hatch "would have gotten eaten alive" by the *Survivor II* players, according to one of the show's hosts. This was intended to be a meaner *Survivor*, with what the show's creator, Mark Burnett, calls "real suffering." "The level of suffering in this season—it would make you cry," Burnett said. He was talking about physical suffering, but, the show's commentary also suggests suffering of the soul.[7]

Other reality TV programs play off the basic formula of *Survivor* but are even meaner. *The Mole* was based on a surreptitious wilder who doesn't reveal his identity while sabotaging others. Hatch may have acted like a mole, but he was up-front about his intentions.

In *Temptation Island*, another hit reality show, the whole point was to test and subvert real-life relationships by enticing participants into infidelity with sexy other partners, with millions of viewers as titillated voyeurs. Tammy, a 27-year-old banker who is an addicted fan, says, "It seems so wrong to me, this whole concept of bringing these singles in to tempt the couples. But it's kind of like a car accident. I couldn't stop watching." Getting rid of people is in the mix here, too, since *Temptation Island* not only plays off the disposability of modern relationships (mates as live-in temps) but also involves repeated votes by participants to jettison others off of the show.[8]

Temptation Island is also a twisted mirror image of *Who Wants to Marry a Millionaire?* Millionaire Rick Rockwell offered millions to a contestant who would actually marry him on TV. While *Temptation Island* broke up relationships through seduction and intrigue, *Millionaire* presented relationships as a strategy for getting rich. Darva Conger, the beautiful blonde nurse who married Rockwell on air, broke down and left him almost immediately, proving that the whole concept was somehow inhuman. But she kept the car she won, went on to pose nude, and turned herself into a celebrity.

The parallels between reality TV and the Ik are almost too obvious to mention. Among the Ik, survival is the only game in town. Relationships are pure manipulation and love is seen as absurd, an impediment to staying alive. The Ik have learned to get their greatest pleasure from duping and betraying their neighbors; every Ik is a cynical strategist, and Richard Hatch would find himself strangely at home among them.

Reality TV, in fact, creates a virtual culture that imitates the wilding culture of the Ik. The only way to survive on *Survivor* is to act like an Ik—that is, to find a way to cheat and ultimately dispose of everyone around you. Among the Ik, this is necessary because everyone is a competitor for the food one needs to stay alive—and, therefore, it's kill or be killed. On *Survivor*, the survival strategy is essentially the same because the producers wrote the rules that way. The question is why the scenario works in the richest country in history, a matter to be addressed shortly. Suffice it to say, *Survivor* sells because it mirrors a survival strategy that millions of Americans have embraced.

Lost, House, and *The Shield*: TV Wilding for Men

"Three people on that island have been killed in cold blood, and they're quote-unquote good people who you're rooting for every week," says Paul Scheer, a 29-year-old fan of the popular ABC series *Lost*. It includes some rough men who end up on an island after a plane crash, battling for survival. But it is even rougher than the reality show version. One of *Lost*'s main protagonists, Sawyer, is an alcoholic narcissist who has no sympathy for Michael, another character who is trying to find his kidnapped son. Sawyer offers the show's moral code: "It's every man for hisself."[9]

Networks like Spike TV, owned by Viacom, interviewed thousands of American males to see what they want to watch on television. The answer is characters like Vic McKay in *The Shield*, who shoots a corrupt fellow officer directly in the face. The actor playing McKay, Michael Chiklis, won an Emmy for his performance in that episode, which received the highest audience rating in the history of the FX network.[10]

Spike TV producers have responded quickly to the demand for sociopathic male heroes. There is Michael Scofield in *Prison Break*, who plots to help his brother escape from jail. Dr. Gregory House, in the show bearing his name revels in popping drugs like Vicodin. Vic McKay, in *The Shield*, is happy to brutalize suspects in his custody. The code of the actors in all these programs, according to Brent Hoff, 36, another fan of *Lost*, is, "Life is hard. Men gotta do what men gotta do, and if some people have to die in the process, so be it."[11] Such characters are becoming staples on the TV landscape. Denis Leary, in *Rescue Me*, plays Tommy Gavin, a firefighter who helps plan the revenge murder of a man who had run over and killed Gavin's son. Gary Randall, a producer who helped create *Melrose Place*, is currently developing a show for Spike TV called *Paradise Salvage*, also starring antiheroes with wilding sensibilities. Randall says that the networks are creating these antisocial stars to get men in touch "with our Neanderthal, animalistic, macho side," in an era when men are supposed to be both more sensitive and more aggressive. The antiheroes help men deal with their internal conflicts and feel better: "You think, 'It's O.K. to go to a strip club and have a couple of beers with your buddies and still go home to your wife and baby and live with yourself."[12]

Scheer, the *Lost* fan, who is an actor himself, says that realistic portrayals on television today do not make traditional moral judgments even about extreme violence. "You don't have to be defined by one act," he says, even if it is murder. Referring to the three people killed on the island in *Lost*, he concludes, "You can say 'I'm messed up and I left my wife, but I'm still a good guy.'"[13] Journalist Warren St. John, whose writing I have drawn upon extensively in this section, notes that the new male heroes are obviously different from earlier good guys like Magnum or Barnaby Jones. "They are also not simply flawed in the classic sense: men who have the occasional affair or who tip the bottle a little too much. Instead," notes St. John, "they are unapologetic about killing, stealing, hoarding and beating their way to achieve personal goals."[14]

Pancho Mansfield, the head of original programming for Spike TV, says he sees network television going the way of *Scarface*. Dr. Robert Thompson, director of the Center for the Study of Popular Television at Syracuse University, says that the new characters can be seen as "an improvement in the sophistication and complexity of television," portraying real-life moral dilemmas more honestly. But he acknowledges that "you could see the proliferation of these types of characters as an indication of the decline of American civilization."[15]

Downtime: A New Wilding Recipe

As the price of happiness ratchets up, the ability of the average American to pay is falling. The great contradiction of today—and a recipe exquisitely designed for wilding—may be the increasing gap between bigger American appetites and shrinking American wallets.

The 1990s were billed as one of the great economic booms in history. The new dot-com economy, with its combination of magical technology and ruthless global corporate restructuring, helped fuel the creation of astonishing new wealth. Many college students, like other young Americans, came to believe that they should be rich by 30, that this was their birthright, and that they had a golden future as millionaire dot-com entrepreneurs.

But the collapse of the dot-com economy and the high-tech Nasdaq in 2000, and the serious economic slowdown that followed, put the fabled new economy in a different light. The fantasy that everyone can become rich in the information economy has soured in the new reality, and now many wonder whether they will keep their jobs or be able to meet their rent and pay off their credit cards. We also learned that the boom never really did reach millions of Americans, since the bulk of the new wealth created in the 1990s was pocketed mainly by the very rich. Moreover, much of the new wealth turned out to be pure illusion, paper wealth that could vanish as magically as it had appeared.

A look back into recent economic history shows that the boom was always contradictory, putting the bigger dreams of most Americans on a collision course with the reality of the American economy. In 1973, for the first time ever, the real wages of the American worker began falling. By 1998, the real wages of the average American worker and the real income of the typical U.S. household had barely risen at all. In other words, 25 years of the Reagan and Clinton "booms" had done very little in real economic terms to help the ordinary American, a sad reality compounded by a big increase in job insecurity and a decrease in pension plans, health coverage, and other employee benefits.[16] Between 1973 and 2000, average real income of the bottom 90 percent of Americans fell 7 percent. As noted in Chapter 1, this trend has continued every year through 2005, with real wages and income of ordinary Americans continuing to stagnate or decline on an annual basis.

Americans were learning to dream big, but only a tiny fraction actually could afford to live big. The richest 1 percent of Americans skimmed off most of the new wealth created by the new economy. While the bottom 90 percent saw their real income decline by 7 percent between 1973 and 2000, the top 1 percent saw their real income increase in the same period 148 percent, the top 0.1 percent saw their income rise 343 percent, and the top 0.01 percent saw their income rise 599 percent.[17] Although wealth was being created rapidly, it was being distributed more unequally than at any time since the 1920s. By 1996, the United States had become the most economically unequal country in the developed world, and the richest 1 percent owned more than 40 percent of the nation's wealth, a near-record high. By 2000, U.S. median wages had declined well beyond those of most European countries, and the U.S. rate of poverty was triple that of northern Europe. Much of this decline reflected the successful attack on unions unleashed by President Reagan in 1981 and taken up enthusiastically by George W. Bush. Corporations have exploited labor weakness in the new global economy by rushing to find cheap labor overseas while breaking union contracts and cutting wages and benefits at home.[18]

While much of the boom has always been an illusion for ordinary Americans, they continue to be glued to the Dream Machine, creating the paradox that *Business Week* calls the "money illusion." They keep spending as if they are "getting the kind of real raises" that they used to get "in the 1960s." Something is profoundly out of kilter, the magazine suggests, because in a period of "crushing new constraints, the average American appears unable to lower his sights."[19]

Of course, the contradiction cuts more or less deeply, depending on where the dreamer sits on the economic ladder. For those on top, whether business executives or fabled dot-commers, there is the problem, as the *New York Times* reported, of "feeling poor on $600,000 a year." The *Times* describes the misery of young Wall Street financiers and New York doctors and lawyers who feel strapped by the costs of their million-dollar co-ops. The pain is tolerable, however, as author Kevin Phillips writes, because Reaganomics (and Clintonomics) unleashed an upsurge of riches to the wealthy that "has not been seen since the late nineteenth century, the era of the Vanderbilts, Morgans, and Rockefellers." As the economy declines, the rich can keep dreaming big dreams.[20]

Where the contradiction draws blood is at the bottom. The poor, no less than the rich, stay tuned in to the Dream Machine in bad times as well as good. They are always the "last hired and the first fired," so every business cycle wreaks havoc with their dreams. Their boats did not rise with the Clinton boom, and they became dangerously poorer, partly due to the cutting of the social safety net under Reagan and the first Bush, and partly due to Clinton's willingness to follow the leadership of Speaker Newt Gingrich and his Republican colleagues in shredding it further. After Clinton's dismantling of welfare, millions of poor people were left without housing, medical care, jobs, or educational opportunities; 6 million children—one of every four kids under six years of age in America—were officially poor. Mired in third world conditions of poverty while video-bombarded with first world dreams, rarely has a population suffered a greater gap between socially cultivated appetites and economically available opportunities.

Blood has been drawn in the great American middle as well. As they work longer and harder to get their share of the Dream, middle-class Americans are sinking. *Business Week* says that Joe Sixpack "plunged into debt, thinking 'Buy now, before the price goes up again.' With a little luck, he figured, his next raise would keep the credit-card bills and the mortgage covered."[21]

Unable to "lower his sights," Joe kept "borrowing. He now own[ed] a house, a big Japanese color TV and VCR, an American car, and a Korean personal computer—all bought on credit." By now, Joe had 10 credit cards, which he used to live well above his means, spending $1.03 or more for every $1.00 he earned. This credit-financed binge gave Joe the illusion of living the American Dream, and he wasn't alone: all across America, consumers were piling up unprecedented credit-card debt, with the number of Americans declaring bankruptcy in 2000 about double that in 1990. Total credit-card debt skyrocketed to $735 billion in 2004 compared with $243 billion in 1990, almost tripling.[22] The transfer of debt from government to ordinary citizens has been one of the great revolutions in the new economy.

Joe Sixpack's wife is working, which helps pay for the "children's orthodontist bills and family entertainment, but it falls short of what they'll need to send the kids to college." Judith Bateman, the wife of a Michigan Bell Telephone dispatcher, told *Business Week* that she and her husband run a big weekly "deficit, but until times get better, which she keeps hoping will happen, she says, 'We enter a lot of sweepstakes.'"[23]

Young and Wild: Drinking, Cheating, and Other Campus Sports

The young are among the more exuberant wilders in America. Progeny of the Reagan-Bush I-Clinton-Bush II era, and the most vulnerable to the slings and arrows of economic fortune, they are an ominous harbinger of America's future.

Boston University professors Donald Kanter and Philip Mirvis report that a clear majority of youth under age 24, in contrast to only 43 percent of the population as a whole, are "unvarnished cynics" who view "selfishness as fundamental to people's character." Most students do not disagree with this assessment of their generation. On the first day of one semester, I asked a class of about 40 college students, most of them economics majors, whether the average student on campus would agree or

48

disagree with a series of highly charged statements about selfishness and self-interest. Their answers were not reassuring. Sixty-five percent said that the average student would agree that "there is nothing more important to me than my own economic well-being," and 72 percent said that the typical student would agree that "I am not responsible for my neighbor." Seventy-five percent said their generation believed that "it's everyone for himself or herself in the American economy," and 88 percent said their fellow students would agree that "in our society everyone has to look out for number one." A stunning 96 percent thought their generation believed that "competition is the most important virtue in a market society," and 65 percent expected a typical student to agree that "people do not let moral scruples get in the way of their own advancement." In discussion, they explained that most students were apprehensive about their economic prospects, fearing that they would not do as well as their parents. If they wanted to succeed, they said, they would have to focus all their energies on "buttering their own bread."[24]

On the positive side, significantly lower percentages of the students, ranging from 30 percent to 50 percent, said that they personally subscribed to the selfish sentiments cited. This is an indication that a significant sector of the younger generation remains committed to moral principles. My impression as a teacher is that a large percentage of today's college students remain generous and decent, although increasingly confused and torn between "making it" and remaining faithful to their moral ideals. Unfortunately, many sacrifice their intellectual loves to make big money, such as the student with a profound passion for the study of history who decided to give it up and become a corporate lawyer so that he could live the high life.

Growing student cynicism has led to an explosion of wilding on campuses across the country, a phenomenon that started over a decade ago. A report by the Carnegie Foundation for the Advancement of Teaching released in 1990 found "a breakdown of civility and other disruptive forces" that are leaving campus life "in tatters." Of special concern was an epidemic of cheating, as well as a mushrooming number of racial attacks, rapes, and other hate crimes. Words, the currency of the university, have been increasingly "used not as the key to understanding, but as weapons of assault."[25]

Campuses are no longer ivy-walled sanctuaries but increasingly have become sites of theft, sexual assault, property damage, and other crimes. The epidemic of alcoholism among students—70 percent qualify as binge drinkers at some colleges—has contributed to these rising crime rates. A study of 104 campuses conducted by the Harvard School of Public Health identified 44 colleges in which a majority of the students were binge drinkers. On these campuses, 9 out of 10 students said that they had suffered assaults, thefts, or other forms of violent intrusion, often by drunk students.[26]

Much campus crime, however, is committed soberly by cold, calculating student wilders. A Harvard University student pleaded guilty in 1995 to stealing $6,838 raised at Harvard for the Jimmy Fund, a charity to help kids with cancer. Joann Plachy, a law student at Florida State University, was charged in 1995 with hiring a professional killer to murder a secretary who accused Plachy of having stolen a copy of an exam. In 2001, Joseph M. Mesa Jr., a 20-year-old freshman at Gallaudet University, reportedly confessed to killing two other students living in his dormitory, one four months after the other. He stabbed one classmate and fatally beat the other. His motive: petty robbery involving a few hundred dollars.[27]

The view of the campus as a haven from violent crime or other societal wilding is now as obsolete as the notion of the family itself being a safe haven. Ernest L. Boyer, the Carnegie Foundation's president, said that college promotional material "masks disturbing realities of student life" that mirror the "hard-edged competitive world" of the larger society.[28] Desperate for good grades, huge numbers of students routinely plagiarize papers and cheat on exams. Studies on many campuses, including Indiana University and the University of Tennessee, show that a majority of students admit to submitting papers written by others or copying large sections of friends' papers. A majority also confess to looking at other students' answers during in-class exams. "You could check for cheating in any class and you'd certainly find a significant portion of the people cheating," one M.I.T. student said, adding casually, "it's one way of getting through M.I.T."[29]

A controversy brewing in 2000 about fraudulent college admission essays shows that the cheating begins early in academic careers. Mothers, fathers, and other relatives often ghostwrite their childrens' essays, and professional entrepreneurs are making entire careers off of the new trend. Michele Hernandez, who used to work for admissions at Dartmouth, opened a dot-com that caters to applicants who need somebody to craft a college admissions essay for them. For $1,500, she will help write and polish the essay; if you come from a rich enough family, you can pay her $4,500 to complete your entire application.[30]

Technology, especially computers, has also made life easier for the new generation of student cheaters. Students routinely ask their friends for copies of old course papers on computer disk. It doesn't take much effort to rework a paper on a computer for a new class. One student at an elite Boston university said that nobody on campus thinks twice about the morality of such high-tech cheating. Students can buy online term papers about popular texts, including *The Wilding of America.*

Books on how to cheat are hot sellers on campus. Michael Moore, 24, has written a primer, *Cheating 101*, which has sold briskly on campuses around the country. He describes how to stuff crib sheets filled with useful facts into one's jeans or under one's baseball cap. He offers tips about how students can communicate answers on multiple-choice tests by shifting their feet under desks in a prearranged code. About cheating, Moore says that "everyone's doing it" and that he's making an "honest living." About his decision to make an "honest living" by writing a how-to book on cheating, Moore says, "I'm just exercising my First Amendment rights."[31]

Although a significant minority of students are idealistic and intensely concerned about others, the majority appear to be increasingly cynical about their studies and their futures. They want to "invest as little time in their studies as possible," the Carnegie report suggests, while collecting their meal ticket and moving on to the professional gravy train. Fifty-five percent of faculty members complain that "most undergraduates . . . only do enough to get by." Carnegie Foundation President Boyer, however, noted that faculty are complicit in the problem by pursuing "their own research at the expense of teaching." He might have added that some faculty and administrators are the worst role models, as can be seen by looking at the growing faculty research scandal. In the 1990s, Congressman John Dingell uncovered science fraud in the biology labs of M.I.T. as well as unlawful diversion of research overhead expenditures for such things as "flowers, country-club memberships, and going-away parties for departing deans" in many of the nation's most famous universities, including Harvard, Stanford, and the California Institute of Technology. Stanford University President Donald Kennedy resigned after the media reported the extensive diversion of Stanford overhead funds to pay for such extravagances as a yacht. The reputation of Nobel laureate, David Baltimore, one of the country's foremost cancer researchers and president of Rockefeller University, has been tarnished by the National Institutes of Health's conclusion that a member of Baltimore's own laboratory falsified data.[32]

In 2000 and 2001, controversies broke out about biotech and medical researchers making lucrative deals with pharmaceutical giants. This is just one sign of the growing presence of big corporations in university life. More professors are seeking equity stakes in companies or creating their own start-ups that give them a vested financial interest in how the data come out. As corporations fund bigger slices of academic research and the dot-com fever spreads among students, more professors sacrifice teaching quality and even research integrity to pursue their own fortunes. In February 2001, the dean of the Harvard Medical School ordered a broad review of the relations between the medical school and corporations funding research, including companies in which the university itself has equity. Dean Joseph Martin acknowledged that serious institutional bias may arise as universities and individual professors favor research linked to companies that can return the highest profit. Campus life breaks down as students, faculty, and administrators follow the narrow paths of their own careers and financial interests.[33]

Grand Theft Auto, Doom 3, and *Custer's Revenge*: Video Wilding for Fun and Profit

In the wildly popular video game *Grand Theft Auto III*, players can carjack a vehicle and then run over and kill pedestrians.[34] Players can also work for a crime boss and kill rival gang members. They can even pick up a prostitute, have sex, and then murder her in order to get back their money.[35]

Grand Theft Auto III, created in 2001, is just one in a series, including a blockbuster sequel, *Grand Theft Auto: San Andreas*. In *San Andreas*, one of the requirements to advance in the game is to murder a police officer. In the next sequel, *Grand Auto Theft: Vice City*, players join up with a Haitian or Cuban gang, then secretly team up with the other side, and use racial hate language as they enjoy murderous shoot-outs.[36]

Grand Theft Auto is just one of a huge number of computer and video games that are among the most popular ways to have fun in America. They are especially popular among young people, including college students. When I asked my own students what they would include in this new edition of wilding, many of them put at the top of their list *Grand Theft Auto* and related games (second on their list was use of steroids and other drugs in sports, a suggestion made even before the new sensational allegations that slugger Barry Bonds had used multiple performance-enhancing drugs for years to move to the top of the all-time best home run hitters).[37]

Violence is the common denominator of the video games. The Interfaith Center on Corporate Responsibility warns of the 10 most violent games: *Doom 3*; *Grand Theft Auto: San Andreas*; *Gunslinger Girls 2*; *Half-Life 2*;

Halo 2; *Hitman: Blood Money*; *Manhunt*; *Mortal Kombat: Deception*; *Postal 2*; and *Shadow Heart*. *Doom 3* is the ultimate monster murder game, based on Mars, where the player goes through hell while perfecting his strategies to kill off blood-thirsty demons.[38] *Mortal Kombat* is a martial arts series drenched with blood that rewards players with a "Fatality" move, where you get to kill a defeated opponent in a particularly savage way.

While extreme violence of all kinds is the hallmark of these games, sexual violence and pornography are particularly notable. In *Custer's Revenge*, an early example released in 1983, the player moves a nude General Custer across the screen until he can mount a naked Native American female tied to a cactus or pole. In *BMX XXX*, players who win the game are rewarded with video footage of topless strippers. Embedded within *Grand Auto Theft: San Andreas* is a minigame allowing the player to engage in interactive sex.[39]

The remarkable popularity of the games suggests a widespread appetite among Americans for a kind of violence that can only be characterized as full-blown wilding. The main reward in these games is the sheer thrill of brutal killing and sexual violence, forms of expressive wilding. Of course, violent themes have played out in cowboy and Indian films and other movies for a long time. What is new is the incredible savagery of the violence and the direct personal engagement that the technology makes possible. In *General Custer*, for example, the player himself moves the general toward the naked Native American woman, becoming part of the rape scene. Computers and video sticks turn the spectator into the active protagonist in games like *Grand Auto Theft* so that he becomes the perpetrator of multiple murders. The earlier spectator of cowboys-and-Indians films is now the actor, with virtual violence blurring the distinction between game and life.

Controversy rages whether games like *Grand Theft Auto* or *Doom 3* actually incite violence or simply reflect its legitimacy and prevalence in social institutions. Either way, they can be seen as part and parcel of a wilding culture. Some studies suggest that players of the most violent games become more aggressive and violent, a matter of widespread concern after Columbine and other school shootings but also a matter of considerable debate among researchers.[40] The U.S. military now uses games like *Grand Theft Auto* as a recruiting tool.[41] This approach may suggest that the military sees the games as good measures of who is likely to want to become a soldier or to become a good killer in real combat.

Institutions, including the military, are developing their own video games to teach recruits both skills and a worldview, according to Professor James Gee, a video game expert and professor of education at the University of Wisconsin. In the game *America's Army*, soldiers learn how to carry out combat operations. Other violent organizations, including neo-Nazi groups like National Alliance, have developed their own recruiting and training games. In the National Alliance's game, *Ethnic Cleansing*, "a player runs through a rotted city, killing blacks, Latinos, and Jews." To promote critical reflection on contemporary U.S. culture, Gee says, "People ought to use *Grand Theft Auto* in the classroom to think about values and ideology."[42]

While the players are mostly engaged in expressive wilding, it's a different matter for the companies who make huge profits off the sales. Gee points that the gaming industry makes more money than Hollywood.[43] Corporations such as Rockstar Games, which produces *Grand Theft Auto*, are less concerned with the thrills than the bottom line and financial killing, the core of instrumental wilding. Companies that sell murder and rape, particularly for the enjoyment of young people, are certainly good candidates for what I call "corporate wilding."

In the recent film *The Corporation*, based on a book of the same name, the creators ask how a psychiatrist would diagnose a corporation if it were a person.[44] The answer: a psychopath. Psychopaths have no moral qualms about doing harm to others to make money or get power. This would seem a fair characterization of the corporations, such as Rockstar, that make the most violent and vicious video games. Whether it is also a fair characterization of the giant firms at the heart of the global and American economy is the subject of our next two chapters.

All-American Drug Dealing: Unattainable Goals and Illegitimate Means

"I spend long hours, night and day, in crack houses and on drug-copping corners, observing, befriending, and interviewing street dealers, addicts, and anyone else who will pause to talk to me." Those are the words of anthropologist Philippe Bourgois, who spent five years living in an East Harlem tenement. Though he was not looking to score a big drug deal, he was trying to get inside the minds of crack dealers to see what makes them tick. His conclusions are remarkable, suggesting that inner-city children bear a greater resemblance to careerist college students than anyone had imagined. Wilding at the bottom springs from the same basic recipe as wilding higher up.[45]

Bourgois describes a broken social world reminiscent of the Ik. Violence is everywhere, especially among people working or living with each other. Jackie was eight months pregnant when her crack-dealing husband, a drug lord of substantial means, was caught and sentenced to jail. Before he left, she shot him in the stomach in front of his associates. Instead of leaving her money before he was sent to prison, he had been squandering thousands on young women and "bragging about it."[46]

Jackie's violence so impressed the new drug lord that he hired her. At about the same time, Jackie started dating Julio, another dealer, who was being stalked by the lover of his ex-girlfriend, Rose, for refusing to pay for her abortion after Julio had gotten her pregnant. Julio knew how to deal with violence, for he had been hired to guard a crack den where murderous stick-ups were common. On one occasion, Julio admitted "that he had been very nervous when robbers held a gun to his temple and asked for money and crack." Julio impressed his boss when he successfully hid some of the stash in a hollowed-out statue of a saint. But he did not tell his boss the whole truth. Julio "exaggerated to his boss the amount that had been stolen; he pocketed the difference himself."[47]

Julio had started out straight, working as a messenger for a magazine. There were no career possibilities for him there, and when he needed money to support a new crack habit, he realized he needed a better job fast. Like other crack dealers Bourgois got to know, Julio had become fed up with the "low wages and bad treatment" of the jobs available to him. He had bigger dreams of a career "offering superior wages and a dignified workplace," and he found it in the underground economy. After he started dealing crack, the money and new sense of "responsibility, success, and prestige" allowed him to kick his own crack habit.[48]

Bourgois concluded from his talks with Julio and other dealers that the view that the poor have been badly socialized and do not share mainstream values is wrong. On the contrary, ambitious, energetic inner-city youth are attracted to the underground [drug dealing] economy precisely because they believe in the rags-to-riches American Dream. Like many in the mainstream, they are frantically trying to get their piece of the pie as fast as possible.[49]

Drug dealers such as Julio, Bourgois finds, are meticulously following the "model for upward mobility" of the era, "aggressively setting themselves up as private entrepreneurs." Their dreams of wealth and success are precisely those of other youngsters tuned in to the glitter of television and videos. Rather than abandoning their dreams when the hard reality of their economic position sets in, they adopt an ambitious strategy consistent with the opportunities open to them.

Bourgois hints that it is hard to distinguish these street entrepreneurs from those in business schools and on Wall Street. They are equally dedicated to "making it" and equally ruthless in their business dealings. They are prepared to take unusual risks to realize their dream of fast money. The successful ones enjoy the same lifestyle, speeding "around in well-waxed Lincoln Continentals or Mercedes-Benzes." They invite friends and acquaintances "out to dinner in expensive restaurants almost every night." When a dealer parks his car on the street, "a bevy of attentive men and women . . . run to open the door for him."[50]

"Using the channels available," Bourgois writes, people such as Julio can be seen "as rugged individualists on an unpredictable frontier where fortune, fame, and destruction are all just around the corner." Widely presumed to be the archenemies of the American way of life, inner-city drug wilders are instead among the purest products of the American Dream.[51]

In 1995, William Adler published a book about ghetto children and drugs that conveys the same sad truth. Adler focused on the four Chambers brothers, originally from rural Arkansas, who moved to Detroit and built a gigantic cocaine business with all the trappings of a Fortune 500 corporation. The Chambers brothers were arrested and sent to jail, but not before they had created a conglomerate grossing at least $55 million—tax-free—a year.[52]

The Chambers story is not about inner-city youth as drug consumers, but as capitalists. The brothers promised their young employees, recruited from both cotton fields and the inner city, that they could get rich in a year, but only if they would give up their girlfriends and work hard. The crack company enforced strict discipline and work rules, and it offered health and benefit plans, performance bonuses, and quality improvement incentives. When the Chambers brothers were put in jail, other young crack entrepreneurs quickly took their place. After all, for thousands of inner-city youth, crack dealing is the only path to the American Dream.[53]

4

U.S. Business vs. Us

Global Capitalism and Corporate Wilding

*What do you mean **we**, kemo sabe?*

—Tonto to the Lone Ranger

A Fish Rots from the Head First

In January 2001, the U.S. Department of Labor reported that a clothing plant, Daewoosa Factory, in American Samoa—a U.S. territory in the Pacific—that produced for J.C. Penney, Sears, and Target was abusing hundreds of workers who were held as indentured servants. A Labor Department investigator said that many workers, who looked like "walking skeletons," lived "36 to a room and received bare-bones meals." The National Labor Committee (NLC), a New York–based public interest group, carried out its own detailed investigation, reporting that workers were beaten; sexually harassed; threatened with deportation; starved; forced to work 12- to 18-hour days, seven days a week; and made to live in rat-infested dormitories.[1] In 2003, Mr. Kil Soo Lee, the owner of the factory, was convicted by the Justice Department of holding more than 200 workers in "involuntary servitude." He faces life in prison after being found guilty of 14 of the 18 charges against him, in the largest human trafficking case ever investigated by the FBI and prosecuted by the Justice Department.[2]

On February 18, 2001, a report on the TV program *60 Minutes* detailed some unseemly facts about the diamonds we associate with love and marriage. Brutal wars are fought in Zaire, Sierra Leone, the Congo, and other African countries to control access to the diamond mines. *60 Minutes* focused on the role of giant corporations that allegedly help finance these wars, which are among the most brutal in recent memory (the Sierra Leone war is fought mainly by children whose fate when captured is to have their hands cut off). The *60 Minutes* report also explained why diamonds are so expensive; it is not because they are naturally scarce but because the largest companies exercise monopoly power to restrict supply and extract huge profits.

On May 10, 1993, a toy factory near Bangkok burned to the ground, killing 188 workers, mostly teenage girls. One surviving worker who had jumped out of an upper-story window told investigators that she and some of the other workers had tried to escape down the stairs but had been commanded by supervisors to get back to work. Her sister also had jumped but died. The 188 deaths made this the worst industrial accident in history, exceeding the 146 garment workers killed in New York's Triangle Shirtwaist garment factory fire in 1911. But while the Triangle fire helped inspire an era of regulatory reform, the tragedy in Thailand stands as a symbol of a new age of unregulated global wilding.

The Thai factory was owned by Kader Industrial Toy Company, a giant, global manufacturing conglomerate that contracts with Toys "R" Us, J.C. Penney, Fisher-Price, and other major American companies. *New York Times* columnist Bob Herbert wrote that the company had been running a sweatshop with young girls who were "semi-slave laborers." Calling it "terror in toyland," Herbert said that workers such as these girls slave for "grotesquely low wages and in disgusting and extremely dangerous conditions."[3]

We have focused thus far on wilding by individuals, but wilding by corporations and governments plays a huge role in our growing crisis. Such wilding, as discussed in Chapter 1, involves behavior by institutions that enhance their own wealth and power by harming workers, citizens, and communities. Our new wilding crisis—in the United States and increasingly in the world at large—is fueled by the predatory behavior of multinational firms that seek fast profits at any price. Such corporations collude with governments and are driven both by the financial markets and by unfettered greed.

This chapter's focus on corporate wilding helps make clear that wilding starts from the top. The leaders of giant corporations and their political and intellectual allies are at the heart of the wilding crisis. They create the institutional conditions and reigning ideologies that catalyze wilding at all levels of society.

A thin line has always divided the capitalist quest for profit from economic wilding. John D. Rockefeller, Andrew Carnegie, and the other robber barons of the late nineteenth century who built American capitalism were spectacular economic wilders, famous for their brutal treatment of workers and corrupt, monopolistic practices. In the famous 1893 Home-

58

stead Steel strike, Carnegie ordered his workers shot. Since then, we have suffered repeated cycles of wilding—the Roaring Twenties, with its huge speculative binges and political scandals, for example—that have chipped away at the nation's moral fabric.

The tenuous line between business success and wilding is being even more dangerously blurred by two fundamental changes. The first is the institutionalization of the radically individualistic political economy ushered in during the 1980s and championed now by President George W. Bush. The Reagan revolution enshrined a new privatization and deregulation, worshiping business and profits and demonizing labor unions and government. It has become the dominant ideology of our times and is fanning the flames of wilding from Wall Street to Main Street.

The second change is the rise of global capitalism, the most fundamental economic shift of our times. The new global system threatens to destroy the social dikes against corporate wilding that national governments, labor organizations, and communities have struggled to build throughout the last two centuries of the Industrial Revolution.

Capitalism vs. Community: Sociological Prophets and Global Profits

The making of a global economy is the real business of the twenty-first century. Huge multinational companies are spreading their wings for global flight, capitalizing on technological and communications revolutions to produce and market their wares from the Amazon to the Pacific Basin. Wall Street is eagerly financing the new global system, helping create the financial markets that send trillions of dollars across the globe every day at lightning speed. Meanwhile, America's political leaders, both Republican and Democratic, are sponsoring a torrent of free-trade treaties, from the North American Free Trade Agreement (NAFTA) and the Free Trade for Africa Agreement to the proposed new Free Trade Agreement of the Americas. The World Trade Organization (WTO)—the target of the turbulent 1999 Seattle protests—is laying the legal groundwork for a new economic world order.

Globalization is being created by a new "corpocracy"—a worldwide nexus of financial markets and corporations that now dominates the world. There are more than 45,000 corporations in the world today, but the 200 largest companies rule, with sales comprising more than 25 percent of the world's total gross domestic product (GDP). Financial institutions are especially important, with the 100 largest banks controlling $21 trillion in assets, about three-fourths of the world's wealth. The biggest companies, such as Citigroup, General Electric (GE), and General Motors (GM), are global empires with no national loyalty. They are larger and more powerful than most countries; GM's annual sales are greater than the entire GDP of Poland; Wal-Mart's are greater than the GDP of Israel or Denmark.[4]

The rush toward a global economy is the most revolutionary development of our times. It has the potential to bring many benefits, including a more robust world economy, dynamic growth in corners of the world that have known only poverty and despair, and even the development of a new world community. But in its current form, it threatens to pit the interests of businesses against those of their host societies, creating a new predatory capitalism based on worldwide economic wilding.

Concepts developed a century ago by the founders of sociology are powerful tools for understanding this new wilding threat. As we saw in Chapter 1, the great French sociologist Émile Durkheim argued that early industrial capitalism, by destroying traditional communities and encouraging individual ambition and mobility, endangered social solidarity and the survival of society itself. The burgeoning industrial era bred a culture of egoism and anomie—egoism reflecting the loss of community and anomie, the rise of socially unregulated dreams and passions. Egoism and anomie are fertile breeding grounds for wilding, spawning self-interest, greed, and violence that can spiral out of control and subvert society.

Globalism promises to further weaken the social ties and values that civilize both individuals and business. Unencumbered by national loyalties, corporations now roam the world searching for the cheapest labor in desperately poor countries. As corporations move overseas, U.S. communities themselves become more vulnerable, with shuttered plants and industrial ghost towns becoming fixtures of the American landscape. Thrown into competition with workers in developing countries, millions of U.S. workers face an uncertain future, and many become "temps," unable to find steady, full-time employment. In the words of some observers, the multinational corporation is itself becoming a virtual, or hollow, community, with transient "contractors" replacing permanent employees. This erosion of community intensifies both egoism and anomie, transforming growing numbers of employees into rootless, atomized "entrepreneurs," constantly seeking reemployment. At the same time, the multinationals and their top managers are increasingly liberated from governmental regulation, free to pursue unbounded appetites for global power and vast worldwide profits.

Although the twentieth century proved Karl Marx's predictions about capitalism's death to be folly, globalism eerily vindicates Marx's view of the potential for capitalist wilding. The market's function of reducing all behavior to the cash nexus and naked self-interest becomes increasingly relevant in a global economy. Employees who must act as entrepreneurs find no shelter from the market and survive only by embracing relentless self-promotion. Major American corporations, seeking bonanza profits, pursue child labor in India and prison labor in China.

Marx recognized that the great moral problem of capitalism is the incentive of business to make money by exploiting its employees. In a global economy, this problem assumes a new scale. The core of the current wilding threat arises from the intensification of appetites whetted by the new fantastic global possibilities and from the ingenious new multinational corporate strategies for realizing them.

The Musical Chairs of Global Business: The New Corporate Wilding

The key is a game of global musical chairs—a master strategy for maximizing profits by pitting national workforces against one another. Corporations able to hire cheap labor around the world can threaten to leave a community unless workers submit to lower pay or local governments agree to various incentives to keep companies from pulling up stakes. Such intimidation has long been one of business's trump cards, played 50 years ago by Massachusetts and New Hampshire textile mill owners, for example, who relocated from New England to the South after northern workers unionized. But musical chairs becomes a game plan for unparalleled wilding when the theater shifts from the nation-state to the world—and the mill owners can relocate to South Korea or Mexico.

Here, the analyses of Durkheim and Marx converge. Musical chairs in the national arena has been a regulated game, with national governments playing the role of arbiter and community protector of last resort. Such national regulation restricts the degree of egoism and anomie that can arise from the economic game and limits exploitation by prohibiting child labor, enforcing minimum wages, and protecting the environment. Within U.S. national capitalism, labor agreements and government programs created during and after the 1930s New Deal era helped ensure that higher profits for companies translated into higher wages for their workers and more resources for their host communities. This linking of corporate and community interests lent some credibility to the corporate manifesto expressed in the 1950s by the president of General Motors: "What's good for GM is good for America."

Under global capitalism today, however, there is no effective regulatory watchdog for the world community. As an unregulated game, global musical chairs opens societies all over the world to a purely egoistic and anomic world economy. The danger is that such a game veers, as we shall see in the rest of this chapter, toward new rules that allow businesses to maximize profit by undermining the health of their host societies. As the global economy regresses back to the raw capitalism of an earlier era, the social protections built up over two centuries are jeopardized.

Global economic wilding is the fruit of active collaboration between multinational companies and national governments. Markets, whether national or global, are always shaped by those with power, and while it may seem strange that national governments would collaborate in their own demise, they have, during the last two decades, played a major role in subverting their own authority as they help write the rules of the new global game. This collaboration reflects incestuous entanglements among multinationals and political elites in both developed and developing countries who have struck deals that too often subvert their own societies. These deals have triggered a downward competitive spiral—a "race to the bottom," as some global observers have dubbed it—among economies around the world, pushing much of America toward third-world wages and working conditions while intensifying the misery of already-impoverished masses in poor countries.[5]

Wilding around the World: The Third World as Global Sweatshop

On the campus where I teach, a Vietnam-style revolt has mushroomed in recent years. Students have been outraged about Boston College (BC) caps and sweatshirts allegedly being made in sweatshops in Indonesia, Mexico, and El Salvador. As my students have pushed the university, with considerable success, to stop using sweatshop products (the BC bookstore now sells only BC sweatshirts and caps produced by plants certified to be "sweat-free"), similar protests have spread like wildfire across many other campuses throughout the country. Sweatshops have become the symbol of the economic wilding at the heart of the new global economy.

Some students may have read about the famous Gilded Age journalist, Upton Sinclair, who ventured into the terrifying meat factories of Chicago. In his classic book *The Jungle*, published in 1906, he described a world of 16-hour workdays, in which laborers were paid pennies per hour to work in slaughterhouses producing poisoned meat rotting with blood and hair. A century later, Sinclair's graphic sketch of the sweatshop economy still scorches the brain and shapes our understanding of economic wilding of an earlier age.

The Upton Sinclair of today's global economy is Charles Kernaghan, the New York–based muckraker most famous for his exposure of sweatshops in El Salvador making clothes for Kathie Lee Gifford's clothing line. Kathie Lee claims to have broken down in tears when she listened to Salvadoran workers who had stitched the clothes bearing her label. Most workers were young girls, aged 14 to 24, and they outlined their 20-hour shifts from 6:50 A.M. to 3:00 A.M. the next morning, with one 40-minute break in the day at noon for lunch. The girls described death threats for attempted unionizing, mandatory pregnancy tests, forced overtime, and starvation wages of 60 cents an hour. Managers refused to let them get up or move from their worksites, or to permit more than two daily bathroom visits. The girls also told of bosses cursing and yelling at them to sew faster and exceed the very high production norm of 100 to 150 pieces an hour. Their plants are behind barbed wire and look like prisons.

Ground zero of the global workshop is China, with its 1 billion–plus workers. In December 2005, after numerous trips to Chinese factories, Kernaghan's organization, the NLC, reported on its own intensive research on sweatshops in China, with a particular focus on Wal-Mart's Chinese contractors. One 2005 report on the Lungcheong factory, which produces toys for Wal-Mart, was carried out over a four-year period, and concluded that sustained violations included "child labor, paying below China's minimum wage, forced overtime . . . , women denied their legal paid maternity leave, termination of workers injured on the job, production quotas of painting 2,000 toy trucks a day, 250 an hour, one every 14.4 seconds, workers paid just 18 cents for each $64.97 truck they assume for Wal-Mart, workers housed 12 to each primitive, dark and gloomy dorm room, and fed food they describe as awful."[6] Kernaghan describes an equally grim picture at another Chinese factory, where workers reported producing toys for Wal-Mart:

> At the Huangwu No. 2 Toy factory, workers are forced to work 15 to 19 hours a day, from 7:30 A.M. to 10:30 P.M, or even until 3:00 A.M., seven days a week. Workers must complete one operation every three seconds, repeating the same

furious motion 10,000 times a day. The constant repetition wears off their skin, leaving them with sore, blistered and bleeding hands and fingers. It is not a pretty sight, but Wal-Mart says it has a code of conduct and everything is fine in its suppliers' factories in China, which is why, we imagine, Wal-Mart continues to hide its fine factories.

Kernaghan concludes, "Workers are kept in a state of terror, knowing that if they were to say a single truthful word about abusive factory conditions, they would be immediately fired. Wal-Mart's monitoring is a sham. Wal-Mart's bargains are based on misery."[7] Wal-Mart has responded that in recent years it has expanded its in-house global monitoring program to address such abusive practices, a claim that I will examine shortly.

Abusive labor practices are not limited to the giant Wal-Marts of the world. Even a company such as New Balance, which prides itself on its sensitivity to outsourcing and its social responsibility, is not immune. In a January 8, 2006, NLC report, Kernaghan writes:

> Workers making New Balance sneakers at the Hongyuan Shoe factory in China are being paid just 41 cents an hour, while they are forced to work grueling 14.5 to 15.8-hour shifts, six and seven days a week. There is no regularly scheduled day off. Workers are routinely at the factory 96 hours a week. Workers are forced to work 36 hours of overtime each week, but then cheated of their legal overtime pay. Workers are fined 1.5 hours' wages for each minute they are late. Workers who bring "outsiders into the factory," disseminate "rumors" or encourage strikes will be immediately fired and face criminal charges. Workers are housed in primitive, crowded dorm rooms sleeping in triple-level bunk beds. Women workers must shower in front of the men. The sickening smell of plastic fumes hangs heavy in the factory air, and in some departments the noise level is so high workers have to shout and gesture with their hands to be understood. Workers say factory food is so awful they have to force themselves to swallow it—including rice contaminated with rat feces. Workers must pay for the water they drink in the factory.[8]

Despite the claim by workers that many of their products carried New Balance labels, New Balance denied contracting with the Hongyuan plant, although it acknowledged contracting with another Chinese facility owned and operated by Likai, the parent company of the Hongyuan plant, where it claims such abuses do not exist. It will be important to see how New Balance, a company that permits independent inspections of contractor plants and brands itself partly around its responsibility to workers, responds to these allegations.[9]

China is not the only offender. Most developing countries have established special "export processing zones" or "free-trade zones" that offer "tax holidays" to multinationals and exempt them from environmental codes and labor laws. Sometimes walled off behind barbed-wire fences, these zones—where corporations locate their sweatshops and get state protection for every manner of economic wilding—have been described as "huge labor camps," often controlled by special police forces. The most famous of these zones, and among the most important to American companies, is along the U.S.-Mexican border, which is the site of the *maquiladora* plants that now reach well into the Mexican interior.[10]

Growing out of the Border Industrialization Program of 1965, the *maquiladoras* are a classic instance of collaboration between multinationals and government. The Mexican government offered corporations favorable land deals, waived custom clearance and import duties, and agreed to low taxes and, tacitly, the right to run their businesses with a free hand, exempt from environmental and labor laws. The U.S. government did its share by running political interference for U.S. companies and giving them technical assistance and tax breaks for going south of the border. The passage of NAFTA in 1993 facilitated the huge American corporate exodus to south of the border, swelling the ranks of displaced Mexican workers in agriculture and other industries that cannot survive American competition.[11]

The NLC has documented labor rights violations in Mexico and other Central American countries by Alcoa, Wal-Mart, and other global companies that, like the practices in China, are full-blown corporate wilding. Regarding Alcoa's practices, which were also discussed on CNN's *Lou Dobbs*, on July 22, 2005, Kernaghan writes that "Alcoa workers in Mexico, manufacturing auto parts for export to the U.S., earn a base wage of just $1.21 an hour, trapping them in deplorable living conditions. In Piedras Negras, many Alcoa workers sell their blood plasma twice a week in order to eke out an existence. In Acuña, Alcoa workers live in primitive one- and two-room cinderblock huts, lacking windows and potable water." Kernaghan continues:

> In the race to the bottom in the global economy—and moving from NAFTA to CAFTA—even these wages are too high and these living conditions too extravagant. Alcoa has shifted 2,500 jobs from Mexico to Honduras and is now threatening its Mexican workers, "We can hire three Hondurans for every one of you Mexicans." Alcoa is trying to slash wages and benefits in Mexico by 25 percent. Alcoa workers in Honduras earn 68 cents an hour. Like their colleagues in Mexico, they have no rights to freedom of association or to organize. Anyone even suspected of doing so will be fired and blacklisted.[12]

Alcoa defends its wages, saying that it pays among the highest in the region and that if it paid even higher salaries, it would lose business to rivals paying less. It is true that we need systemic change to put a global floor on wages, so that workers around the world are protected against such brutal conditions and assured a living wage. But wages are such a small percentage of costs that Alcoa could increase wages without increasing its prices even under the current global system.

Labor violations in Central and Latin America are all too familiar to a whistle-blower at Wal-Mart, who has asserted that Wal-Mart's monitoring of factories for labor or human rights violation is a sham. James Lynn, who is suing Wal-Mart after he claimed the company fired him for whistle-blowing (Wal-Mart denies this), was in charge of certification of monitoring for Central and Latin American Wal-Mart contractors. Fired in 2002, Lynn monitored Central and Latin American factories sourcing to Wal-Mart before his dismissal. He told his story to the NLC and to the *New York Times*. Kernaghan writes that Lynn documented a consistent pattern of gross women's and human rights violations and harsh sweatshop conditions. In factories producing for Wal-Mart, Lynn found mandatory pregnancy testing, pat-downs, locked fire exits, workers fainting from excessive heat, forced overtime including 24-hour all-night shifts, filthy bathrooms lacking even toilet paper and soap, no clean drinking water, workers docked two to three days pay for taking a sick day, and an atmosphere of repression and fear in which workers knew that if they dared to speak the truth about factory conditions, they would be immediately fired. Wal-Mart's factory certification visits had to be announced at least three days in advance, which often translated into several weeks notification as travel plans had to be confirmed. Spot checks or surprise visits were not allowed. Wal-Mart monitors had to follow a strict script. They did not visit the factories at night or on holidays to see if the workers were being forced to work overtime. They did not visit the workers' homes or speak with workers in a safe location. They never asked about the workers' legal rights to freedom of association and to organize a union.[13]

Wal-Mart argues that it monitors its overseas contractor plants with a comprehensive certification program and that it carried out 12,500 inspections in 2004 alone. It claims to have addressed the cases Lynn raised in his reports to the company, and it argues that it takes labor violations seriously and is beefing up its in-house global monitoring program.[14] But unlike New Balance, Wal-Mart does not permit independent audits or inspection by outside groups and does not publicly disclose location of its contractor plants.[15] This casts serious doubts on its commitment, as do the persistent reports of abuse by workers.

Mexican labor lawyers who have independently investigated sweatshop conditions have concluded that the failure to reinstate striking workers fighting for an independent union is the central issue. The absence of unions has meant a continued slide in Mexican wages and working conditions that began after the passage of NAFTA in the early 1990s and has continued for many years thereafter. In October 2000, Oscar Chavez Diaz, an Alcoa employee in Acuña, Mexico, showed a *New York Times* reporter a weekly pay stub for $60. Diaz lives with his wife in the rusting shell of a school bus and says he lacks money for food and clothing. Ruth

66

Rosenbaum, a social economist who has studied the purchasing power of 11 border communities, says the misery is getting worse: "You study these wages for a while," she says, "and it makes you sick to your stomach." Another assembly-line employee at Alcoa, Isidro Esquivel Sanchez, said, "They work us like donkeys, and we come back to this" as he pointed to his one-room, dirt-floor hovel. According to the *Times* reporter, "In Acuña, as in other border settlements, Mexican workers earn such miserable wages and American companies pay such minimal taxes that its schools are a shambles, its hospital crumbling, its trash collection slapdash and sewage lines collapsed." More than 50 percent of the border workers have no indoor bathroom.[16]

Alcoa is a highly profitable company chaired by Paul O'Neill, before he became George W. Bush's first secretary of the treasury from 2001 to 2002. He presided over Alcoa during some of its worst abuses of worker rights in Mexico. In his role as treasury secretary, O'Neill was a central player in shaping U.S. trade policy with Mexico, which emphasizes, as it has all over the world, enforcement of property rights and bailouts of rich investors, while dismissing labor rights and environmental standards.

Another very serious form of global economic wilding, long visible in the *maquiladoras*, is the sexual abuse of young female workers. Young women between the ages of 14 and 26 make up more than two-thirds of the workforce in most free-trade zones. Labor lawyers and social workers in the *maquiladoras* report that young women are often propositioned by their male supervisors and can lose their jobs if they don't sleep with them.[17]

Corporate wilding also includes massive environmental abuse. *Maquiladoras* have dumped millions of tons of raw sewage into rivers, many flowing up into the United States. A study by the AFL-CIO found the water supply on the border to be massively polluted; indiscriminate dumping of toxic waste in unsafe, often clandestine, sites threatens fish and wildlife with extinction and the ecosystem as a whole.[18]

In addition, workers are subjected to toxic conditions inside the plants. Anthropologist Maria Fernandez-Kelly, who worked in the plants in Ciudad Juarez, reports that workers' health tends to deteriorate rapidly because of the brutal work pace, unsafe machinery, and hazardous fumes, with the most frequent complaints being "eyesight deterioration, and nervous and respiratory ailments." A survey conducted by the University of Massachusetts at Lowell found widespread musculoskeletal disorders related to the pace of work and poor workplace engineering. Many studies have found serious health problems caused by toxic chemicals and other unregulated pollution.[19]

Foreign companies are producing wealth and a booming border economy, but most of the wealth flows back into the corporations' own coffers.

Gustavo Elizondo, the mayor of Juarez, says that the sad reality of his community is that it is "a place of opportunity for the international community," but one that has left the local government unable "to provide water, sewage and sanitation." According to the 2000 Mexican census, 75 percent of Mexicans live in poverty today, compared with 49 percent in 1981. "Every year we get poorer and poorer," the Juarez mayor concludes, "even though we create more and more wealth."[20]

The prevailing subhuman conditions in the plants and the surrounding communities are a product of coordinated repression by multinational corporations and the Mexican government, which has intervened repeatedly, using the police and the army to suppress labor protests and permitting multinational companies to evade environmental and labor laws. Wages and working conditions have declined as the multinationals have expanded because the huge firms have worked so effectively with the U.S. and Mexican governments and with company-sponsored unions to erode workers' rights and community social protections. These are neither free nor fair markets but rather the predictable outcome of a global game of musical chairs gone wild.

Globalization without Wilding: The Future of Globalization after the Battle of Seattle

In December 1999, the streets of Seattle became a fiery battleground with U.S. tanks on the streets, Nike windows shattered, and tear gas shots heard around the world. Fifty thousand protesters—many of them college students teaming up with workers and environmentalists ("Teamsters for Turtles")—rallied to shut down the meeting of the WTO. Their goal was not to end globalization but to challenge the WTO—which helps make the rules of the global economy—to make new regulations protecting human rights as well as protecting money.[21]

Seattle was a Constitutional Moment, a recognition that financial elites from the richest nations are making basic rules that will determine how the world is run for decades to come. The protesters, who want globalization without wilding, have shown their determination; they have mounted electrifying protests since Seattle at nearly every meeting of the financial elites who make the rules. As these elites look for places to meet in quiet

68

secrecy (choosing in 2001 to hold the WTO meeting in the Mideast dictatorship desert of Qatar), the protesters defy efforts to be deterred by police violence and armed fortifications. At the 2001 meeting of the World Economic Forum in Davos, Switzerland, many protesters actually skied in to evade blockades at the border and on the streets.

As noted at the beginning of this chapter, globalization could be organized in a different way to reap the benefits of global specialization, production, and trade without inflicting harm on millions of the world's workers and communities. Why then, have our political leaders allowed globalization to proceed in its current form? And how might the global economy be restructured and regulated to balance the enormous power of multinational corporations and contain their greed?

The United States will retain significant influence in the web of global institutions, from the International Monetary Fund (IMF) and the World Bank to the WTO. But the players gaining the most power in the new world economy are not governments but the multinationals themselves. The reason both Republican and Democratic presidents acquiesce to the multinationals' agenda is simple: Both political parties are dependent on business funding to win elections and are not prepared to risk opposing huge global corporations on issues of central importance to them. Five hundred of the largest U.S. corporations have offices in Washington and employ thousands of lobbyists, as do 400 of the largest foreign multinationals. Together, these corporations constitute by far the largest and most influential special-interest group in Washington. Ultimately, business sets the parameters for economic policymaking in America because of its lobbying efforts and because members of the U.S. corporate elite themselves occupy the highest governmental economic posts, thereby controlling the money and investment decisions essential to the survival of both the population and the government.[22]

Students and other Seattle protesters have already shown that their actions can force change. The protests in 2000 and 2001 triggered a major crisis among the financial elites, with corporations rushing to embrace an image of social responsibility. The former president of the World Bank, James Wolfensohn, claimed after the protests that he was redirecting his agency to focus on the needs of the global poor. The U.S. government has pulled back some of its support for institutions such as the IMF and indicated a concern with introducing labor and environmental rights in trade agreements.

The aim of the protesters is to turn globalization into a means of empowering people and dignifying their lives. One approach is to promote global labor movements that will represent the interests of the new global workforce and balance the power of the multinationals. Both American workers and employees in developing nations need strong unions to prevent the horrendous exploitation of global sweatshops and contingent employment. But the U.S. government has avoided any identification with American unions and has done nothing to support the embryonic movements for independent unions in Mexico, Indonesia, and other developing countries. President George W. Bush, with his long anti-labor record, has abandoned even the small steps that President Clinton took to promote unions and labor rights around the world, including the effort to introduce provisions for worker and environmental rights into NAFTA and at WTO negotiations.

American unions are starting to develop new international strategies. These unions now realize that when corporations are allowed to operate sweatshops abroad, workers will begin to encounter sweatshop conditions at home. After years of hostility to foreign workers and foreign labor movements, the AFL-CIO labor chiefs have begun to speak about international labor solidarity and to put their money where their mouths are. John Sweeney, current president of the AFL-CIO, has provided vocal support and funding for organizing efforts in the *maquiladoras* and other trade zones. As early as 1994, workers in a Ford truck-assembly plant in St. Paul, Minnesota, voted to send funds to Ford workers in Mexico to support a union drive in the *maquiladoras*. The American workers, who recognized that wretched Mexican wages and working conditions affected their own jobs and security, wore patches on their jackets saying "Cross-Border Solidarity Organizers." A growing number of labor unions—such as the U.S. United Electrical Workers, with help from the Teamsters—have begun to contribute to independent labor organizing in the *maquiladoras*.[23]

The rise of new international labor confederations—in coalition with student groups, environmentalists, and other human rights groups—could help prevent multinationals from playing one country's workers against another's in a race to the bottom. It could also help create new controls over the unchecked lightning-fast movement of speculative capital around the planet. As the Asian crisis of 1998 showed, such fast money can easily destabilize the economies of entire continents and erode the ability of nations to protect their own people. We need foreign investment and trade, but only when there are speed bumps and checks that allow nations and communities to control their own destinies.[24]

Ultimately, a new democratic coalition must become a major player at the tables where the new constitution of the global economy is being written. The finance ministers of the rich nations and the corporate advisory teams who meet regularly at the WTO, IMF, and World Bank will have to make room for a whole new set of worker and citizen representatives. Global rules will have to shift from their exclusive focus on protecting property rights and free trade. The new mission is to create a democratic model of globalization, centered on respect for human rights and a fair distribution of wealth between rich and poor nations, as well as between corporate CEOs and their global workforce.[25]

This may seem a long, steep climb, but one immediate step along the way is to build codes of international labor standards and corporate conduct that would set a humane global floor for wages and working conditions. The European Union (EU) has established a European Social Charter that sets minimum wages, health and safety standards, and other social codes to be honored by all the member nations. The International Labor Organization (ILO) has a code of global labor rights that now needs to be toughened and enforced in all nations and corporations, with sanctions imposed on companies that wild by ignoring the codes. Although President Clinton negotiated NAFTA with side agreements to protect labor and the environment, most observers criticized them as being pitifully weak. Citizen and labor groups are pushing for far stronger agreements that are consistent with or stronger than current United Nations and ILO standards, and for a robust social charter for *maquiladora* businesses.[26]

Apparel companies such as Nike and Reebok have banded together in the Fair Labor Association to form their own corporate codes of conduct, promising to avoid use of child labor or prison labor and to pay the prevailing wages in each country in which they operate. Such corporate codes across an entire sector can be an important first step toward ending corporate wilding, although the Fair Labor Association is viewed by some critics as hopelessly co-opted by the corporations who participate.[27] It will take public action to make the companies accountable and truly end the new wave of global economic wilding. Students in the antisweatshop movement have proved that even huge companies such as Nike can be forced to change by consumer boycotts. Across the nation, students have become more careful about their own buying habits and mounted visible boycotts at Nike stores that have helped to change Nike policy. They also forced their universities to break ties with companies that operate sweatshops around the world, and they have helped create new monitoring and enforcement agencies to ensure that these companies do not continue to wild on the sly.[28]

Multinational companies in the United States and elsewhere have used globalism to escape their social responsibilities and weaken the accountability that the workers and governments of their own nations historically have imposed on them. This approach will lead to a permanent regime of corporate wilding unless a new social covenant is negotiated between multinationals and the workers and citizens of the world. Building a new world community through the struggle for global employee rights and democratic and accountable multinational corporations may prove to be the most important new social movement of the coming era.

Enron

Systemic Wilding in the Corridors of Power

The Enron drama in 2001, culminating in the 2006 trial of founder Ken Lay and CEO Jeff Skilling, was one of the great business scandals of the modern era. This was not simply because Enron was the seventh-largest American corporation, nor because an even bigger company, the telecom giant, WorldCom, went bust a few months later and became the biggest bankruptcy in history. Nor was it because 570 other corporations were accused of corporate fraud in 2002, constituting one of the largest corporate crime waves in history. Rather, Enron was important precisely because so much of the wilding it represented was perfectly legal and because it involved not only huge corporations but Wall Street, the accounting and legal professions, and much of Washington, D.C. It was a crisis that undermined public faith in the integrity of the market system, suggesting that a systemic wilding event was shaking the capitalist order and opening up the possibility of unforeseen change in the system itself.

In this chapter, we consider the meaning of systemic wilding, which goes beyond the wilding of particular individuals or even of specific institutions. President George W. Bush framed the crisis as the wilding of a few corporate executives. He said that there are always a few "bad apples" and that the executives who committed crimes at Enron, WorldCom, and other companies would be aggressively prosecuted. But as the crisis unfolded, it became clear that this was not just about a few "bad apples" or even the specific companies they directed. This was a case of the barrel itself being rotten, infecting nearly all of the apples in one way or another. If a few "bad apples" is a metaphor for individual wilding or the wilding of a small number of companies, a rotten barrel evokes the meaning of systemic wilding, which can only be fixed by constructing a new barrel.

Systemic wilding is the wilding that emerges from a set of corrupt intertwined business and government institutions at the core of our economic and political order. While presumably acting as checks or watchdogs on each others' conduct, these institutions are becoming increasingly melded together into a monolith of power that inflicts severe harm on ordinary people as it siphons wealth to the elites it represents. The only solution to systemic wilding is systemic change. Here we use the Enron crisis to look at the major institutional players who collaborate to create systemic wilding and to show the new forms of accountability that will be required to make things right.

Enron and Systemic Wilding

The whistle-blower at Enron who blew open the entire scandal was an unlikely hero. Sherron Watkins, a 40-something accountant and a devoted Enron employee, told a rapt congressional panel about going to her boss, founder and chairman of Enron, Kenneth Lay, and telling him point-blank that Enron was on the brink of financial disaster because of deceptive accounting practices. Watkins testified that she told Lay that the chief financial officers of the company, including CEO Jeffrey Skilling and CFO Andrew Fastow, had concocted a shadowy network of Enron-funded off-book financial entities that were shielding massive and growing Enron debt. If the process continued, Watkins warned, Enron would quickly descend into insolvency and might face serious legal liability. The mysterious special financial entities, with bizarre names such as Chewko, Raptor, LJM Cayman, and LJM2, were allegedly being used by Skilling and Fastow to skim off big money (Fastow made more than $45 million from the LJMs alone). Chewko, Raptor, and the LJMs also cleverly fogged the view of investors, workers, and the public about Enron's increasingly desperate financial situation. Ken Lay dithered and Enron's board of directors dallied, later pleading ignorance but essentially underwriting the orgy of deception and fraud.

Enron was a company that was accustomed to big profits. Within 10 years, it had transformed itself from a small, stodgy energy business into a "new economy" financial company that gambled on global energy trades and acquisitions. The ethos of fast money and high living attracted executives such as Fastow, whom a high school teacher once called a "budding wheeler-dealer." Fastow was known at Enron as "an intimidating and single-minded self-promoter," embodying the Enron culture of "me first, I want to get paid."[1] Fastow pled guilty in 2005 to two counts of conspiracy and was sentenced to 10 years in jail after agreeing to cooperate with prosecutors. In the 2006 climactic Enron trial, Fastow became the star witness against his bosses, Ken Lay and Jeff Skilling, whom he claimed knew of and approved his deceptive financial practices.

As Enron got deeper into the speculative world of trading, its executives saw themselves as a special breed. They gambled on high stakes with happy abandon and employed strategies "close to the edge." The *Wall Street Journal* reported that the prevailing corporate culture was "to push everything to the limits: business practices, laws and personal behavior."[2] Enron executives showed off by paying over $5,000 for choice company parking spots, spending money on expensive Porsches, and celebrating successful deals by going down to local strip clubs and throwing lots of money on the table. *Fortune* magazine reported that a dancer at the Treasures strip club said that a group of Enron execs marched in after one deal and announced that they had $10,000 to spend on the best girls.[3]

The debt deception and profit skimming by executives was just one component of the web of wilding engulfing Enron. An Enron executive pled guilty to conspiracy to drive up prices in secret and illegal energy deals orchestrated by Enron in California that led to disastrous electric power shortages, blackouts, and massively inflated prices for California consumers. Enron engaged in similar extortionary energy trading practices in the United Kingdom and around the world, going abroad to reap tax advantages and government subsidies while concealing debt. Enron's power plant operations in India and its proposed pipeline operations in Bolivia both exploited political connections—in India they used these connections to crack down on dissent from workers, and in Bolivia they used them to silence local communities concerned about their environments. In what created the most public outrage, Enron locked its workers into pension funds invested exclusively in Enron stock even as the executives were selling off their own Enron shares and cashing in their stock options, knowing that the stock would collapse soon and leave many of their workers without a penny for their retirement. Thousands of workers were devastated by this loss.

In the heady world of the dot-com economy and the 1990s market bubble, scores of big companies plunged headlong into their own "creative accounting." Driven by greed and the new relentless demands for higher earnings on Wall Street, executives at WorldCom, Qwest, Global Crossing, Imclone, Kmart, Adelphi, Tyco, Cendant, and Martha Stewart Enterprises have all been indicted for fraud, inside dealing, or similar charges. Among those that have been convicted and sentenced to jail are WorldCom CEO Bernie Ebbers, guilty of orchestrating an $11-billion fraud, the largest corporate fraud conviction ever; Tyco CEO Dennis Kozlowski, guilty of stealing

$600 million from his company; Adelphia Communication's founder John Rigas, guilty of conspiracy, bank fraud, and securities fraud; and Martha Stewart, guilty of conspiracy, obstruction of justice, and lying. As for Enron, based on the convictions and testimonies of other Enron executives, including convicted CFO Andrew Fastow, founder and Bush buddy, Ken Lay, and his colleague, CEO Jeffrey Skilling, were convicted of 29 criminal charges. Skilling was convicted on 19 of 28 counts including one count of insider trading. Lay was convicted on all six charges of conspiracy, securities, and wire fraud in his corporate trial.

The intense Wall Street pressure on the companies for big profits and soaring stock prices does not justify corporate deceptive conduct, but it does point to the systemic character of the wilding and explain the spread of the crisis across the entire economy. Numerous other companies, notably Harken Energy, the company on whose board George W. Bush served as a director, and Halliburton, the energy firm once run by Dick Cheney, all came under investigation for allegedly hiding debt, inflating profits, or pulling insider sweetheart deals for top executives, many paying the CEOs unconscionable options and bonuses even as the corporate ship was going down.

Arthur Andersen: Master of Unaccountable Accounting

The accounting profession may not seem glamorous, but the green eyeshaders are vital to the integrity of the free market system. They are essential watchdogs who vouch for the honesty of financial reporting and help sustain faith in the markets. By partnering with Enron to create its deception and fraud, accountants (along with bankers, lawyers, and politicians) helped transform one company's wilding into the nightmare of systemic wilding.

Arthur Andersen was one of the Big Five, the great accounting firms who audit Fortune 500 companies and put the Good Housekeeping seal of approval on their financial statements. But only months after the Enron scandal broke, Arthur Andersen became the symbol of accounting gone wild. Andersen had been the auditor not only for Enron but also for WorldCom and many of the other firms that have been investigated for "misstatements," including Cheney's Halliburton. Cheney had made a video testifying to Andersen's integrity that would come back to haunt him.

Andersen became a key target of Justice Department investigations and was indicted for numerous violations, including obstruction of justice for shredding Enron-related material. A Houston jury that convicted Andersen of obstruction watched a video in which an Andersen manager tells the Enron audit team that destroying documents even the day before the litigation is "great" because anything useful to the courts was gone. David Duncan, the chief Andersen accountant on the Enron audit team, confessed that he personally destroyed documents and testified that, just before the trial, Andersen employees worked overtime to delete hundreds of computer files and shred "tons" of documents, in the process overloading the shredding machines and causing them to malfunction.[5]

While Andersen top executives continued to maintain that they had nothing to hide, the shredding hinted that Andersen was up to its eyeshades in Enron's financial fraud, helping craft the infamous special partnerships and signing off on statements affirming their legality. Governments and creditors have filed numerous suits against Andersen to punish it for fraud and to redeem Enron-related losses. Texas revoked Andersen's license, and the Justice Department filed its first major criminal charge in the Enron case against Andersen for covering up and destroying documents and e-mails.

Andersen CEO, Joseph Berardino, admitted that "what was done was not in keeping with the values and heritage of this firm. It was wrong." But Berardino also said that only a few Andersen employees had erred.[6]

In December 2004, the Supreme Court reversed a Houston jury's conviction of Anderson for its role in the Enron affair based on the prosecution's failure to prove that Anderson accountants and executives knew their behavior was criminal. Nonetheless, as *Fortune* business writer Bethany McLean wrote, Anderson knew its practices were "high risk" and went along with Enron because it "didn't want to lose Enron's business."[7] The fact of technical legality in the face of such obvious complicity in Enron's misleading accounting practices only highlights the structural conflicts of interest that can lead to wilding without risking going to jail. But when Anderson collapsed after the original conviction, its 28,000 employees all lost their jobs, victims of the wilding built into the fabric of our corporate order.

The problem was a systemic conflict of interest between truthful accounting and making money. Accounting firms have become not only auditors but also consultants, making fortunes off of their new expansive roles. Had Andersen not played ball with Fastow and Skilling, signing off on the deceptive Chewko, Raptor, and LJM entities, Enron would have found another accounting firm willing to play the game. To blow the whistle in their auditing role would have not only jeopardized their fees as accountants but also forfeited the millions Andersen made in its other role as consultant to Enron. Andersen symbolized the structural conflict of interest that threatens the integrity of all of today's green eyeshaders.

Merrill Lynch and Wilding on Wall Street

The Enron crisis could not have occurred without the complicity of the biggest players on Wall Street. Their role is critical to understanding systemic wilding, since the big banks lie at the center of the capitalist system. The investment banks' relations to Enron and other corporate clients have become clouded with conflicts of interest—sometimes criminal but mostly legal—a hint of wilding that is integral to the system itself.

On July 28, 2003, J.P. Morgan Chase and Citibank agreed to pay $300 million in fines for helping Enron misrepresent its financial condition. The banks advised Enron on structuring the off-the-books partnerships that deceptively inflated earnings and concealed debt. In February 2003, the Securities and Exchange Commission (SEC) fined Merrill Lynch $80 million for two transactions also involving Enron's secret partnerships. The SEC also charged four Merrill executives with aiding and abetting fraud related to a sham 1999 Enron deal involving LJM2, a key Fastow partnership, in which 100 Merrill employees personally invested funds.[8] Several British bankers, including three at Greenwich NatWest bank, have also been indicted for Enron-related fraud.[9]

Why would banks get involved in financing and marketing off-book schemes that might be used for concealing debts or inflating profits? By doing so, the banks consolidated a web of profitable relationships with Enron and other companies, enriching themselves by helping the companies enrich themselves.[10] According to a 2002 class-action suit filed by Enron shareholders (led by chief claimant, University of California, and still being litigated at this writing), Merrill Lynch, Citigroup, and J.P. Morgan Chase not only helped design Enron's debt-concealing entities, but also invested heavily in them and profited from the deceptive accounting schemes. Merrill Lynch allegedly raised $390 million for LJM2 and invested $40 million in another Enron secret entity called Zephyrus. As determined by the SEC in its Merrill Lynch settlement and alleged by Enron bankruptcy examiner, attorney Neal Batson, in a February 14, 2003 court report, these big banks that invested in Enron stock were involved in deals that concealed debt from investors and made money off Enron's soaring reputation and stock prices, inflated by the Raptors, LJMs, and other secret partnerships, as well as by the misleading and optimistic reports of analysts employed by the banks themselves. Batson's report, which is thicker than the Manhattan phone book and is known as the "St. Valentine's Day Massacre," is the first of two bankruptcy reports alleging grounds for indicting Wall Street bankers who were in bed with Enron executives—quite literally in the case of one fired Texas-based Merrill Lynch banker, Schuyler Tilney, whose wife, Elizabeth, was an Enron marketing executive known for inventing Enron's infamous crooked E logo. Schuyler Tilney is one of the four Merrill Lynch executives already charged by the SEC for aiding Enron fraud.[11]

On April 28, 2003, a Senate governmental affairs subcommittee accused Merrill Lynch of helping concoct a 1999 sham deal relating to the sale of Nigerian barges that inflated Enron's profits by $12 million, a deceptive Fastow LJM2 deal that is also the basis for the SEC charges against the four Merrill Lynch bankers. On another matter, the subcommittee found that when Enron threatened to cancel business with Merrill Lynch after a negative Merrill Lynch analyst report, Merrill Lynch replaced the analyst with a new one who promptly upgraded Enron stock, leading Enron to award Merrill Lynch more than $2.5 billion in new underwriting business. Senator Peter Fitzgerald (R-Ill.) concluded that "it's clear that Merrill Lynch has been investment banker to a big Ponzi Scheme."[12]

As a team of *Frontline* investigators summarized it, the big investment banks tied to Enron "were involved in designing the structure of these hidden partnerships, and then made money from investing in them." The banks' profits from Enron stock soared along with the stock price itself, inflated by the fraudulent partnerships and analysts' "buy ratings." The banks simultaneously profited from lucrative underwriting fees that were part of their intertwined, multifaceted relations with Enron.[13]

The Wall Street analysts' conflict of interest has become one of the biggest Enron-related stories. Like the accountants, Wall Street analysts play a vital role in sustaining faith in the integrity of the market system, with their research on companies presumed to be "objective" and their buy and sell recommendations considered the gold standard for investor judgment. But through much of the Enron crisis, as Ken Lay was exuberantly touting the health of Enron stock (while secretly liquidating many of his own Enron holdings), analysts were issuing deceptively optimistic "buy" recommendations.

The analysts' wilding was especially dramatic in the WorldCom debacle. Jack Grubman, one of Wall Street's most respected analysts, issued glowing recommendations about WorldCom stock just days before the telecom giant collapsed. Subsequent e-mail revelations showed an intimate collaboration between Grubman and Bernie Ebbers, the WorldCom founder and chairman, with Grubman coaching Ebbers on business strategy and on how to calm analyst and public concerns about WorldCom as it began to unravel. The touted independence and objectivity of the analyst were obviously fictional, a point made more graphic in another scandal when Grubman acknowledged that he had elevated his rating of AT&T stock because AT&T's boss had helped Grubman's twin daughters get into an exclusive nursery school.[14]

On April 28, 2003, the SEC and state regulators reached a $1.4-billion settlement against 10 of Wall Street's biggest banks for proffering misleading advice to the public. Almost all the advice involved recommendations to buy when the company was in trouble. As one of the most far-reaching and damaging legal settlements ever won by the SEC, it specifically accused Citigroup's Salomon Smith Barney, Merrill Lynch, and Credit Suisse First Boston of fraud, while implicating nearly every other major Wall Street bank in the duping of investors "to curry favor with corporate clients."[15] Analysts' compensation is tied to the amount of banking business they help bring in, partly through buttering up executives by issuing rosy reports on their companies. Ninety-eight percent of analyst recommendations are to buy, reflecting the cronyism among analysts, the banks that employ them, and the companies they do business with. This problem, finally acknowledged by Wall Street itself, long preceded Enron and is clearly a form of systemic wilding. Analysts were constrained in telling the truth about companies such as Enron and WorldCom because the banks that employed the analysts had sunk commercial loans into these companies and were desperate to hold onto the huge lucrative underwriting business that a gloomy analyst report might jeopardize. The analysts' work inevitably became a thinly veiled con job, leading Morgan Stanley analyst, Barton Biggs, to write that Wall Street "may at times have seemed like a casino, but at least it was an honest casino." Now, as in Las Vegas, small investors are left to wonder whether the house always wins and whether they are "players in a loser's game."[16]

This systemic wilding emerged from the deregulation of Wall Street and the breakdown of the "Chinese wall" that had historically separated commercial from investing banking, as well as banking of both types from research and analyst services. After the 1929 financial crash, where similar crony relations had contributed to loss of faith in the markets, President Franklin Roosevelt passed the Glass-Steagall Act and other regulations preventing commercial banks from engaging in investment banking, brokering sales, or other financial services. In the 1990s bubble, these regulations were systematically dismantled, and new financial giants such as Citigroup and Merrill Lynch gobbled up business on both sides of the toppled Chinese wall. Investors are already shunning the advice of the Wall Street analysts, moving to more unbiased sources in independent companies, and many Wall Street firms are eliminating their analyst services or separating their analyst and research divisions completely from other banking services. The only answer to this particular component of systemic wilding on Wall Street is to rebuild the wall.

George W. Bush and the Corporate State: Systemic Wilding in Washington, D.C.

After the Enron crisis hit the headlines, George W. Bush proclaimed that corporate criminals would go straight to jail, but then he appointed Harvey Pitt as head of the chief watchdog agency, the Securities and Exchange Commission. Pitt was a lawyer for accounting firms, well known for protecting the rich. The Pitt appointment was just the tip of the iceberg of the political protection system that both Republican and Democratic administrations have lavishly supported. The Bush administration, with a cabinet drawn heavily from the big business community, is the embodiment of the corporate state, which is a melding of corporations and the political class that pursues profit over people. The corporate state helps fuel systemic wilding today, and it continues to grow under both Republican and Democratic presidents.[17]

The close relation between George W. Bush and Kenneth Lay, Enron's CEO, exposed America's corporate state to the glare of public scrutiny. Bush and Lay were longtime golfing buddies, and Bush scribbled notes addressed to "Kenny boy." Enron was the top contributor to Bush personally over his career, donating $623,000 to him by January 2001. In the 2000 campaign alone, Enron gave $1.5 million to Republican candidates for federal office and the GOP National Committee.[18] Lay was also one of Dick Cheney's energy advisers and was once rumored to be Bush's choice for secretary of the treasury. Moreover, many of the Bush administration's top officials had worked for Enron, whose board of directors had long been full of Bush cronies. Wendy Gramm, former secretary of labor and wife of the former powerful Texas senator Phil Gramm, had served on Enron's audit committee. Secretary of the Army, Thomas White, who resigned in 2003, had been Enron's point person in its deceptive and disastrous California operations in electric power trading.

The massive contributions of Enron to Bush paid off richly in Washington. Enron had long sought to dominate a deregulated energy market, and Bush was the great champion of energy deregulation. The Bush administration deregulated the energy future contracts market (Enron's most lucrative business) nationally. More broadly, it turned a dull system of regulated markets into a "free for all of energy companies selling electricity back and forth like pork bellies," while resisting efforts by states to regulate Enron's business. Enron helped pick Bush's head of the Federal Energy Regulatory Commission, who then prevented California from imposing essential price controls on this disastrous free-for-all. And to seal the deal, in five secret meetings, Enron executives helped Vice President Dick Cheney craft the Bush administration's overall energy program, which included a major role for Lay in the plan to tap Arctic oil. Cheney invoked executive privilege to avoid making the contents of those meetings public.[19]

Nonetheless, there still remained the SEC, the crown jewel of the regulatory system, a commission charged with defending the public from Enron-like abuses. In the five years preceding the collapse, when Enron-mania was driving up Enron's stock value by 40 percent each year, the SEC never audited Enron. After the crisis, when it became impossible to ignore the company's wilding, Bush promised to crack down and increase the investigatory powers of the SEC. But when he appointed Pitt as head of the SEC, it became clear that the corporate state was going to protect its own. Pitt's appointment was such a blatant display of corporate influence that it created a huge public outcry, eventually leading to his resignation. The SEC today, however, still lacks the will or resources to prevent future Enrons. It is charged with reviewing the statements of 17,000 public companies and has about 100 lawyers to do it, with the number of senior experts able to decipher the more technical details being far smaller. The SEC lacks enough staff even to just read the glossy annual reports of the 17,000 companies, let alone vet the detailed technical statements, supervise the vast mutual funds empire, oversee the financial exchanges, and monitor insider trading. SEC lawyers are paid about one-third less than those in other federal agencies, and their turnover is over 30 percent—double that of other government agencies. While the

SEC launched hundreds of new probes after Enron, most are fading away, dying for lack of will and resources in a Bush regime of, by, and for the corporation.[20]

It would be a mistake though, to imagine that a Democratic administration would be much different. The corporate state is indifferent to whether the donkey or the elephant is sitting in the White House. Consider that Enron in 2002 had made contributions to 71 of 100 senators as well as to 187 members of the House. The top recipients included Senator Charles Schumer, a Democrat from New York, and Senator Joseph Lieberman of Connecticut, who ran for vice president in 2000 on the Democratic ticket with Al Gore. In the Clinton years, Enron developed close relations with Ron Brown, Clinton's top trade official, who continued Bush Sr.'s practice of helping Enron win lucrative energy contracts in India, the Philippines, Chile, Colombia, and many other countries. Throughout the Clinton years, Enron was a major political force in Washington, spending money all over K Street (the heart of the lobbying industry) and wielding major influence over the White House, Congress, both political parties, and major lobbies such as the U.S. Council for International Business and the National Foreign Trade Council.

Enron is just one of hundreds of huge corporations throwing their weight around Washington, and is in fact, low on the list of the biggest political contributors. The Enron case is thus a dramatic but small instance of the larger crisis of the corporate state. The corporate state has become the domineering institution of our times, undermining the prospect of true democracy and running roughshod over the interests of ordinary people. A marriage of corporations and the political class, the corporate state is the engine that drives systemic wilding. It shapes a political and economic system designed to reward the rich at the expense of the general public. The Enron crisis is important mainly because it exposes the wilding dimensions of the corporate state and the larger social system it creates and protects.

The solution to systemic wilding is democracy. Enron was a huge unaccountable corporation, with its top executives wheeling and dealing without having to answer to anyone: its board of directors, federal regulators, its own workers, or the public. Enron, though, simply symbolizes the lack of accountability built into the larger system in which it was embedded. All the major players—accountants, regulators, and politicians—worked together to insulate their collective wilding from public view or control. How can such a system be made accountable? This will happen only if the public decides that enough is enough and begins to take the constitutional creed of democracy seriously. The corporate state will continue to be an engine of wilding—siphoning power and wealth from ordinary citizens to the rich—until people turn off their corporate-programmed televisions, shrug off their couch-potato identities, and decide to throw the CEOs out of Washington. Then, they will face the task of rebuilding a true democratic system—something that will require imagination, hope, and dedicated activism in a new generation that may be inspired to act by the memory of Enrons past and the frightening prospect of those still to come.

Wilding in the Church

Unaccountable Brethren and Voices of the Faithful

While the Enron scandal was sending shock waves throughout America and the world, a new scandal was shaking the nation. Sitting in my office at Boston College (BC), I was watching it unfold just a few blocks from me. For weeks, I saw television and radio crews, along with police officers, lined up outside the vast seminary buildings and homes where Cardinal Bernard Law—a great prince of the church—lived, just down Commonwealth Avenue from BC. The reporters were waiting for the cardinal to come out and give them an account of what he had known about priest sexual abuse and when he had known about it. The police were there to keep order as angry groups of laity congregated to demand Law's resignation. And every morning, when I sat down to breakfast and opened my *New York Times* and *Boston Globe*, I read another headline about the sickening litany of abuse cases and the alleged coverup by Law and the other esteemed leaders of the church.

As I read the papers, I often saw one story about Enron and another about the church on the same page. A reader (especially a sociologist) could hardly avoid seeing some parallels. Here were two of the world's great institutions—the corporation and the church—imploding in sensational scandals. In both cases, the leaders at the top faced charges of gross ethical and criminal misconduct. They had protected themselves at the expense of those who had put their trust in them, and they had been getting away with it for years. When the truth began to spill out, they had launched massive coverups. In both cases, leaders had hijacked their institutions from the "laity" and had faced no accountability. Both cases were institutional wilding on a grand, systemic scale.

Wilding in the church is in many respects more shocking than in the business world. We expect greed and deception in the business world. But the business of the church is morality, and we expect the church to model the highest standards of conduct. Societies look to their great religious institutions to teach and inspire moral commitments, and when they fail to do so, societies themselves are at risk of unraveling. This has been part of the central teaching of the social theorists who created the modern discipline of sociology. Émile Durkheim argued that collective moral codes have been the glue of societies throughout history. The agents of these moral codes may change over time, and Durkheim thought that the professions and a new division of labor in the economy might supplant traditional religious institutions as the most important sources of solidarity and moral cohesion. But sociologists since Durkheim have seen religious institutions as integral to the survival of morality and society itself.

Wilding in the church is then, arguably, the most dangerous type. If it signals a broad decline in the integrity of religious institutions, it could turn wilding into a social epidemic, triggering the type of complete breakdown of moral restraint found among the Ik. The wilding in the Catholic Church is frightening because it appears to mirror wilding in the corporate world, in the government, and in other core American institutions, suggesting systemic wilding on a very broad level. And it has the potential to destroy the faith of Americans in anything but looking out for number one.

I need to caution here that my observations in this chapter are about the church as a social, political, and administrative institution, not about Catholicism as a faith or doctrine. Teaching at a Catholic institution has reinforced my sense of the power of the Catholic faith to inspire courage and commitment to social justice. I see this demonstrated by my students, mostly Catholic, who impress me every day with their humanity and dedication to making the world more compassionate and just. My wilding story here is not a reflection on Catholic faith but a commentary on how the power hierarchies that corrupt so many of our institutions have corrupted the institutional church. And as at Enron, the solution involves creating institutional accountability by empowering the laity, something that I show is entirely consistent with the canonical law of the church.

Pedophilia, Sexual Abuse, and Rape: Wilding among the Priests

In 2002, the *Boston Globe* Spotlight Team, a group of crack investigative journalists, broke the story. In a series of devastating reports, they showed that hundreds of priests in the Boston archdiocese had been committing repeated acts of sexual abuse against the young boys and girls entrusted to them. One of the early priest offenders was John J. Geoghan, a now-convicted child molester who became the victim of brutal wilding himself when he was allegedly strangled to death in jail on February 22, 2004, by a fellow inmate in the Massachusetts prison where he was serving his sentence.[1] Eighty-six people have filed civil lawsuits against Geoghan and his superiors, claiming that he had assaulted them over a period of almost 35 years, and more than 130 people have testified since the mid-1990s that Geoghan had molested or raped them as he was moved around six Boston parishes over three decades. Almost all of the alleged victims were young boys in elementary schools when Geoghan assaulted them, one as young as 4 years old.[2]

In the 1980s, Geoghan targeted his victims by approaching young Catholic mothers, often single parents, working overtime to hold their large families together. Geoghan would offer to help by taking the kids for ice cream or helping them pray in their bedrooms. *The Globe* reported that one of the victims, 12-year-old Patrick McSorley, was lured by ice cream. In the car, after buying ice cream for Patrick, Geoghan "patted his upper leg and slid his hand up toward his crotch." McSorley said, "I froze. I didn't know what to think. Then he put his hand on my genitals and started masturbating me. I was petrified." Geoghan then began masturbating himself. When he let Patrick out of the car, he said this was a secret between the two of them and that "we're very good at keeping secrets."[3]

Another horrific story involves the priest, Paul Shanley, who was transferred to a parish in California after reported abuses in the Boston archdiocese. Church records show allegations of Shanley's abuse of children dating back to the 1960s. In May 2003, Shanley was indicted for raping a 6-year-old multiple times. Shanley has been accused of raping at least 26 children, including Gregory Ford who alleges he was raped from the time he was 6 to 11. Ford's attorney, Roderick MacLeish, said of Shanley, "This man was a monster in the archdiocese of Boston for many, many years." Ford called Shanley's long service to the church a "reign of terror."[4]

A remarkable feature of the Shanley story is that Shanley had openly advocated sex between men and boys for years. In the 1970s, he had explicitly embraced this position in an address to the North American Man-Boy Love Association (NAMBLA). Moreover, after the Boston archdiocese transferred him to St. Anne's parish in San Bernardino, California, Shanley and another priest, John J. White, opened up a bed-and-breakfast inn for gay customers while still on the payroll of the church. Shanley, a former street priest, and White operated a substantial business, including multiple motel cabins on two plots of property in Palm Springs called Whispering Palms and the Cabana Club resort.

More than 1,200 priests have now been accused of criminal sexual or other abuse. These include a priest accused of beating and terrorizing a housekeeper, one who traded cocaine for sex, and one who enticed teenage girls into having sex, comparing himself to Jesus Christ. At this writing, a growing scandal about rape of girls as well as boys is threatening to add more fuel to this never-ending fire.[6]

Cardinal Bernard Law and the Coverup: The Church as Institutional Wilder

The sexual exploitation of young children is a horrific form of expressive wilding by individuals, made worse when carried out by priests entrusted with tending to their spiritual needs. The numbers of priests and victims is overwhelming, and were this the whole story, it would be tragedy enough. But the more important dimension of the story for our purposes is not the individual wilding by priests but the institutional wilding carried out by the top of the clerical hierarchy. The conduct of the clerical princes reveals that the church itself, viewed not theologically as a faith but sociologically as a complex organization, is an engine of institutional wilding, a matter of the gravest concern in what many view as the most important moral institution on the planet.

Cardinal Law, one of the most powerful and esteemed American clerics before the crisis, who had close ties to the Vatican, tragically illustrates the transformation of the institutional church into a wilding system. On September 18, 2002, 27 people who claimed to be sexual assault victims filed a civil lawsuit accusing Cardinal Law, other top bishops, and the archdiocese itself with covering up sexual abuse by priests for 50 years. The cardinal, who denied the charges almost to the end, resigned three months later, unable to sustain financial contributions to the diocese or maintain his moral authority in light of the facts coming to the courts. Outrage about Law's conduct spread from the victims to leading Catholics in the business community, universities, the media, and the political establishment.

Ultimately, Law was forced to admit in court that he had known of many of the priests who had repeatedly raped and abused young children—and that he had not reported the facts to the courts or prevented the repeat-abusers from continuing to do pastoral work among young people. Law defended his behavior by saying that in some of the cases priests had received counseling and that in others there was insufficient evidence to make a conclusive decision about guilt. He also expressed belief in the redemptive power of faith and healing for priests, and the responsibility of the church to help them.

Law's pattern of behavior was to protect the abuser-priest rather than the victim, typically by shuttling him to a new parish. Geoghan was a glaring example, with Law transferring him from St. Paul's parish in Hingham in 1974, from St. Andrew's in Jamaica Plain in 1980, and from St. Brendan's in Dorechester in 1984. In each case, there were voluminous records in the archdiocese showing molestation, as well as rumors widely spread among priests and housekeepers about Geoghan bringing altar boys into his rectory rooms and sexually abusing them in the showers.[7]

Law not only repeatedly reassigned Geoghan to new parishes but also added grave insult to injury by having his aides tell traumatized victims to remain silent. Bishop Thomas Daily, a top Law aide, acknowledged that he "may well have" encouraged seven abuse victims of Geoghan who lived in Jamaica Plain to "keep quiet." They had a responsibility to do this, he said, to protect the church from scandal.[8]

Protection for priests who abuse was also proffered to Paul Shanley. Though the Boston archdiocese had received allegations and reports about Shanley's sexual abuses and open advocacy of sex between men and boys, it continued to reassign him to new parishes. In 1990, Law's top aide, Bishop Robert Banks, wrote a letter to a San Bernardino, California, diocese vouching for Shanley's good record and integrity, despite internal reports in the Boston archdiocese that he had allegedly molested three boys. An attorney for a victim claimed that the archdiocese was doing anything possible to keep Shanley out of Boston, hoping to spare Cardinal Law the embarrassment and potential liability of Shanley's presence.[9]

Geoghan and Shanley were only the tip of the iceberg. Cardinal Law kept the Reverend James D. Foley on active parish service even after he knew that a woman had died of a drug overdose following an evening of sex with the priest. After a conversation with Reverend Jay Mullin, who had been accused of several molestations and removed from several parishes, Law reinstated Mullin in 1998 as parish vicar without telling the new congregation that the church had paid a secret settlement of $60,000 to settle an earlier abuse case against Mullin. While the cardinal continued to deny knowing about or reassigning abusive priests, church records turned over to a Boston court after a civil suit filed by victims in 2002 showed otherwise. Judge Constance M. Sweeney wrote that more than 11,000 documents showed clear evidence that the church reassigned priests who were abusers. Meanwhile, records showed that the church had paid thousands upon thousands of dollars to victims in secret settlements over the past two decades to buy their silence.

The archdiocese went to great lengths to keep its records out of view of the courts and the public, claiming legal immunity for charitable institutions and arguing that the constitutional separation of church and state created the right of the church to keep its records secret. Judge Sweeney called this "an increasingly dreary effort" by church lawyers to hide documents. On July 24, 2003, after a 16-month investigation, Massachusetts attorney general Thomas F. Reilly concluded that Cardinal Law and his subordinate bishops had facilitated abuse and protected abuser-priests for years. "The mistreatment of children was so massive and so prolonged that it borders on the unbelievable," Reilly said. The church leaders, he said, "in effect, sacrificed children for many, many years."[10]

Cardinal Law's protection of priests over victims is unfortunately not a unique practice but a pattern increasingly being revealed in dioceses all over the country. Some are run by protégés of Law in Wisconsin, New Hampshire, and New York, but victims have alleged similar coverups in archdioceses from California to Florida. As the crisis became national, the U.S. Conference of Catholic Bishops convened to develop a new policy, and the Vatican itself began to get involved. The bishops promised a new policy of zero tolerance, but the laity and public have yet to be convinced, not unreasonably since Cardinal Law had pronounced such a policy in 1994.

Enron, the Corporate State, and the Church: Wilding and the Collapse of Institutional Accountability

In the previous chapter, I showed that Enron's wilding grew out of a hijacking of the corporation by its chief executives, who ran it without accountability to their workers or the public. There is a striking parallel with the Boston archdiocese and the institutional church more broadly. Top church administrators run their organizational empires with virtually no accountability to their laity. Sociologically, the wilding that follows is an entirely predictable outcome of vesting exclusive power in the princely brethren.

Enron became a major crisis because the one group to which the executive brethren were legally accountable—the shareholders—were key victims of the scandal. The Enron crisis showed that the accountability to even this legally enfranchised group had collapsed. This created a crisis of legitimacy about capitalism among investors whose faith is essential to the operation of the system.

The church crisis has an eerie parallel. The mission of the church is to serve the spiritual needs of the laity, a group similar to the shareholders and workers in the Enron crisis. As I detail shortly, there are elements of canon law that specify that the clerical brethren are, in fact, accountable to the laity, organizationally as well as spiritually. But the current crisis shows that, as with Enron, the brethren have captured the institution for themselves and are prepared to protect their own at whatever cost to the laity they are supposed to serve.

Priests have made this argument forcefully. The Reverend James J. Scahill, pastor of St. Michael's parish in Springfield, Massachusetts, wrote a public letter to his bishop, Thomas L. Dupre, scolding him for dragging his feet on removing a priest convicted of abusing boys. The bishop accused him of disobedience, but Scahill believes that the hierarchy of the church wanted a dangerous type of authority. "The kind of obedience he's looking for," Scahill said, "is the obedience of the soldiers of Hitler—a blind, myopic obedience."[11] Scahill charged that the top bishops are seeking, for their own ends, to keep the institutional church immune from scrutiny by the laity, the public, and the courts. "The bishops are spending more time with their lawyers than with their consciences."[12] Regarding the brethren's efforts to protect themselves by invoking the constitutional separation of church and state, he says, "I don't hold the institutional church to be superior to justice. It's made me ashamed to be a Catholic."[13]

Scahill offers a keen observation about the core of the problem: the hierarchy's disposition to "protect the institution at all costs." The historical example he uses is startling. "In some real way, we're the last of the landed gentry. They give us beautiful houses to live in, housekeepers to clean. Who else has that? . . . I think priests have become content with their little fiefdoms . . . and I think that's the reason for the silence."[14]

This remark hints at the parallel between the Enron crisis and the church's. In both cases, the princely "brethren"—whether CEOs or archbishops—have hijacked an institution, eliminated any countervailing power, created a culture of secrecy or nontransparency, and used their unaccountable authority to serve their own interests. To protect their privileged lifestyle, they have been willing to sacrifice their respective laity, whether shareholders or parishioners, rendering them mute. Without a voice, the laity has become vulnerable to horrible abuse that can only be described as institutionalized systemic wilding.

The similarity between corporate and church wilding is not sociologically surprising. The church is one of the world's great corporate empires, historically one of the wealthiest institutions, possessed of vast land-holdings, great buildings, and thousands of employees. The material wealth of the institutional church remains formidably large, and the princes of the church enjoy enormous privileges of lifestyle, status, and political power. They consort closely with business and political elites in the corporate state, a part of the broader social elite in America. They have embraced the organizational structure of the other great hierarchal institutions, including the corporation and the military. And as in these other institutions, they have succumbed to the inevitable temptations to monopolize power and information to help themselves and protect their own. As they disenfranchise the laity, it is sociologically entirely predictable that the lack of accountability leads to wilding. Tragically, self-interest and exploitation are becoming as integral to the structure of the institutional church as they are to the corporation and the corporate state.

How to End Wilding in the Church: Empower the Laity

Reverend Scahill concludes that "there needs to be other voices out there. A healthy church requires change."[15] The institutional church is not exempt from the structural imperatives essential to any vast complex organization. To heal itself from the wilding curse, it needs the same remedy as Enron and the corporate state in Washington, D.C. It must reconnect with the laity and empower them with knowledge, voice, and governance authority. The unaccountable institutional system is predisposed to become a cesspool of uncontrollable wilding.

In the corporate world, preventing institutional wilding means putting worker and public representatives on the board of directors, flattening the corporate hierarchy, institutionalizing transparency, and creating an entirely new system of public regulation and accountability. This, of course, means nothing short of democratizing the corporation and its captive government in Washington. Both the corporation and the government must become institutions of, by, and for the people.

But is such a democratic system of accountability possible or even desirable in the institutional church? Many might conclude that both history and doctrine make the institutional church unique, one that must inevitably be a hierarchy ruled by the princes at the top. Others disagree, and some of the most interesting voices are those of the faithful that are emerging in the wake of the current crisis.

In Boston, the epicenter of the crisis, a bold group of laity formed to demand that the church listen and change to ensure that sexual abuse never again occur in the church. Calling themselves the Voice of the Faithful, they have become a global organization of more than 30,000 practicing Catholics.[16] They see themselves as "mainstream" Catholics, but they conclude that the institutional church needs to end its culture of secrecy and empower the laity to prevent future scandals. They see this new transparency and empowerment as entirely consistent with their faith and with the vision of the institutional church expressed in the Second Vatican Council, a historic papal initiative between 1962 and 1965 that called for more social justice and democratic church reforms.

A fundamental principle of Voice of the Faithful is that "the Church should respect the dignity and intelligence of the laity . . . and work for active and meaningful engagement of the laity in the operations of the Church." Drawing on Vatican II, the organization proposes "to empower an active Parish Pastoral Council in every parish." It also proposes creating "parallel Lay councils on intermediate levels such as the vicariate and the region." Voice of the Faithful sees the participation of the laity in church governance as central to preventing future abuse and regards the church's current culture of "secrecy and exclusion" as incompatible with the church's health.[17]

Organizations seeking to bring more openness, democracy, and accountability to the church have existed long before the current crisis. The Association for the Rights of Catholics in the Church (ARCC) is a federation of the laity in many European countries, including France, Germany, Great Britain, Ireland, Italy, Belgium, and others. The ARCC is affiliated with the European Conference for Human Rights in the Church and is also inspired by the vision of the Second Vatican Council. It is part of a worldwide movement to promote social justice and democracy inside and outside the church.[18]

The ARCC believes that "the message of the Gospel mandates a concern for justice in the Church, as well as in the world." Thus the rights of Catholics must be respected and embodied in the structure of the institutional church as well as in the broader society. It believes the rights of Catholics in the church "derive both from our basic humanity as persons and from our baptism as Christians."[19]

The ARCC's Charter of Rights includes sections on basic rights, decision making and dissent, due process, and social and cultural rights, as well as ministries and spirituality. It reads remarkably like the 1948 U.N. Declaration of Universal Human Rights and is essentially a manifesto for democratizing the institutional church. Regarding decision making, it proposes that "all Catholics have the right to a voice in all decisions that affect them, including the choosing of their leaders." Should there be any doubt that this is a call for democratic accountability, the Charter's sixth provision is that "all Catholics have the right to have their leaders accountable to them."[20]

The fascinating feature of the ARCC is that it explicitly roots these Catholic rights in the church within canon law, the body of official codes that governs the institutional church, although it views canon law as only a "partial" statement of the necessary just relation between the church and its faithful. The right to participate in all decisions is rooted in Canon 212.3 of the 1983 revised Canon Law code, which mandates that the faithful "have the right, and even at times a duty" to express their views. The right to accountability is drawn from Canon 492, which mandates in each diocese a finance council "composed of at least three members of the laity," and from Canon 1287.2, which states that "administrators are to render an account to the faithful." The ARCC references many other canon laws that spell out the rights of the laity to form associations and express their views freely on all matters within the church.[21]

The ARCC, drawing on the social justice teachings set forth in Pope Paul VI's "Populorum Progressio," says that justice requires "the renewal of the Church's own structural organization." Underlying the entire Charter of Catholic Rights is the principle that "all Catholics are radically equal." This is rooted in Canon 208, which states, "There exists among all the Christian faithful, in virtue of their rebirth in Christ, a true equality with regard to dignity and activity."

While one of his great concerns was the separation between church and state, Thomas Jefferson articulated the same philosophy of radical equality in the Declaration of Independence, and there is a similar vision of human rights in the Bill of Rights to the Constitution. The United Nation's Declaration of Rights is more expansive than Jefferson's in its vision of social and economic rights and more parallel to the philosophy of comprehensive rights now being articulated by the church's rising "voices of the faithful." While they should be kept separate, the institutional church and the corporate state must be renewed with a similar vision of rights and democratic accountability if they are to prevent the princely brethren, corporate and clerical, from dominating both spheres and plunging us further into a systemic wilding epidemic. Fortunately, new grassroots movements are rising to challenge the princes in all the great hierarchies of society and offer hope of a more democratized and moral order.

Killing Society

The Ungluing of America

A nation never falls but by suicide.
—Ralph Waldo Emerson

An American Dream that does not spell out the moral consequences of unmitigated self-interest threatens to turn the next generation of Americans into wilding machines. In a pattern already visible today, Americans could turn not only on each other but also society, being too self-absorbed to make the commitments and observe the moral constraints that hold stable communities together. There is already abundant evidence that a wilder generation of Americans is assaulting and abandoning society, allowing the guarantees of civilized behavior and the most vital social institutions to languish and die as this generation pursues its own selfish dreams.

The breakdown of society that I describe in this chapter—from violence on the streets to state violence, from broken schools to broken politics—is a cause as well as a consequence of the wilding crisis. The wilding culture poisons families, workplaces, and neighborhoods, which in their weakened form are fertile spawning grounds for more wilding. There is no first cause in this chicken-and-egg causal chain; the wilding virus creates social breakdown and simultaneously grows out of it.

Wilding in the Streets

America's culture of wilding, at its extreme, is triggering an epidemic of bizarre and terrifying violence. The new violence constitutes a direct assault on society, threatening the social infrastructure that sustains civilized life.

On February 1, 2001, police arrested a 9-year-old boy who allegedly attacked four of his schoolmates with a hypodermic needle. Running through the gymnasium in Public School 66 in Brooklyn, New York, he reportedly stabbed two boys and two girls, who had to be rushed to the hospital.[1] A yet more bizarre needle attack took place on New York City streets some years earlier, when 10 teenage girls were arrested and "charged with jabbing women with pins in dozens of unprovoked attacks on the Upper West Side over a one-week period." The girls "thought it was fun to run down Broadway," Deputy Police Chief Ronald Fenrich said, and stick "women with pins to see their reactions." The girls expressed some remorse, Fenrich reported, although mainly "they were sorry they got caught." Meanwhile, the neighborhood residents, although they had seen more vicious crimes, told reporters that they found the pinprick attacks an "intolerable invasion, both because of the cavalier manner in which the attacks were carried out, and because rumors spread early that it was possible the jabs had come from AIDS-infected needles."[2]

American cities have always been violent places, but the pinprick attacks are emblematic of a new, more menacing violence and a more profound breakdown of social life. Like the expressive wilding in Central Park, the attacks involve taking pleasure in the inflicting of pain and complete indifference to the sensibilities of the victims. The potential targets—anyone walking the street—need to become hyper-vigilant and assume that every pedestrian is a potential threat.

The horrifying image of children killing children has helped define our era. In 2004, Lionel Tate pleaded guilty to second-degree murder for killing a 6-year-old girl in 1999, when he was 12, while practicing wrestling moves he had seen on television.[3] Just two weeks later, Massachusetts police arrested an 11-year-old boy for stabbing another boy to death in a Springfield movie theater. Less than two years earlier, a 10-year-old Massachusetts boy was charged with murdering a 5-week-old baby.

The epidemic of kids murdering kids first grabbed public attention in the 1990s. In October 1994, two Chicago boys, ages 10 and 11, threw 5-year-old Erik Morris to his death from a fourteenth-floor window. The reason: Erik had refused to steal candy for them. Erik's 8-year-old brother had desperately tried to save him but was overpowered by the bigger boys.

A month earlier, Chicagoan Robert Sandifer, age 11, was killed by two boys, ages 14 and 16, who feared that Sandifer would squeal about their gang activities to police. Shortly before his own murder, Sandifer had killed a 14-year-old girl, Shavan Dean, when he fired a volley of bullets into a group of teenagers playing football. Young Sandifer was buried with his teddy bear.

Violent crime throughout the United States peaked in the mid-1990s, but rates of murder, armed burglary, and other violent crimes remain exceptionally high—far higher than in Western European nations, Japan, and other developed countries. A November 2000 survey of 10,000 youths ages 12 to 17 documents that violence is rampant. Funded by 18 federal agencies, the study reports that one out of four students, representing about 5.3 million American children, "told investigators they had either used a gun or knife, carried such a weapon or had been involved in an incident in which someone was injured by a weapon in the past year." Robert Blum, the principal researcher, concluded that "the prevalence of violence is much higher than we expected, particularly when you consider we've taken out all the fistfighting that seventh- and eighth-grade boys do." He might have added that the study also factored out the violence rates among the astonishing number of young people whom we have locked up in federal and state prisons.[4]

School violence is now widely considered a national crisis in itself. On February 29, 2000, a 6-year-old child allegedly fired a .32-caliber pistol at a 6-year-old girl in a classroom at Buell Elementary School near Flint, Michigan. According to eyewitnesses, the boy had tucked the gun in his pants, pulled it out, and fired, striking her in the neck. He then reportedly ran into a nearby bathroom and threw the gun into a trash can. The girl, Kayla Rolland, died 30 minutes later. According to one report, the motive might have arisen out of a scuffle between the two on the playground the day before.[5]

The U.S. Centers for Disease Control and Prevention reports that almost 10 percent of children bring a weapon to school. School violence peaked in the early 1990s, but incidents with multiple fatalities have increased, the most famous being the 1999 massacre at Columbine High School in Littleton, Colorado. At Columbine, two students in black trench coats opened fire with semiautomatic machine guns and killed 15 people and wounded more than 20 others. As in many of these incidents, the motives for this expressive wilding involved jealousy and revenge for being excluded from the most popular circles—the rage of the outcast. But they also mirrored the violent culture of the school that they hated. Columbine put the toughest football players on a pedestal, honoring physical force. The Columbine area also has a strong military presence, and the young killers had grown up infatuated with war and surrounded by guns.

The chronicle of school violence in the last decade is stupefying. On December 6, 1999, a 13-year-old student in Fort Gibson, Oklahoma, came to school and shot at least four of his classmates with his father's nine-millimeter semiautomatic weapon. A few weeks earlier, a 12-year-old boy in a Deming, New Mexico, middle school shot and killed a female class-mate, age 12, in the schoolyard. On May 15, 1998, a 15-year-old student in Springfield, Ohio, killed two classmates in the school cafeteria. On May 21, 1998, police reported that three sixth-grade boys had a "hit list" and had been plotting to kill many of their classmates in a sniper attack at school during a false fire alarm. A few months earlier, in a high school in West Paducah, Kentucky, a 14-year-old student killed three students and wounded five others while they were participating in a prayer circle in a school hallway. And a few months before that, a 16-year-old student in Pearl, Mississippi, shot and killed his mother and then shot nine students at school.[6]

Children themselves are terrified in many schools and neighbor-hoods. Fourteen-year-old Chirll Rivers is a Boston student who says she's scared: "I don't want to die. You have to watch your back every day. Someone could mistake you for someone else and shoot you. I could be the wrong person."[7] Another kid, forced to walk home from a youth program after a van broke down, collapsed in a panic, crying, "I can't walk home, I just can't walk home. Someone got killed on my street. I'll get killed too." The *Boston Globe* reported that this youth did get home, running all the way, but that in the next eight days, three young men did not have the same luck—they were killed on the same street—while a fourth was fatally shot through the window of his mother's apartment. The result of this unprecedented epidemic of violence, the *Globe* said, was that "increasing numbers of city youths are arming them-selves, carrying small knives and pistols tucked into their waistbands or inside their coats."[8]

A new wave of school violence erupted in Boston schools in 2001, cre-ating a crisis in the city. On January 19, 2001, a parent attacked a first-grade teacher, who was sent to the hospital with a black eye and fractured cheekbone. Within three weeks of this incident, an eighth-grader punched an assistant principal, and a knife-wielding ninth-grader chased a track coach. A week later, assailants with knives stabbed boys in two different schools. According to the National Center for Education Statistics, despite a reduction in juvenile crime rates, the national percentage of students saying they felt too unsafe to go to school at least once per month grew to 5.2 percent in 1999, compared with 4 percent in 1997. And, according to another study released in 2001, a majority of U.S. teenagers used vio-lence in the last year, and one in five boys brought a weapon to high school. "The seeds of violence," said Michael Josephson, president of the Institute of Ethics, which funded the study, "can be found in schools all over America."[9]

Falling Bridges, Potholes, and Peeling Schoolroom Paint: The Abandonment of Society

Journalist Tom Ashbrook, returning from a long trip to Asia, records his initial impressions of Los Angeles. "Hello Occident. Cracked highways, no service. Hotel is heavy on glitter and self-promotional hype, light on everything else. Construction quality shabby. Rusting metalwork. Cheap materials. . . . Rich next to poor. Slick by shabby. Twitchy bag ladies and a legless panhandler croaking 'Aloha'. . . . Korean cabdriver complains road repairs take ten times longer than in Seoul."[10]

"An American homecoming," Ashbrook groans, "is a journey into shades of disarray." It is downright "scary for a recent returnee." Ashbrook, who is returning from a 10-year sojourn in Asia, learns that his brother-in-law "sleeps with a large pistol in his nightstand and an alarm system that can track a burglar room by room." Turning on the radio, Ashbrook hears of "Los Angeles drivers taking potshots at one another on the freeway, American schoolchildren scoring at the bottom of the first-world heap in key subjects. Drug lords reigning over urban fiefs, Alcoholics Anonymous and its ilk as a new religion. Wall Street sapping the economy." Fresh into his hotel, Ashbrook's son flicks on a Saturday morning cartoon: "Hey, fella! This is America," booms the wisecracking voice of an animated hero. "I've got the right to not work any time I want."[11]

"Our cracked highways and rusting bridges," writes Ashbrook, "seem physical reflections of falling standards, organization, simple care in the performance of jobs—of lost resolve." He concludes that a "returning American comes home with trepidation," hoping that his or her sense of the breakdown of America "is exaggerated, fearing that it might not be, subtly prepared to accept it as fact."[12]

Ashbrook is seeing the unmistakable signs of a looming breakdown in both the physical and social infrastructure necessary to keep a society viable. America's physical infrastructure—its grid of roads, bridges, railways, ports, airports, sewer systems, and communications nodes—is in serious disrepair. The failure to maintain the levees in New Orleans may have been the most dramatic example. As I flesh out in Chapter 9 on Hurricane Katrina, the flooding of the city could have been prevented had the government been willing to rebuild a crumbling infrastructure of levees and dams that New Orleans leaders and citizens had long recognized as a catastrophic threat to the city's survival. That failure stands as the most powerful indictment of a society abandoned by its own national leaders from both political parties.

But well before Katrina, the erosion of the U.S. infrastructure was clear to ordinary Americans—for example, to the folks in Covington, Tennessee, where a bridge over the Hatchie River collapsed, sending seven motorists to their deaths; or people in upstate New York, where the collapse of a bridge killed 10 people. "Forty percent of the nation's bridges have serious deficiencies. Highways are strained beyond capacity, while potential mass transit options go unexplored. Water delivery systems are so antiquated that some cities still transport water through nineteenth-century wooden pipes." California Democratic congressman Robert T. Matsui says, "The problem is absolutely catastrophic." Rebuilding the national infrastructure, Massachusetts transportation secretary Frederick P. Salvucci says, "is the greatest public works challenge since the pyramids were built."[13]

Ripping the Social Fabric: Wilding in Health Care and Education

As the physical infrastructure erodes, the social infrastructure is being quietly starved, creating an emergency in basic health care, education, and the social services required to sustain the social fabric. The crisis of affordable housing has now yielded "over three million homeless people," writes journalist Michael Albert, "who wander our backstreets eating out of garbage cans and sleeping under tattered newspapers in bedrooms shared with alley-rats."[14]

About 13 percent of Americans have fallen through the slashed social safety net and are poor, partly reflecting the unpleasant reality of an economy churning out a high proportion of extremely low-wage jobs. More than 45 million Americans have no health insurance. This includes one-fifth of all American children, contributing to America's life expectancy being lower, and the infant mortality rate higher, than in all Western European nations.

The health crisis, a product of political policy that redistributes taxpayer money from social welfare benefits to corporate handouts, has four dramatic symbols—all of which involve institutional wilding. One is the collapse of public health after Katrina, where according to CNN reports, staff members of New Orleans' Memorial Medical Center repeatedly discussed killing some of their own terminally ill patients. Parish coroner Frank Minyard said investigators in New Orleans went further and told him that "someone was going around injecting people with some sort of lethal medication" to commit euthanasia.[15] This reflected a lack of preparedness in the face of the huge storm and a broader breakdown of public health care in the nation, particularly in urban hospitals serving the poor.

A second symbol of the health crisis is the failure to protect Americans and people around the world from lethal plagues such as AIDS or a potential global avian bird flu disaster. In the case of AIDS, big drug companies have resisted allowing poor countries, especially in southern Africa where AIDS affects up to one-third of the population of some countries, to use generic versions of drugs or cheaper imports. Big Pharma, the most profitable industry, relies on global patents extended by the WTO, to resist requests for cheaper prices, although some have given concessions in response to global pressure. In regard to a potential avian flu pandemic, the one company (Roche) that produces Tamiflu, the most important antidote, has wielded its intellectual property rights to limit rivals and governments from producing enough of a supply of the drug to protect the public. New York senator Charles Schumer, who finally had succeeded in getting Roche to license production rights to other companies, observed that the drug companies' view, even in the face of an emergency, is "You have a patent, you cling to it. That's what patent law allows." When hundreds of thousands are dying from any pandemic, enforcement of such patents constitutes legal wilding. The U.S. government's failure to produce vaccines and its late start in offering federal incentives for drug companies to produce vaccines, for avian flu or other pandemics, may be an even more important part of the crisis.[16]

Governments collude in public health wilding by privatizing the health care system and investing in expensive technologies for specialized care, while ignoring the necessity of producing low-profit vaccinations, as well as by failing to pass the clean water and clean air measures that could save millions.

A third health crisis centers around fraud or bias in drug research and publishing—a serious form of corporate wilding that drives up drug costs, making crucial medicine unaffordable—and creating biased research sponsored by the drug companies themselves, controlling the public dissemination of which studies will be published. The drug companies also promote the proliferation of other super-profitable drugs, such as psychiatric meds for children, or drugs prescribed to adults that are hyped through advertising to doctors and the public, have serious side effects, and may be unnecessary in the first case.

The greatest public health crisis is in the planet's environmental sustainability and creation of environmental conditions that could breed an irreversible disaster. In service to mining, energy, timber, coal, and other industries that helped finance President Bush's elections, the Bush administration systematically seeks to unravel environmental protections on everything from wetlands and national forests and national parks to the Clean Air and Clean Water Acts. More fundamentally, the conditions for the sustainability of a livable planet are being ignored by the failure to address the crisis of global warming, the ultimate form of wilding against the human community past and future in the name of protecting jobs and profits for the energy and, specifically, the petrochemical complex. The president and vice president have their closest corporate links to the oil companies. The current corporate regime, beyond the Bush-Cheney administration, is dominated by the auto, oil, and broader petrochemical complex, making its profits a core imperative of all regime policy and a source of its greatest economic and environmental wilding. This is manifested most clearly in the administration's failure to sign the Kyoto Protocol controlling global carbon emissions, or even to acknowledge that global warming is an established scientific fact.[17]

The crisis in the educational infrastructure is also dramatic. The collapse of American public education is yielding an average American public high school student who not only has difficulty locating France, Israel, or even the United States itself on a map, but who scores lower across the board on standardized tests than students in virtually all other advanced industrialized countries. This is well understood by American parents, who shun the public school system when they can afford to do so. An estimated 9 out of 10 Boston parents send their children to parochial school or any place other than a Boston public school.[18]

In response to growing public concern, Bush steered through his No Child Left Behind program to help fund basic reading and writing programs in urban schools. But this turned out to be mainly rhetoric, with both Republican and Democratic governors complaining that Bush and the Republican Congress did not follow through with the necessary funding. In 2003, the bipartisan National Governors Association voted to characterize the No Child Left Behind program as an "unfunded mandate," one of those federal programs that governors believe unfairly saddles states with public obligations that they have no funds to implement.[19] Meanwhile, Jonathan Kozol, in his latest and most searing indictment of public education, showed that segregation is re-emerging in American public schools, in both the North and the South, with a growing percentage of schools either overwhelmingly white or overwhelmingly black, and the black schools starved for funding.[20]

Parents recognize that American public schools are literally disintegrating. A 1995 report by the General Accounting Office (GAO) showed that 25,000 U.S. schools housing 14 million children need extensive physical rehabilitation, including New York City schools that had exposed asbestos, rotting roof beams, and broken plumbing; Montana schools where water leaks have led to collapsed ceilings; and a New Orleans school where termites have eaten books on library shelves, and then the shelves themselves.[21]

This abject unraveling of the social fabric is the ultimate manifestation of the new wilding culture, an abandonment of society consciously engineered by the country's political leadership and passively endorsed by the majority of voters. The cost of maintaining and reconstructing its physical and social infrastructure is well within the reach of the world's still-richest country; however, in what may be the greatest act of domestic-policy wilding, recent presidents, while continuing to pour billions into the Pentagon's coffers, have refused to support the public spending that would halt and reverse the crumbling infrastructure. This refusal is rationalized under the umbrella of "free-market" ideology—to wit: rolling back taxes, deficits, and "big government." In contrast, Western European countries such as Belgium, France, Germany, and the Netherlands, all less wealthy than the United States, have managed to preserve much of their social infrastructure by spending a substantially higher percentage of their gross national product on health care, education, and a wide range of other social programs.[22]

Government for the Rich: Compassionate Conservatives, New Democrats, and Political Wilding

George W. Bush campaigned as a "compassionate conservative" who would "leave no child behind." While the rhetoric is appealing, the reality behind the words is less palatable. About one in every five children in America is poor, and it will take billions in education and social services to help lift them out of poverty. But by making huge trillion-dollar tax cuts the center of his presidency, in the name of cutting "big government," Bush has undercut the children. His tax cuts will require taking money from the poor and middle class and redistributing it to the rich. Moreover, as the president himself acknowledged, social spending by most federal departments will have to be slashed to make the tax cuts possible, meaning that social programs for the needy will be sliced in order to return huge sums to the wealthy.

Massive tax-cutting for the rich, in a period of history when the income and wealth of the richest 1 percent of Americans is growing far faster than that of all other Americans, creating the greatest gap between rich and poor since the 1920s, has become a prime and enduring symbol of the new public-policy wilding. Cynically fueled by politicians from both parties (Democrats in 2001 advocated a "modest" tax cut of almost $1 trillion), the so-called tax revolt has created the political space that leaders need to reward their wealthy patrons who finance their campaigns. Cutting taxes has become the respectable political vehicle for lashing out at the poor and ultimately abandoning both government and society itself. Future historians may come to view American leaders playing the tax revolt as a sequel to Nero playing his fiddle as Rome burned.

As will be described shortly, tax cuts for the rich are the centerpiece of George W. Bush's presidency, with Bush seeking to complete the revolution inaugurated by Ronald Reagan. Tax cuts for the wealthy were at the heart of the 1980s Reagan revolution, with Reagan, in the name of attacking "big government," cut marginal tax rates for multimillionaires and billionaires from over 90 percent to 37 percent. As discussed shortly, Reagan actually expanded government, but to serve the rich rather than the middle class and poor. Newt Gingrich and his Republican colleagues, who took over Congress in 1995, followed in Reagan's footsteps, putting tax cuts for the wealthy at the center of their Contract with America, and proposing drastic cuts in nearly all social spending, from education to health care to welfare.

The billions being returned to the people through tax cuts go overwhelmingly to the very rich, through ingenious schemes not well understood by the public. Bush's proposal to create new savings accounts into which well-to-do families can put $60,000 that will never be taxed is a radical and little discussed step to end taxation on wealth.[23] His cut in the dividend tax is another huge giveaway to the rich, masquerading as a tax cut for all. And his massive income tax cuts, amounting to $10 trillion over 10 years, are a shameless bonanza for the wealthy, sold falsely as fair tax relief for all Americans. Under the Bush plan of 2002, the poorest 20 percent of the population in 2002 received an average income tax cut of $15. The middle 20 percent got an average cut of $170. The cut for the top 1 percent averaged $13,469. As for whether Bush's overall tax-cut plan offers compassion for the ordinary worker, secretary Luwaunna Adams, a Pennsylvania mother who makes $20,400 a year, got a tax benefit of $117 a year, or $2 a week. She appeared in a press conference with New Jersey multimillionaire senator Jon Corzine, who said he would get an annual tax benefit from Bush's plan of $1 million.[24]

The Democrats illustrated this huge gift to the rich when Democratic leaders Richard Gephardt, House minority leader, and Tom Daschle, Senate minority leader, appeared on Capitol Hill with a black Lexus sedan and an old, beat-up replacement muffler. Senator Daschle said that the car "was just like the Bush tax cut—fully loaded. If you're a millionaire, under the Bush tax cut, you get a $46,000 tax cut, more than enough to pay for this Lexus. But if you're a typical working person, you get $227, and that's enough to buy this muffler."[25]

The wilding dimension of the tax cuts has been highlighted, ironically, by outspoken opposition to Bush's plan from some of the world's most famous billionaires. Warren Buffet, the nation's second-richest person; George Soros, the world's premier global investor; and William H. Gates Sr., head of the Gates Foundation and father of Bill Gates, joined dozens of other super-rich individuals attacking the Bush plan. They zeroed in on Bush's proposal to repeal the estate, or "death," tax. Gates Sr. says that "repealing the estate tax would enrich the heirs of America's millionaires and billionaires while hurting families who struggle to make ends meet." Buffet said Bush's plan "would be a terrible mistake," the same as "choosing the 2020 Olympic team by picking the eldest sons of the gold-medal winners in the 2000 Olympics. . . . Without the estate tax," Buffet concluded, "you in effect will have an aristocracy of wealth, which means you pass down the ability to command the resources of the nation based on heredity rather than merit."[26]

In fact, only 2 percent of the richest Americans pay the estate tax and would thus receive all the benefits of the repeal. Bush's own new head of faith-based giving, John J. DiIulio Jr., has himself opposed a repeal, since he agrees that the net effect would be to undermine the tax's financial incentive for charitable giving.[27] But the Republican House of Representatives nonetheless approved repeal of the tax in 2005 and voted to make the repeal permanent, part of an overall effort by the Bush administration to sell permanent tax cuts for the rich. The Bush administration has been successful in presenting tax cuts as beneficial for all Americans, even though its tax agenda has been mainly a bonanza for the wealthiest Americans and has created extreme and dangerous polarization between America's rich and poor.[28]

Presidents from Ronald Reagan to George W. Bush, who have spearheaded the revolution against "big government," are not telling you the truth. They do not really want to shrink government because the capitalist economy and, especially, the super-profits of large corporations themselves depend on very big government. Presidents Reagan and W. Bush are radicals who have massively expanded the size of government and created the biggest government deficits in history by cutting taxes while spending vastly more money on corporate handouts to the petro-chemical and the military-industrial complexes, along with other sectors of big business. When Ralph Nader ran for president in 2000, one of his main aims was to blast "corporate welfare"—the vast giveaways and subsidies doled out to big business. Without such help from "big government," corporate profits would rapidly decline.

Texan Justice: Political Wilding and the Prison-Industrial Complex

The rich also need government to provide the police, prisons, and military security that protect them from the left-behinds both at home and abroad. As elites increase corporate welfare and use "trickle-up" tax policies to redistribute money to themselves, government leaders depend ever more on the use of force to contain the unrest of millions who languish in poverty, get downsized, and accumulate credit-card debt that threatens their ability to live the American Dream. In this section, we see that the massive increase in police and prisons reflects the effort to hold together by force a society that is deeply fractured by race and class.

State violence is political wilding when it involves the use of governmental force, for power or money, that ends up harming innocent people. State crime and violence have become hot political topics in the new century. Nations around the world now seek to hold leaders accountable for war crimes, such as those committed by Serbia's deposed dictator, Slobodan Milošević, who, prior to his death in 2006, was forced to appear before the International Court of Justice for masterminding genocidal campaigns of "ethnic cleansing." Central Intelligence Agency (CIA) coups against democratically elected foreign leaders, such as the one in 1973 that deposed Chile's president, Salvador Allende, are another very important form of state violence that goes unpunished but constitutes egregious political wilding.[29]

The main concern here though, is wilding practiced by the U.S. government and the "prison-industrial complex" at home (see Chapter 8 for a separate discussion of military and CIA wilding, both abroad and at home, tied to the war on terror). One prominent form is police brutality, symbolized most famously by the beating of Rodney King—an African-American—that triggered the Los Angeles riots in the early 1990s. The tape of the King beating, replayed on television sets across the country, showed police officers hammering King 61 times in 87 seconds with metal batons, then continuing to kick and hit him as he lay face down and motionless on the ground. Struck initially by two police Taser darts carrying 50,000 volts of electricity each, King suffered a broken leg and several broken bones in his face.

Police brutality is just one expression of an epidemic of U.S. government violence against its own citizens, especially the poor, minorities, and immigrants. Sociologist Max Weber wrote that the state can be defined as the institution vested with a monopoly of the tools of official violence, including the military, police, courts, and prisons. When governments resort to police and prisons to repress racial minorities or disadvantaged groups, or to inflict excessively harsh force against any citizens (as in the famous Waco tragedy), they commit political wilding.

The movement of George W. Bush from the Texas governorship to the U.S. presidency has focused attention on the huge expansion of, and violence in, the prison system in the last decade. When Bush was governor, Texas built more prisons and executed more people than any other state. "Texan justice" is seen by many as an oxymoron, since so many of the Texans that are locked up and killed are African-Americans, and so much cruelty and capriciousness are built into the system.

As governor, Bush approved the execution of Karla Faye Tucker, a confessed murderer who had undergone a deep religious conversion and been a model prisoner for two decades. Supported by thousands of religious and other civic leaders, Tucker, who had become a national symbol of redemption and humility, unsuccessfully sought Bush's pardon.

During the presidential debates, a spectator asked Bush whether he was proud of all the executions he had overseen, and Bush said no. But many were looking for a more thoughtful response. The death penalty is outlawed in every European country, and many Europeans' first reaction to Bush's election involved commentary about the barbarism of state execution and shock that Bush, a symbol of American cruelty, had been elected.

In 2000, after a prisoner sentenced to death was proved innocent by DNA tests, the Republican governor of Illinois, George Ryan, suspended all executions in his state. His bold action catalyzed similar decisions in other states, where public opinion has begun to turn against the death penalty as immoral, a position long held by the Catholic Church. Whether the death penalty itself constitutes political wilding can be debated. But most agree that sentencing to death potentially innocent people who lack the money for fair legal representation and who have not been proven guilty by DNA testing and multiple other checks is unjust state violence. Moreover, experts on Texas courts and prisons have generally concluded that these flaws are blatantly evident in the Texas system and in many of the executions supervised by Bush when he was governor.

The death penalty controversy is only the tip of a rapidly escalating crisis of the prison system. More than 2 million people in 2000 were locked up in U.S. prisons, the most of any nation in the world and eight times the number incarcerated in 1970. Of these 2 million, 70 percent are minorities and half are African-Americans. One of every eight black men between the ages of 18 and 24 is in jail. "A black man in the state of California," University of California professor Angela Davis tells us, "is five times more likely to be found in a prison cell than in one of the state colleges or universities."[30]

America can barely build prisons fast enough to meet the demand. Corporations have leapt into the breach, building and operating hundreds of new prisons in the fastest-growing industry in America. Critics such as Davis have begun talking about the new "prison-industrial system." The term connotes a new melding of economic and political wilding, in which racism and poverty help fuel the growth of a huge, disadvantaged prison population and the attendant prison system that returns billions of dollars in profit to wealthy investors.[31]

The raging controversy about "racial profiling," in which police target minorities for random drug checks, shows that wilding begins in the prison "recruitment" process. While African-Americans consume 13 percent of illegal drugs, they comprise 74 percent of the drug offenders sentenced to prison. This figure reflects not only racial profiling but also massive disparities in sentences for crack compared to powder cocaine, as well as the practice of police department drug-busting on urban streets rather than suburban parking lots. For most offenses, minorities are disproportionately likely to be arrested, sentenced, physically abused by guards, or denied medical treatment in jail.[32]

The prison-industrial system is not only racist but also class-biased, being deeply punitive to the poor. White-collar and corporate criminals steal billions more than street burglars. Yet the percentage of corporate criminals who go to jail is far lower. The prison-industrial system returns fat profits to corporate elites who own and run the jails. Much of the profit is extracted from prisoners forced to work for wages as low as 10 cents an hour.[33]

Wilding continues upon a prisoner's exit from the system, since many states deny released felons the right to vote and some, illegally, even deny the franchise to those convicted of misdemeanors. Fourteen percent of African-American men in the United States have lost their right to vote for alleged criminal offenses, and in some states the percentage is much higher. One-third of all black men in Alabama are disenfranchised, evoking memories of Jim Crow days and the slave-era South.[34]

The flawed Florida election count in 2000—as well as the controversial election results in Ohio in 2004, where majority-black precincts had fewer machines and far longer waits for voters in the rain—puts a new light on these data. As Derrick Jackson writes of the 2000 election, "In Florida, where Al Gore lost by 537 votes, 31 percent of African-American men, 200,000 of them, cannot vote because of felony convictions. For the Florida Republican Party, that was not enough. They hired a firm to purge the rolls even more, wrongly slashing thousands of people who were guilty only of misdemeanors."[35]

Meanwhile, a more recent investigation in 2004 by the GAO, showed that fraud could have swung the results of the election in Ohio, and thus the entire 2004 election. The GAO concluded that voting software and machines were vulnerable to many forms of hacking, tampering, and altering of votes.[36] These findings do not prove that massive fraud occurred and that the results might have been different. But, taken in conjunction with other findings of disproportionate problems involving registration, proof of identification with official photo, long wait times, and voting irregularities in black precincts, the GAO conclusions were consistent with the arguments made by African-American leaders, such as Jesse Jackson and Representative John Conyers (D-MI), who argued that election officials had excluded or miscounted black votes in Ohio, as they had in Florida four years earlier.[37]

The 2000 presidential election, especially as it was played out in the Florida recount farce, is a case of one form of political wilding multiplied by another. At the very peak of the U.S. internal security system, which includes the judiciary as well as the prison-industrial complex, sits the Supreme Court. Bush ultimately became president because five members of the Supreme Court ruled that the Florida recount could not continue. Dissenters on the Court and hundreds of law professors have decried the decision as a historic stain on the entire judicial system.

The slim Supreme Court majority ruled that variation in counting methods in different Florida counties constituted a violation of the Fourteenth Amendment's equal-protection clause, originally passed, ironically, to protect the civil rights of freed slaves. But former Los Angeles deputy district attorney Vincent Bugliosi notes that "varying voting methods have been in use for two centuries; the Court has never hinted there might be a right that was being violated." Bugliosi's conclusion is stark. "These five justices," he writes, referring to the bare majority who ruled for Bush, "are criminals in every true sense of the word, and in a fair and just world belong behind prison bars." Even if one rejects Bugliosi's conclusion, there is the undeniable hint that judicial partisanship among the nation's highest judges subverted the will of the American people in electing a president. It is hard to imagine a more serious and frightening form of political wilding.[38]

Political Decadence: A Wilding Culture of Cronyism and Corruption

In the fall of 2005, House Majority Leader Tom DeLay, Senate Majority Leader Bill Frist, and President Bush's most important adviser, Karl Rove, were all being investigated for corruption. DeLay, the most powerful Republican leader in Congress, was indicted by two grand juries in Texas for money laundering of campaign contributions. The Securities and Exchange Commission (SEC) subpoenaed Frist's financial records in an investigation of insider trading. Along with I. Lewis "Scooter" Libby, Vice President Dick Cheney's chief of staff who was already indicted (see Chapter 8), Rove was one of 11 senior White House officials under investigation for a serious and criminal breach of national security: leaking to journalists the name of a CIA officer, Valerie Plame, as punishment for her husband's public opposition to the Iraq war. And the scandals hovering around these three leading officials were just the tip of an iceberg of a system of cronyism and corruption that can only be viewed as political and societal wilding on a grand scale.

As investigations and indictments of leading players in the administration unfolded, it suggested something like the "Enronization" of the entire political system. Ironically, one of the leading operatives of the Bush administration, Ralph Reed, a central political figure in the religious right, had once been a lobbyist for Enron, and he may be under investigation by various state and federal authorities for lobbying activities and his role in sensational scandals involving Indian casinos linked to his close associate, Jack Abramoff.[39] The murky financial dealings of Frist, whose family owns and operates Hospital Corporation of America (HCA), the largest for-profit hospital corporation in the world, seemed to replicate the shady financial reporting and conflict of interest in the Enron crisis. Abramoff, a leading lobbyist with numerous top-level ties to the Bush administration, was indicted for illegal contributions to DeLay and fraudulent activities with

Tyco, one of the companies that imploded around the same time as Enron in a similar massive corruption scandal. As will be shown shortly, the Abramoff affair mushroomed into a prime symbol of America's new systemic "culture of corruption."

Political corruption has been around ever since the founding of the republic. In the first edition of this book, I detailed massive criminal fraud during the Reagan years in the Pentagon, the Department of Energy, the Department of Housing, the Department of Health and Human Services, and nearly every other major government agency, linked to huge Enron-like financial scandals such as the Michael Milken junk bond conviction and the multitrillion-dollar savings and loan debacle of the late 1980s. Corruption is hardly a Republican monopoly; as far back as New York City's infamous Tammany Hall and the Daley political machine in Chicago, which was notorious for finding dead voters to cast deciding votes in tight elections, Democrats also have been famous for their own corrupt political machines. During the Clinton years, allegations of financial fraud in the Whitewater affair engulfed the Clintons, and many Democratic officials have had their own sleazy connections to lobbyists and corporations as well as an insider system of political hacks and favoritism.

Nonetheless, the pattern that emerged in the Bush years had a new, meaner, and more systemic flavor. The phrase "culture of cronyism and corruption" became a household label for the incestuous dirty dealing and strong-arm tactics that seemed to characterize the administration from the very top. Its aim was absolute federal power at the price of the conservative principles—including fiscal responsibility, limited government, and moral integrity—that the administration publicly embraced. It is hardly surprising to find systemic cronyism and corruption in the corporate-dominated regime, beginning with Reagan. But while we have focused earlier on wilding where corporations spearheaded massive corruption that engulfed captive politicians, the pattern in the Bush years shows that wilding also flows in the other direction, as a conservative political machine strong-armed its own corporate allies and built a culture of routinized shakedowns, fraud, political hack appointments, criminal influence-peddling, and propaganda. For an administration elected on its promise to resurrect the moral values of the nation, this had the awful stench of moral hypocrisy in the name of morality itself.

Tom DeLay, known as the "the Hammer," was a leading designer and enforcer of this most recent political wilding machine. Texan prosecutors indicted DeLay for laundering corporate contributions to Texan politicians through the Republican National Committee (RNC). Texas law prevents corporate contributions to state political campaigns, so DeLay allegedly arranged for companies to donate to his Leadership Political Action

Committee (PAC) or to the RNC and then illegally funneled the money back to Texan Republicans, all during a period when Delay had engineered a gerrymandering scheme to secure permanent Republican control of the Texan legislature. The scandal surrounding these charges forced DeLay to step down permanently from his position as House Majority Leader.

DeLay's wilding goes far beyond the money-laundering charges to what is known as the "K Street Project." Beginning more than 10 years ago, with Senator Rick Santorum (R-PA) and the Republicans' leading antitax activist, Grover Norquist, DeLay sought to purge Democrats from the 35,000 members of the lobbyist community housed along K Street in Washington, D.C., essentially requiring that corporations and other groups seeking favors in Congress politically align themselves with the Republican majority. The new game in D.C. was known as "pay to play."[40]

Here's the way it worked: Because of their dominance of all branches of government, the Republicans were able to shake down the corporations for huge political donations in order to preserve Republican dominance. Because the companies and their trade associations depended on federal handouts and corporate-friendly trade, fiscal, and social policies, they needed to ante up to the Hammer's machine. And the antes were steep, DeLay being famous for raising millions of dollars for his PAC and the RNC. The *Texas Observer* offers one small illustration: "In early June 2002, DeLay held a two-day golf tournament. . . . The cost of attending the event was a corporate contribution of $25,000 to $50,000. Five energy companies were invited. . . . The golfing took place just before a House-Senate conference on an omnibus energy bill."[41]

The pay-to-play machine operated not only through illegal money laundering but also through perfectly legal extortion. Industries put literally millions of dollars each year into paying their lobbyists and the requisite money to the machine. In 2004 alone, the drug industry anted up $123 million for its lobbyists' role in the game; the broadcast media industry, $35 million; telephone companies, $72 million—to name just a few.[42]

While lobbyists routinely greased the machine with outrageously large, but entirely legal, contributions to get paybacks for their industries, the level of incestuous cronyism and greed frequently led to criminal excess. In October 2005, David Safavian, former administrator of the Office of Federal Procurement Policy, former chief of staff of the General Services Administration, and also a former lobbyist who had worked closely with Abramoff and Norquist, was indicted on multiple perjury counts as well as obstruction of justice. Safavian's offices oversaw $300 billion of federal contracts, a key part of the machine that rewards the companies that ante up with their paybacks from the game.[43]

Safavian's case is intertwined with that against DeLay and DeLay's "dear friend," Jack Abramoff, who helped pay for DeLay's lavish vacations to Korea and Scotland, and who extorted kickbacks and contributions to Republican organizations from Native American tribal casinos that needed Republican support for their business ventures. In January 2006, Abramoff pleaded guilty to charges of fraud, conspiracy, and tax evasion, which involved defrauding Indian tribes, bribing congressional officials, and engaging in other forms of illicit influence-peddling. His agreement to cooperate with prosecutors and spill the beans about his deals with lawmakers sent tremors through Congress and the Republican Party. Polls in early 2006 suggested that a majority of the public was fed up, agreeing with poll statements that the Abramoff case was a "major scandal." Fifty-three percent of the public called for big changes in Washington, citing corruption as a primary issue in 2006 midterm elections, along with Iraq and the economy.[44]

Ultimately, the novel feature of such systemic corruption involves its engulfment of a regime claiming to defend the deepest moral values of the nation against Middle East terrorists and East Coast liberals. In this sense, it creates the same shock as unrestrained wilding by the church, discussed in Chapter 6. We are not so surprised by corporate wilding since corporations are all about money. But wilding by the church, which is presumably all about morality and spirituality, seems like it could lead to the death of society itself.

The Republican Party is hardly the church, but its mass base is Christian conservatives. Republican operatives such as Ralph Reed and Karl Rove brilliantly orchestrated Bush's winning campaigns in both 2000 and 2004 on an appeal to the moral sensibilities of evangelical Christians and others committed to strict biblical principles and traditional values. What will these core Christian constituencies do if Rove is indicted? What will they do if Reed is indicted? The tension between moral rhetoric and moral conduct has become too explosive to be ignored. If conservative religious communities accept this regime's political decadence, they will have become key political sponsors of the very moral decay that they claim is the source of their political engagement. Pay or play may be the way of Washington, but it is not the way of the righteous.

8

War and Wilding

Iraq and the War against Terrorism

The great sociologist Max Weber defined the state as the institution with a monopoly on official violence, and Hans Morganthau, the famous political theorist, argued that states always act in their own self-interest. If states use their monopolies on violence to wage war for naked self-interest or corporate profits, this would appear to make war one of the most catastrophic forms of institutional wilding. We have already defined state violence for greed or power at home as political wilding, and in a world exploding with war for power and profit, it is hard to imagine a more dangerous and sociologically important species of wilding.

In this chapter, we consider two American wars: the war against Iraq and the "war on terrorism." In focusing on American-led wars, it is important to keep in mind that the United States is the greatest military power in world history and the sole superpower today. The United States spends more on the military—approaching half a trillion dollars annually—than all the other nations of the world combined. Many view the United States as an empire, exceeding in its power even the Roman or British empires. Sociologists such as Immanual Wallerstein and Giovanni Arrighi offer a framework known as "world system theory" for understanding the American empire as a wilding system. Looking back on the last 500 years of colonialism, world system theorists argue that the world economy has been organized by a dominant or "hegemonic" power, such as Britain during the late eighteenth and nineteenth centuries, that ruled over much of the world for profit and glory. The United States is the successor hegemon to Britain, with even greater power.[1]

Hegemony, as conceived by the Italian social theorist Antonio Gramsci, is power dressed up in universal values, such as freedom and prosperity. Gramsci wrote that governments always use such soothing rhetoric as "the white man's burden" to "manufacture consent," since naked coercion is an expensive and inefficient mode of control. During the British empire, the British claimed to bring civilization to the whole world, as did the ancient Romans to their conquered provinces. During the Cold War, the United States claimed to defend the entire "free world" against the evil of communism. Arrighi and other world system theorists observe that with the collapse of the Soviet Union, American hegemony is increasingly organized around claims to defend the whole civilized world against the evils of terror and chaos.

Hegemons increasingly turn to military force when their economic power and legitimacy begin to wane. The United States is in the early phases of hegemonic decline, associated with a long-term crisis in the global economy and the rise of a speculative "casino capitalism" that yields short-term profits at the expense of long-term growth. We can expect that the United States may move toward increasing militarism to secure its endangered global wealth and power, leading to the kind of mayhem and wilding witnessed during the decline and fall of the Roman and British empires.[2]

War in Iraq

When Baghdad fell on April 9, 2003, U.S. newspapers and TV news programs showed jubilant Iraqis dancing in the streets. Iraqis embraced and kissed American soldiers, stomped on pictures of Saddam Hussein, and with the help of U.S. Marines, toppled the huge iron statue of Saddam in central Baghdad. This was the reaction that President Bush had promised. Although no weapons of mass destruction had been found at this point, the Iraqi celebration seemed to nail down Bush's claim that this was a war of liberation, a just war destroying a barbaric regime and bringing freedom and democracy to a suffering nation.

Just after Baghdad's collapse, surveys suggested that most Americans agreed with the president. A poll released on April 10, 2003, showed that about 75 percent of Americans supported the war. Even those who had earlier protested the war were rethinking their opposition, wondering whether the end of a horrific despot justified the destruction inevitably wrought by war. One thoughtful student in my class raised his hand and said that the obvious joy of many Iraqis at the downfall of Saddam made him question whether his earlier opposition to the war was ignorant.

But while Americans watched images of Iraqis celebrating in the streets, Arabs were opening newspapers with headlines blazing "Humiliation!" and "Colonialism Is Back!" The images Arabs saw were of dead Iraqi children killed by bombs, starving Iraqi families screaming at U.S. soldiers for water or food, Iraqi soldiers lying dead on the highway, hospitals without electricity or medicine overflowing with wounded Iraqi civilians, widespread looting and mayhem, and fires burning out of control in many Iraqi cities. While there was no love lost on Saddam Hussein, Arabs all over the Mideast were horrified at the prospect of an American military occupation of Iraq.

Talal Salman, publisher of *Al-Safir*, a leading Lebanese moderate newspaper, grieved the loss of the richest Arab civilization to a "colonial power." Iraqis, he wrote, are now moving from "the night of tyranny" under Saddam Hussein to the "night of foreign occupation" under U.S. troops.[3] Ahmed Kamal Aboulmagd, a leading pro-Western member of the Egyptian establishment and a longtime friend of the United States, said, "Under the present conditions, I cannot think of defending the United States. To most people in this area, the United States is the source of evil on planet earth."[4]

These sentiments were shared by many Iraqis, who were grateful to U.S. and British soldiers for ousting Saddam but desperate to survive in the wake of the world's most intense bombing campaigns, and viscerally hostile to a new foreign occupation. The majority Shiite population in Iraq mounted huge street protests demanding that American soldiers get out of their country. Iraqis interviewed in Baghdad and Basra told U.S. reporters that they hated Saddam but equally "resented the foreign troop presence." One Iraqi Shiite cleric said the Iraqis were caught between "two fires": one, the cruel, fading power of Saddam; the other, the looming domination of the Americans. Qabil Khazzal Jumaa, an Iraqi nurse, horrified by the amputated limbs, burned bodies, and rotting corpses among the hundred of civilians he had treated, said that this was "a brutal war. This is not just. This is not accepted by man or God." Iraq did not belong to the Americans who would now govern his country. He said simply, "This is my country."[5]

In the face of these starkly competing images—Iraqis dancing in the streets and a bombed, looted country fearing subjugation to a hegemon occupying its cities and oilfields—how does one decide whether the U.S. war in Iraq was wilding? We can start by asking whether the war was legal and then whether this was a just war. This discussion can be framed from a sociological perspective around the question of hegemony: Did the United States invade Iraq to tighten its hegemonic control over the Gulf and the entire oil-rich Islamic world?

Legality

According to Article 51 of the U.N. charter (which the United States rati-
fied), a country can legally engage in war without U.N. approval if the war
is in self-defense. Right after 9/11, on September 12, 2001, President Bush
redefined "self-defense" in a more expansive way than the charter implied.
Bush asserted that the United States could no longer afford to abide by
conventional concepts in an age of terrorism. We must be prepared, the
president declared, "to strike at moment's notice in any dark corner of the
world . . . to be ready for preemptive action when necessary to defend our
liberty and to defend our lives." The president was very explicit about preemption: "We must take the battle to the enemy, disrupt his plans and
confront the worst threats before they emerge."

In emphasizing that he would act against threats "before they emerge,"
the president was moving beyond preemption to prevention. A preemptive war occurs when a threat is imminent—for instance, when missiles or
planes are detected moving toward one's shores—and when there is a plausible concept of "pre-emptive self-defense" within the U.N.'s legal intent.
Preventive war is a response to threats not yet visible and suggests that
one nation can use the new Bush doctrine to attack almost any other country that it mistrusts, an application of the wilding precept that "might
makes right."

Bush's approach kicked up a firestorm of opposition. Former White
House adviser William A. Galston said that Bush's new doctrine "means
the end of the system of international institutions, laws, and norms that
the United States has worked for more than half a century to build. . . .
Rather than continuing to serve as first among equals in the postwar international system, the United States would act as a law unto itself, creating new rules of international engagement without agreement by other
nations."[6] Princeton political scientist Richard Falk, a leading authority on
international law, writes that "this new approach repudiates the core of
the United Nations charter [outlawing wars that are not based on self-
defense against overt aggression] . . . it is a doctrine without limits, without accountability to the U.N. or international law, or any dependence on
a collective judgment of responsible governments."[7]

When the United States invaded Iraq, it claimed that Article 51 made
the war legal. The U.N. Security Council disagreed, saying that there was
more time for inspection and that the threat was not imminent, meaning
that the war could not be viewed as self-defense. France and Germany,

along with scores of other countries, repeatedly argued that the war undermined the U.N. charter. Russian president Vladmir Putin declared that the doctrine of preemption meant the world would descend into chronic war and the law of the jungle.

Just a few weeks after Putin's prophecy of a new global anarchy, the government of India announced that it was using the Bush doctrine to consider a preemptive attack against its nuclear-armed adversary, Pakistan, because of Pakistan's incursions into the Indian-controlled part of Kashmir. A central problem with the invasion of Iraq—and the legal doctrine on which it is based—is that it offers a wilding license for international chaos.

Although the president invaded Iraq alleging that Saddam Hussein had weapons of mass destruction (WMD), American forces on the ground failed to find any nuclear, biological, or chemical weapons. On April 24, 2003, President Bush suggested that WMD might never be found and might not exist, raising grave new questions about the legality of the war.[8] The president's legal argument for the war had rested on the premise that such weapons existed and constituted a threat to American and global security. But after two years of exhaustive investigation, the president's own official commission on arms in Iraq, led by David Kay and Charles Duelfer, concluded in 2004 that Saddam did not have weapons of mass destruction or any imminent program to build them successfully.[9] This conclusion suggests that there was no threat and no plausible legal justification for the invasion. The clear implication is that Iraq was a war of aggression rather than self-defense.

Whether the president or other members of his administration lied about WMD or about Saddam's relation to Al Qaeda and 9/11 has become a major wilding issue in itself. Lying to create a legal justification for war would be political wilding of the highest order, and widespread suspicion of it has already inspired a mass campaign to impeach Bush led by former attorney general Ramsey Clark. John Dean, President Nixon's legal adviser during Watergate, has said that if Bush lied about WMD, which he sees as more likely than any other explanation of the failure to find WMD in Iraq, it would be a far more serious impeachable offense than Nixon's coverup in Watergate. "In the three decades since Watergate," Dean wrote, "this is the first potential scandal I have seen that could make Watergate pale by comparison. . . . To put it bluntly, if Bush has taken Congress and the nation into war based on bogus information, he is cooked. Manipulation or deliberate misuse of national security intelligence data, if proven, could be a 'high crime' under the Constitution's impeachment clause."[10]

In his 2003 State of the Union message, President Bush claimed that Iraq had 30,000 warheads and the materials to produce 38,000 liters of botulinum toxin, 25,000 liters of anthrax, and 500 tons of chemical weapons. Bush also told the American public in the State of the Union address that Iraq tried to buy uranium from the African country of Niger, even though CIA officials had earlier told Vice President Cheney's office and Bush's National Security Council that the Niger story was an obvious fabrication based on forged documents. The White House acknowledged in July 2003 that Bush should not have included the unfounded allegation about Niger in his speech, a matter that would come back to haunt him in the sensational Valerie Plame "CIA leak" scandal of 2005, which I describe shortly.[11] The specter of a pattern of lying to create the impression that Iraq posed a nuclear threat was reinforced by Bush's public claim that aluminum tubes in Iraq's possession were intended to enrich uranium after the International Atomic Energy Agency had already publicly concluded that the tubes probably had nothing at all to do with a nuclear program. Bush also claimed that Saddam Hussein was supporting Al Qaeda, when both his own intelligence agencies and the U.N. reported little evidence of this.

In Britain, two leading cabinet ministers resigned after the Iraq war, accusing Prime Minister Tony Blair of lying to Britons about WMD. One of the resigning ministers, Claire Short, testified to a parliamentary committee that Blair and Bush concocted a prearranged deal in 2002 to invade Iraq in 2003 no matter what was found about WMD. A smoking gun document, known as the "Downing Street memo," proved Short's accusation to be true, exposing misinformation or lies behind Bush's decision to go to war. Leaked by a whistle-blower in the spring of 2005, the memo is the official minutes of a July 23, 2002, meeting between Richard Dearlove, the head of British MI-6 (UK's version of the CIA) and Blair. Dearlove had just returned from Washington to report to Blair about Bush's plans for war. The minutes state that Bush had made a decision: "Military action was now seen as inevitable. Bush wanted to remove Saddam through military action, justified by the conjunction of terrorism and WMD. But the intelligence and facts were being fixed around the policy."[12]

Those final words, "the intelligence and facts were being fixed around the policy," are as close to an explicit affirmation of wilding as one can expect to get. The head of British intelligence is telling Blair in 2002, with no WMD found, that the U.S. president had already made the decision to go to war and that the United States was fixing the intelligence facts on WMD to justify Bush's decision. The minutes specify that Blair's cooperation is critical and offer various options for British military collaboration.[13]

The Downing Street memo was leaked at about the same time that another crucial leak was boiling to the surface. This was the leak to Robert

Novak and other journalists of the name of Valerie Plame, a CIA agent, by senior officials in the White House. Leaking a CIA operative's name can be a felony, and Bush appointed a special investigator to investigate, with the president claiming that he would fire any of his White House staff involved. But the investigation led right up the White House chain of command toward Karl Rove, the president's leading political adviser, and I. Lewis "Scooter" Libby, Vice President Dick Cheney's chief of staff.

Plame, the agent who was "outed," is the wife of Joseph Wilson, a U.S. career diplomat who publicly wrote a *New York Times* op-ed claiming that President Bush's words in his 2003 State of the Union address about Iraq seeking Niger's uranium were false. Wilson had personally gone to Niger to investigate and had told the administration that the claim was untrue. Wilson's public disclosure of the intelligence deception is believed to have motivated White House officials to leak his wife's name and punish him for exposing the WMD deceptions.

On March 6, 2007, Libby was convicted of one count of obstruction of justice, two counts of perjury, and one count of lying to the FBI. The special Justice Department prosecutor, Patrick Fitzgerald, alleged in the indictment that Libby had disclosed Plame's name to several reporters, the first time in June 2003, only days after Wilson had publicly charged that President Bush had deceived the U.S. public about Iraq's search for uranium in Niger. Libby had allegedly lied about leaking Plame's name to reporters and had obstructed the grand jury's investigation into the leak. Especially noteworthy, Libby had received information about Plame's identity as a covert CIA operative from Vice President Cheney himself, known to be the most zealous official in the administration intent on selling the war based on an Iraqi nuclear threat, the very allegation that Wilson had disputed a few days earlier in his op-ed essay. This led to the questions "What did Cheney know about the leaks, and when did he know it?" More important, did Cheney authorize Libby to reveal Plame's name?[14]

The White House, at this writing in late 2005, was in turmoil about the prospect of additional potential high-level indictments, including a continuing investigation by Fitzgerald into the role of Karl Rove, President Bush's top political adviser, in the same leak involving Plame. The trials following the indictments could create a sensational scandal implicating Libby, Rove, the vice president, or the president himself. The questions about what Cheney knew and whether he authorized Libby's leaks ultimately need to be asked and answered about Rove and President Bush himself. If they are implicated, this matter would be grounds for impeachment. Whatever the legal outcomes, it seems that the Plame leak was part of an orchestrated propaganda campaign by an administration that long ago had decided to go to war without any evidence of an imminent threat. To cover up this illegal action—which constituted the highest form of political wilding—it needed to convince the U.S. public that WMD, along with the false attribution of a connection between Saddam and Osama bin Laden, was the reason.

Justice

The question of wilding goes beyond legality to the broader issue of whether the war on Iraq was a just war of liberation. While the argument that a legal war to remove a tyrant can, under some circumstances, be a just action is true, three arguments based on historical, economic, and political perspectives suggest that other goals were behind this war.

The historical argument is based on planning documents only recently made public. In a 1990 strategy document put together by a team under Dick Cheney in the first Bush administration, the United States announced that it must "preclude the rise of another global rival for the indefinite future," building such an overwhelming military superiority that no other nation could possibly contemplate challenging American power. The Cheney document suggested that the United States needed to create a "democratic zone of peace" in which Americans would be prepared to use force if necessary to ensure "human rights or democracy," even if using force involved violating the sovereignty of another nation that posed no threat to the United States. While Iraq was the test case of the time, the idea of overthrowing Saddam was rejected after the first Gulf War because the U.N. did not authorize a regime change. The Cheney doctrine was shelved as embarrassingly imperialistic.[15] Nonetheless, after 9/11, Cheney's vision became the centerpiece of the new Bush administration's foreign policy, and the Iraq war was a crucial first step toward securing the global dominance laid out in the earlier documentary record.[16]

A second argument that the war on Iraq involved wilding centers around the economic goals of the war. Like all prior hegemons, the United States has two economic agendas. The first is to ensure the stable operation of the world economy, including the guarantee of a cheap supply of Mideast oil. In 1990, when Saddam Hussein invaded Kuwait and threatened Saudi Arabia, the United States launched the first Gulf War to stabilize the entire global economic system, protecting the oil supply not only for itself but also for European and Asian allies. In the 2003 Gulf War, the United

States again acted with broad concern for global economic stability based on securing greater control of Iraq's and its neighbors' oil supplies—still a form of wilding but different from simply grabbing more profit for U.S. oil companies.

Another U.S. economic aim, though, is closer to what the protestors had in mind as they waved their "No Blood for Oil" signs. The corporatized American hegemon sees U.S. national interests as tightly connected to the profitability of politically influential American corporations. The Bush administration, including most notably the president and vice president, is especially close to the energy industries, in which several Bush cabinet members served as corporate executives, as well as to the military-related companies rooted in Texas and throughout the Southwest of the United States. It is predictable that the interests of this sector of American corporations would weigh heavily in the Bush administration's assessment of the national interest.

Evidence that profits for U.S. oil giants and other companies were part of the Iraq war aim comes from the postwar reconstruction contracts, which the U.S. Agency for International Development began to award through a closed bidding process.

Halliburton, the Texas-based oil giant formerly headed by Dick Cheney, was awarded the first major contract for servicing of Iraqi oil wells and fire prevention in the oilfields, estimated to be worth up to $7 billion. This contract is widely seen as a foot in the door for more profitable long-term Iraqi oil contracts, and it has led to discussions of a congressional investigation regarding whether Halliburton poses a conflict of interest, since Cheney still receives compensation from the firm.

The United States has also awarded a leading reconstruction role to Bechtel, the vast construction and energy company with ties to then Secretary of Defense Donald Rumsfeld and others closely connected to the Bush administration. George Schultz, former president of Bechtel and currently on its board, also sits on Bush's Pentagon's Defense Policy Board, which advises the administration about Iraq and other vital matters. Richard Perle, head of that same board and the leading hawk on Iraq, was forced to resign his chairmanship when concerns about potential conflicts of interest were raised about his own business interests. At a time when Pentagon planners and the CIA were predicting major new terrorist attacks as a near certainty in the wake of the Iraqi invasion, Perle's company stood to generate lucrative profits from defense and homeland security contracts.[17]

A third argument that the Iraq war involved wilding concerns domestic political benefits reaped by the Bush administration. Bush entered office without a popular majority and only through a controversial Supreme Court decision about the Florida vote. Even before 9/11 and the Iraq war, critics perceived Bush as a servant of the big corporations whose campaign funding had helped propel him to Washington. In his first moves as president, Bush chose a cabinet led by other former corporate executives, including Cheney, Rumsfeld, and Paul O'Neill, his secretary of the treasury. Bush then pushed a domestic agenda centered around the biggest tax cuts to the rich in history, enhancing his image as a political stand-in for his corporate friends.

Such a corporate presidency is inherently vulnerable to a crisis of legitimacy. Bush's social and economic domestic policies have been consistently opposed by a majority of the American electorate. Karl Rove, the president's political guru, has denied in public that foreign policy decisions are made on the basis of domestic political considerations, but he sent a secret memo to Republican activists during the 2002 midterm elections urging them to "focus on the war." He also acknowledged to reporters during the 2002 campaign that he liked the slogan circulating among Republican strategists, "Are you safer now than you were four years ago?"[18]

Occupation as Wilding

On March 11, 1917, British troops captured Baghdad. That day, the British commander Major General Stanley Maude promised the Iraqis, "Our armies do not come into your cities and lands as conquerors or enemies but as liberators." Maude was not telling them the truth, since the British stayed more than 40 years. The real British aims were to take over Iraq after the crumbling of the Ottoman empire, to control trade routes to India and the Far East, and, as the occupation unfolded, to control the newly discovered oilfields. Although Iraq won formal sovereignty in 1931, the British ruled the country through puppet regimes until a coup in 1958 formally drove them out after a long popular insurgency. T. E. Lawrence, better known as Lawrence of Arabia, wrote in 1920 that the British public was "tricked" into supporting occupation "by a steady withholding of information. . . . Things have been far worse than we have been told, our administration more bloody and inefficient than the public knows. We are today not far from a disaster."[19]

The parallels to the American role in Iraq are painful. Almost three years after the invasion of Baghdad, 170,000 American forces occupied Iraq with no end in sight. The United States is building permanent bases around the country to secure Iraq as a nation friendly to the United States and to

American oil interests. Iraq also offers a staging ground for keeping military pressure on Syria, Iran, and other Middle East nations, and for securing other major oilfields as far away as the Black Sea and the Caucuses.

The U.S. public has been misled in the same manner as the British. Lawrence wrote that the British public had been suckered "into a trap from which it will be hard to escape with dignity and honor." British leaders, Lawrence observed, were not honest about their aims, and occupations are, by their nature, "bloody and inefficient." President Bush proclaimed, "Mission accomplished," in spring 2003, after U.S. Marines reached Baghdad, saying American troops would be showered with roses. But occupations are always unpopular and create inevitable insurgencies that lead the occupier to fight the people they rescued.

The truth is that occupations are almost always systemic political wilding, evoking popular resistance that requires more and more violence against civilians to suppress. The war to save Iraq has already become a war that is killing thousands of Iraqis and pitting Sunni, Shiite, and Kurdish ethnic communities against each other in bloody civil conflict that could spiral into a horrific full-scale civil war between Sunnis and Shiites throughout Iraq and the entire Arab world. The wilding by American occupation forces in Iraq became painfully clear during the U.S. invasion of the Sunni stronghold of Fallujah in 2004, which was seen as an epicenter of the insurgency. Heavily armed American forces demolished whole neighborhoods as they systematically ransacked the city. A quarter million residents evacuated, and the whole city burned in a hellstorm of lethal destruction. Doctors in Fallujah hospitals reported "melted bodies," victims of poisonous gases sprayed by U.S. planes. One resident, Abu Sabah, spoke of "weird bombs that smoke like a mushroom cloud . . . The pieces of these strange bombs explode into large fires that burn the skin even when you throw water over them," which suggested the possible use of napalm by U.S. forces, expressly prohibited by the U.N. in 1980 after its use in Vietnam.[20] The United States has denied using napalm but admits using white phosphorus as an incendiary weapon against insurgents, contrary to its previous claim that it was used only for illumination purposes. White phosphorus, which has a similar effect to napalm on contact with the skin, is a lethal substance banned by international treaty for use against civilians, although the United States is not a signatory to that treaty.[21]

Marines were caught on tape killing a wounded, defenseless man in a Fallujah mosque, and marine officers, according to the *Asia Times*, were on record ordering GIs to "shoot everything that moves and everything that doesn't move;" also, to shoot "two bullets in every body"; and, according to journalist Pepe Escobar, "to spray every home with machine-gun and tank fire before entering them." One Iraqi female blogger on the scene reported, "It's difficult to believe that in this day and age, when people are blogging, e-mailing and communicating at the speed of light, a whole city is being destroyed and genocide is being committed."[22]

The destruction of Fallujah has become a metaphor for the entire occupation. As the trial of Saddam Hussein for crimes against humanity began, the White House became concerned that President Bush could be implicated and face legal problems personally by Saddam Hussein's defense that his own killings of Iraqi civilians or antigovernment terrorists paled in comparison to the lethal violence ordered by Bush in Fallujah and scores of other Iraqi cities. By 2005, official American, U.N., and Iraqi reports, as well as press accounts, hinted at a ravaged country so unhinged by U.S. violence that it might not recover. Johns Hopkins University reports 40,000 Iraqi civilians dead since the U.S. invasion, a number corroborated by the independent Geneva-based Institute for International Studies. In Iraq, 400,000 children suffer from chronic diarrhea and eat virtually no protein.[23] According to the U.N. and Iraqi official Iraq Living Conditions Survey (ILCS), released in May 2005, one-fourth of Iraqi children under 6 years of age are "chronically malnourished," and between 2,100 and 3,500 children were killed in the war in the two years following the U.S. invasion in 2003. After reviewing health, housing, and other infrastructure data, the ILCS concludes that its survey reveals a "tragic situation of the quality of life in Iraq."[24]

These survey findings may understate the wilding crisis as the Iraqi social structure unravels. Many of Iraq's most dedicated doctors say that medical conditions are so hopeless—without stable electricity in hospitals or essential drugs—that they want to quit and emigrate. Young Iraqi boys are forced by poverty into prostitution on the streets of Baghdad. Half a million Iraqis are homeless and sleeping without shelter. A Geneva-based international study reports that ordinary Iraqis are increasingly killing each other with small arms, such as pistols, revolvers, and small mortars.[25]

The most famous symbol of the wilding created by occupation is the horrific images of torture at Abu Ghraib, which led to convictions against military guards Charles Graner, Lyndie England, and five other Americans. Most Americans can still remember the photo seen around the world: an Iraqi prisoner held by the U.S. military, hooded and with electrical wires attached to his arms and genitals. Also circulated on the Internet were photographs of naked Iraqi prisoners draped in a pyramid, forced to masturbate by their U.S. guards; pictures of U.S. military guards leading Iraqi prisoners around by a leash; and pictures of U.S. soldiers using fists or weapons to harm prisoners.

In October 2005, America's premier documentary program, PBS's *Frontline*, ran a program called "Torture in Question" focusing on Abu Ghraib.

It is required viewing for every U.S. citizen. The program is the first in which U.S. military interrogators were interviewed on screen and acknowledged personally using torture against Iraqi prisoners. The interrogators said they had been working under orders to "take the gloves off" to get intelligence "with whatever means necessary." The means included attack dogs, sleep deprivation, immersion of prisoners in ice baths to induce hypothermia, beatings leading to broken bones, concussions, and death. Moreover, the intelligence officials doing the interrogation said torture was rife not only in Abu Ghraib but all over Iraq: in shipping containers, inside Iraqi homes, and in military vehicles, where there were no cameras to watch. Since many of the prisoners had no information to share, the interrogators called it pure sadism, the most virulent form of expressive wilding.[26]

While the commanding officer at Abu Ghraib, General Janis Karpinski, was dismissed from her post and was disciplined, the PBS documentary suggests that she was following orders that went up the chain of command to the central command in Iraq and higher into the Pentagon and White House. Secretary of Defense Donald Rumsfeld made clear to his commanding Iraq generals that getting the "intel" was crucial to stopping the insurgency and that prisoners were not protected under the Geneva Conventions. In a memo released by the American Civil Liberties Union (ACLU), the commanding officer in Iraq, General Ricardo Sanchez, authorized 29 interrogation techniques, many of which were in violation of the Geneva Accords and the army's own rules against torture.[27] Meanwhile, the Pentagon authorized officials from Guantanamo to go to Abu Ghraib. According to Karpinski, one of these officials, General Geoffrey D. Miller, communicated the view that you need to "treat them [the prisoners] like dogs."[28] In addition, private contractors coming into Abu Ghraib were using their own interrogation tactics without accountability to anyone. Abu Ghraib, once Saddam's most feared prison site, became a free fire zone for torture, with Americans doing the torture instead of Saddam.[29]

The War on Terrorism

The attacks of 9/11 were a watershed event. When Al Qaeda operatives hijacked the two jumbo jets and crashed them into the twin towers in New York, they showed that the United States was vulnerable to the devastating violence that many other countries have suffered for decades. Americans have historically felt protected by the oceans and the enormous power of the U.S. military. We know now that tiny bands of terrorists can inflict horrific damage on our country, whatever the size of our military or our hegemonic power.

Is the American-led war on terrorism a form of wilding? If it is truly an international struggle to eradicate groups such as Al Qaeda, then diplomatic, police, intelligence, and military actions designed for such aims may be morally legitimate. But the history of hegemonic powers—and of the United States in particular—offers cautions. During the Cold War, many wars fought in the name of anticommunism, such as the 1954 overthrow of Guatemala's elected president Jacobo Arbenz Guzmán, had more to do with protecting the United Fruit Company's banana plantations than fighting communism. The 1953 CIA overthrow of another democratically elected leader, Iran's president Mohammed Mossadegh, was also an imperialist war. It was called an anticommunist war, but it was waged mainly to protect U.S. oil interests. The Cold War developed into a form of hegemonic wilding, involving scores of greed- and power-driven military interventions by the United States to build the American empire as well as wars by the Soviet Union to build its own empire.[30]

During the period of Roman hegemonic decline, in the fourth and fifth centuries A.D., the rise of terror from the invading Germanic tribes became a central security issue on the Roman empire's eroding boundaries. Similarly, as the British empire declined, it faced terrorist attacks from African colonies, such as Kenya, as well as nationalist attacks from groups such as the Zionists in Israel. If the United States is entering a period of hegemonic decline, then we might expect not only disorder and terrorism but also a "war on terrorism" is entirely predictable, since many declining hegemons have waged such a war to preserve their dominance.

What, then, are the real motives driving the U.S. "war on terrorism" that began after 9/11? One is undoubtedly to destroy Al Qaeda and similar violent, criminal groups that threaten the U.S., and if this were its sole purpose, directed and carried out by the U.N. in coalition with the United States purely for its own and other countries' self-defense, the war might not be wilding. But just as the Soviet threat served a useful function for American leaders during the Cold War, the threat of terrorism helps U.S. elites achieve very different aims than self-defense. In fact, the United States political leadership and its terrorist enemies function like spouses in a long and hostile codependent marriage. They hate each other but need the marriage because it serves crucial functions for each of them. While trying to destroy one another, they also become increasingly reliant on the conflict between them to survive and achieve their own aims.

A key codependent marriage has developed between U.S. elites and Al Qaeda. Both seek to destroy the other but at the same time find each other exceedingly useful in promoting their own ends. The American empire provides Al Qaeda with its most potent tool for rallying Arab popular support and undercutting moderate Islamic groups that could make the radicals irrelevant. Similarly, Al Qaeda offers American political leaders their most powerful case for vastly enhanced military spending and wars that bring profit, power, and political legitimacy at home.

A major covert aim of the war on terrorism is to replace the communist enemy with a new terrorist enemy who provides the cover or justification to dominate the world. Put simply, terrorism (and the war against it) has become a powerful selling point for the global wilding policies at the heart of empire. Without Al Qaeda, the Bush administration could not have diverted so much money to expanding the armed forces, especially in an era of decline in jobs and domestic social services. Nor could U.S. leaders have explicitly proclaimed the doctrines of preemptive war and unrivalled military dominance. Al Qaeda has provided U.S. leaders with an argument to introduce American forces in scores of countries as well as to overthrow governments that have not attacked the United States, which is perhaps the defining feature of an imperial power. Without their hated terrorist partners, American leaders could not have attacked Iraq by falsely linking Saddam Hussein with Al Qaeda, or pursued so blatantly the new politics of preventive war and empire.

Another unacknowledged aim of the war on terrorism, also suggestive of systemic political wilding, has been to increase the political standing of the president at home. As noted earlier, President Bush heads a corporate state. He has not only proposed huge tax cuts for the rich but also increased subsidies for agribusiness, pharmaceuticals, and other big industries; he has proposed drilling in the Alaskan wilderness and other energy policies that were a bonanza for the biggest energy giants; and he has supported deregulation that would enrich telecom, mining, and nearly every other corporate sector. This stance has not played well with the American public. By early 2003, as corporations celebrated the new gifts coming from Washington, half of Americans worried that they might not have a job in a year. Many saw their pension nest eggs vanishing while access to basic health care and education drastically eroded.

The war on terrorism was the answer to the political problem posed by the inevitable public opposition to the domestic agenda of the corporate state. Bush's political vulnerability at home would be shared by any president, Democrat or Republican, who presided over the corporate state, since such a government is structurally committed to policies that do not benefit the majority of Americans. If new corporate presidents continue to rely on the war on terrorism for their political survival, we may be faced with one wilding war after another, fought in the name of antiterrorism for political benefits at home. After the fall of Baghdad, rumors surfaced almost immediately about new potential confrontations with Syria, North Korea, and Iran. Fighting even one war for domestic political gain is a horrific form of political wilding; fighting a whole generation of such wars is systemic wilding on a grand scale.

Torture, Big Brother, and State Terror

Torture at Abu Ghraib is the tip of the iceberg. U.S. military officials have used "water board" torture in Afghan detention centers, where prisoners are strapped down to a board and held under water. In Afghanistan and Guantanamo Bay, other reports of U.S. torture include dog attacks that created severe wounds and leg beatings leading at least one prisoner to die. Based on Defense Department data, the ACLU reported on October 25, 2005, that U.S. guards and intelligence officials had murdered at least 21 prisoners in their custody in Iraq and Afghanistan, a form of wilding by any definition. The deaths occurred during or after interrogation from "strangulation" or "blunt force injuries."[31] In 2005, a large-scale hunger fast at Guantanamo by prisoners protesting abusive treatment led to harsh force-feeding that many attorneys called prisoner abuse itself.

Official torture became part of broader U.S. state terrorism inside and outside Iraq—*all in the name of the war against terrorism itself.* During his 2005 Senate confirmation hearings, Attorney General Alberto Gonzales refused to renounce torture. In 2002, as White House counselor, Gonzales had written that 9/11 had rendered obsolete the old rules—such as the Geneva Conventions—that forbid torture. Senator Ted Kennedy argued that the new thinking "has been used by the administration, the military and the CIA to justify torture and Geneva Convention violations by military and civilian officials."[32]

Prominent British journalist Jonathan Steele has written that torture and other "state terrorist" methods are being incorporated into U.S. policy worldwide. Steele writes "that the Administration sees the U.S. not just as a self-appointed global policeman, but also as the world's prison warder. It is thinking of building jails in foreign countries, mainly ones with grim human rights records, to which it can secretly transfer detainees (unconvicted by any court) for the rest of their lives—a kind of global gulag beyond the scrutiny of the International Committee of the Red Cross, or any other independent observers or lawyers."[33] Confirming Steele's report, in October 2005, the *Washington Post* revealed that the CIA maintained at least eight secret "black site" prisons around the world to hold prisoners indefinitely, without formal charges, and without any restraint on torture or inhumane treatment. These prisons are not subject even to military tribunal review.[34] Beyond these charges are those that American soldiers desecrated and burned the dead bodies of Taliban fighters in Afghanistan, using loudspeakers to taunt Islamic soldiers in nearby villages that they were "ladies" fearful of coming to protect their dead colleagues.

Fear that such charges were true and were damaging America's image led the Senate in October 2005 to pass an antiadministration bill, sponsored by Senator John McCain, prohibiting prisoner abuse, including torture. The Bush administration sought an amendment to exempt the CIA and other counterterrorist agencies, the first time that Bush openly claimed that the United States needed to use torture, something that McCain rejected as failing to produce intelligence and endangering American lives.[35] However, when the president finally signed the bill, he issued an "interpretive" signing statement, indicating that he would not comply with the law when he believed his "constitutional authority" was being infringed, essentially a way of saying he would obey the law only when he viewed it as appropriate. This use of interpretative signing statements—which came to light during the confirmation hearings of Justice Alito, who had argued for such presidential powers when he worked in the Reagan administration—puts the legislative power at risk, not only to ban torture but also to ensure that the president would follow any law that he didn't approve of, a grave infringement on the constitutional separation of powers.[36]

On November 19, 2005, U.S. Army colonel Larry Wilkerson, former chief of staff to Secretary of State Colin Powell, said there "was no question in my mind that we did it" (torture) and "there's no question in my mind that we may still be doing it." He also charged that "the philosophical guidance and the flexibility in order to do so originated in the vice president of the United States' office." Wilkerson said that the man implementing Vice President Cheney's "guidance" on torture was Defense Secretary Donald Rumsfeld. Former CIA director Stansfield Turner also implicated the vice president, calling him bluntly "the Vice President of Torture."[37]

The administration has used 9/11 to launch a horrific assault on American constitutionalism, arguably the most serious form of political wilding that is now completely intertwined with the war on terrorism itself. At the core of the matter is unchecked executive power. The president is using "emergency powers" during crises to gut civil liberties and sacred constitutional protections under the Bill of Rights. "The most profound issue," writes eminent *New York Times* legal affairs journalist Anthony Lewis, "is presidential power. Since Sept. 11, 2001, President Bush and his lawyers have asserted again and again that the 'war on terror' clothes the president as commander in chief with extraordinary, unilateral power—the power, for example, to designate an American citizen as an enemy combatant and imprison him indefinitely, without trial or a real opportunity to demonstrate innocence."[38]

The appointments of John Roberts as chief justice of the Supreme Court and associate Justice Samuel Alito are likely to provide judicial backing of unchecked executive power in the nation's highest court. Just before his appointment, on July 15, 2005, Roberts ruled in the case of Salim Hamdam, a Guantanamo detainee, that the president had the constitutional authority to detain prisoners as enemy combatants without the protections of the Geneva Convention.[39] Roberts and Alito both favor a freer hand for the president to address national security crises as he sees fit, even when it involves suspension of traditional judicial procedure that would protect foreign terrorist and even U.S. citizen suspects. In contrast, departing Judge Sandra Day O'Connor was seen as far less deferential to executive power, writing in an earlier case, that of Yaser Hamdi, that "a state of war is not a blank check for the president when it comes to the rights of the nation's citizens."[40] What is at stake here involves the very question of whether every citizen, including the president, must obey the law, and whether the Supreme Court will maintain our constitutional system of checks and balances as well as the most basic rights of citizens during war. This may be the most critical issue facing America today. Paul Rosenzweig, an analyst for the conservative Heritage Foundation, said correctly that the issues involved here are "the most singularly important set of issues that the country" now faces, referring specifically to the enormous importance of the shift in the balance of the court that Roberts and Alito bring.[41]

In November 2005, Americans learned for the first time that "National Security Letters" issued by President Bush had authorized the FBI to search the phone records of more than 30,000 Americans. To find out whom you called or e-mailed, the FBI does not need to go to any judge but simply issue itself a finding that you might have some "relevance" to an ongoing terrorist investigation. The standard of proof of relevance—an oversight by relevant congressional committees—is, according to Congressman Peter DeFazio, a member of the House Homeland Security Committee, "nil," and it opens the door to wiretapping or spying on dissenting groups, such as peace or environmental activists who have no connection to terrorism.[42] This profound intrusion into privacy and civil liberties is just one of multiple threats posed by the PATRIOT Act, the umbrella legislation passed after 9/11 and renewed in early 2006 by Congress and the president. The meaning of Chief Roberts's and Samuel Alito's appointments, who are both on record favoring an expanded constitutional interpretation of presidential power especially in wartime, means that we may have for years a Supreme Court putting its seal of approval on major threats to the Bill of Rights and our own liberty.[43]

In a major story, the *New York Times* revealed that President Bush had approved National Security Agency (NSA) surveillance of ordinary Americans without court approval over four years. According to official sources:

> The volume of information harvested from telecommunication data and voice networks, without court-approved warrants, is much larger than the White House has acknowledged, the officials said. It was collected by tapping directly into some of the American telecommunication system's main arteries, they said. As part of the program approved by President Bush for domestic surveillance without warrants, the NSA has gained the cooperation of American telecommunications companies to obtain backdoor access to streams of domestic and international communications, the officials said.[44]

Many critics, both Democrat and Republican, believe that Bush broke the Foreign Intelligence Surveillance Act (the "FISA" law), passed in 1978 specifically to prevent such spying on Americans without review by a special secret court set up by Congress. In a major address on January 16, 2005, Al Gore said, "What we do know about this pervasive wiretapping virtually compels the conclusion that the President of the United States has been breaking the law repeatedly and persistently." Gore went on say, "It is this same disrespect for America's Constitution which has now brought our republic to the brink of a dangerous breach in the fabric of the Constitution. And the disrespect embodied in these apparent mass violations of the law is part of a larger pattern of seeming indifference to the Constitution that is deeply troubling to millions of Americans in both political parties."[45]

President Bush claimed that inherent executive powers and the initial authorization by Congress to respond to 9/11 with force entitled him to act on his own to prevent terrorist acts, essentially claiming that as commander-in-chief, he was above the law and that presidential powers could not be limited by Congress when it came to preventing terrorism.[46] But Congress specifically excluded the right to wiretap Americans in its post-9/11 authorization, and many constitutional lawyers and political leaders, including Republican senator Arlen Specter, chairman of the Senate Judiciary Committee, were deeply troubled by Bush's claim, with Specter convening Senate hearings to investigate whether Bush had broken the law or violated the Constitution by authorizing the NSA surveillance. John Dean, also a Republican and President Nixon's legal counselor during Watergate, claimed that Bush was violating the most sacred constitutional principle: that everyone, including the president, must follow the law. Dean said that Bush had admitted to an "impeachable offense," and public interest groups called for additional congressional hearings in 2006 about whether the president should be impeached.[47]

After the Plame leak, the covert CIA prisons, torture, the Downing Street memo, the yellowcake disinformation, and other political wilding discussed earlier, it is not surprising that the new information about wiretapping on a mass scale—which included spying on nonterrorist environmental, labor, and peace groups—promoted widespread discussion of impeachment hearings. A Zogby poll in January 2006 showed a *majority* of Americans agreed with the need for such hearings and potential impeachment proceedings.[48]

This is hardly the first time in history that hegemonic nations have embraced political wilding in the form of torture, and other forms of state terrorism—the use of terrorist tactics by a government—in the name of fighting terrorism. It began at least as early as the Roman empire and has been used today by Russian forces employing terrorist tactics to fight Chechen terrorist rebels and by Israel to fight Palestinian suicide bombers. But state terrorism is wilding used not only against enemies abroad but also against opposition at home. As domestic economic and social dissent grows, and protest against adventurism abroad increases, the Bush administration cracks down with political wilding against citizens at home, trying to curb dissent and create a compliant population.

Fighting Terrorism without Wilding

Nations around the world *do* need to come together to try to prevent terrorism. It is precisely because the threat is real and frightening that it is such a powerful tool for manipulating public opinion. In the face of a very real threat, we need a more effective and honest approach to stopping terrorism. What would such an approach look like? We must begin with something like a Hippocratic political oath—the oath to do no harm—by the U.S. government to end its own practices of state terrorism described in detail in this chapter. The United States must immediately renounce the use of torture, the breaking of international treaties such as the Geneva Convention, and the waging of illegal and unjust wars and occupations.

A country that practices state terrorism loses all credibility to lead a global war against terrorism. Moreover, when it uses the war on terrorism as a pretext not only to use terror but also to justify its pursuit of empire—in the codependent strategy discussed above—its credibility collapses entirely, helping to explain the worldwide distrust and even hatred of the Bush administration shown in many polls.

Beyond taking the political Hippocratic oath, which ultimately requires renouncing the use of terror and pursuit of empire by the U.S. government, a just global antiterror campaign would be based on the following principles. First, it would be directed by the U.N. and the international community rather than by the United States. Second, it would attack the root causes of terrorism, requiring major changes in U.S. foreign and economic policy. This would include a far more balanced American approach to the Israeli-Palestinian conflict, the most explosive issue in the Middle East. The United States could do more to end terror by pushing Israel to end illegal settlements and accept a viable Palestinian state than by taking any other step, since this would erode support for Hamas and other Palestinian extremist groups. This will require more pressure on Israel than Bush has exercised since his introduction of his Roadmap to Peace, which most Palestinians correctly perceive as tilted to favor the Israelis. Ending U.S. military occupation of the region and withdrawing U.S. support for the brutal monarchies and sheikdoms is also essential. This could take place only if the United States renounces its aspiration for global hegemony, acknowledging that empire is incompatible with its own democratic ideals as well as with global peace.

An effective antiterror strategy would imply changing the rules of globalization—which is now the economic expression of American hegemony—such that poor people in the Middle East and around the world are not forced to bear the burden of debt while being denied the means to shape their own development policies. As long as the United States imposes a globalization that does not help the 3 billion people who eat fewer calories a day than the ordinary American's cat or dog, we are going to have more anti-American terror.

A war on terrorism that is not wilding would be political, economic, and diplomatic, rather than military. Police and other agents of coercive force may be required to root out violent groups, but the most effective way to do so requires enacting just global policies and involving the full cooperation of other nations and of publics all over the world. The war on terrorism is, of all wars, the one most dependent on winning the hearts and minds of the people.

What You Can Do

Problems related to torture and erosion of civil liberties in the war on terrorism are only likely to get worse. This is another issue that should mobilize people of good conscience everywhere in the country. Students on campuses have a major responsibility here, and they should play a crucial role in stopping this particularly horrific part of the political wilding crisis.

The issue of torture may be a catalyzing one for students. Whenever I have discussed the question among my own students, most are horrified that their own government is now officially endorsing torture. When they read the actual accounts of prisoner abuse at Abu Ghraib, at Guantanamo, or in Afghanistan, they experience revulsion. They want it to stop.

All kinds of interventions are possible. Students can go on the Internet to learn about organizations such as Amnesty International and Human Rights Watch that provide information about prisoner abuse. They can "adopt" particular prisoners and write letters to their congressional representatives and the Pentagon to stop the abuse. They can stage demonstrations on their campuses, educating their peers about the abomination of torture practiced by American military officials. One of my own students made national headlines when he put on a cloak, donned a hood, attached military wires to his arms and legs, and stood out in front of a local military recruitment station. He was arrested, but the charges were later dismissed, as mass media reports concentrated on the horrors of Abu Ghraib and the importance of young people—who are, after all, the soldiers carrying out the abuse—standing up against these practices.

The issues of civil liberties, more broadly, is arguably the most critical topic for students to address. The university is the one institution in U.S. society based centrally on free expression and critical thinking. If you shut down free speech or dissent on the campus, you doom these principles everywhere in society. Unfortunately, in past historical eras where civil liberties have been threatened, such as the McCarthy era, many universities did nothing or, worse, even collaborated with McCarthyism by singling out left-leaning faculty and students as "Communist" and expelling them from campus. Students cannot allow this to happen again.

This issue of civil liberties and the PATRIOT Act is very much alive on campuses today. Right-wing groups are targeting professors critical of the war on terrorism, paying students to monitor the classrooms of professors for any sign of liberal "bias," and some campus administrators are giving in to the pressure. Campuses are making it more difficult for student groups to protest, moving in the direction of shutting down the most basic First Amendment rights that students, and all of us, depend on for our freedom.

On my own campus, students are required to secure permits for any kind of protest, and a recent group protesting the presence of a military company, Raytheon, at a career fair were prevented from carrying out a silent theatrical "die-in" as a protest. This action stirred up a major storm on campus, with many students the next day going to their classes with a piece of tape over their mouths, symbolizing their belief that they had been censored. They sponsored a forum on campus within the week to discuss protest, censorship, and curtailment of civil liberties on campus. The question of whether students should have to get a permit for passing out literature in dormitories, for assembling peacefully on campus to protest, or for inviting media on campus is critical. If students want to stop political wilding, there is nothing more important that they can do than to get active on their campuses to make sure that free speech and civil liberties are not destroyed in the name of fighting terrorism.

History tells us that political leaders can successfully attack student activists and other dissenters at home only by linking them falsely to enemies abroad and disguising the pursuit of empire in the name of a war against terrorism. Students must respond on both fronts. They must show that by protesting torture, illegal spying, and other violations of the Constitution by the president, they are not aiding "the enemy," but instead expressing patriotism. Likewise, they must become part of the new global peace movement that is trying to reveal the war against terrorism for what it really is: the American pursuit of empire. The fight to preserve the Constitution at home is inseparable from the fight to end the pursuit of American empire abroad. Students on campuses must organize new peace movements for the rapid withdraw of American forces from Iraq, the removal of American soldiers from bases in Saudi Arabia and other Arab countries, and the prevention of new attacks on Iran, Syria, and North Korea. We need a new generation of dedicated peace activists who understand that the pursuit of global power and domination by the United States (or any other country) is a kind of wilding that fatally threatens not only people around the world, but also Americans and our own most cherished freedoms.

Katrina: The Perfect Wilding Storm

On September 29, 2005, the New Orleans Police Department announced that it was investigating 12 of its officers for looting during Hurricane Katrina. Osman Khan owns the hotel where several officers were staying during the storm. "They'd leave nine or 10 at night and come back 4:30 in the morning," said Kahn of the officers. They were carrying "everything from Adidas shoes to Rolex watches." A hotel staff member, Perry Emery, brought towels into the officers' rooms and saw "Jewelry, generators, fans." Kahn said he saw police take one generator from Tulane University Hospital, which was trying to save dying patients. Emery saw other booty: "One time they came back with a bunch of weapons."[1]

Erlaine McLaurin told CNN that she and her father saw two officers walk from their car into an apartment building on their block and then come out loaded with stolen goods. "They done fill up the white car, the police car," she said. "He got a four pack of soda, a microwave, CD player. . . . I know everybody that lives here. Ain't no cops live here." Another resident saw police kick in a door of a Garden District home in a different area of the city. "They got police escorts coming in here, breaking in houses and taking the stuff."[2] A *Times-Picayune* journalist was one of several witnesses who saw police steal items off the shelves of a Lower Garden District Wal-Mart that they were supposed to be guarding.[3]

When police openly loot homes or stores they are sworn to protect, it suggests a collapse of civil society. Hurricane Katrina, a massive hurricane that smashed the Gulf Coast on August 29, 2005, is called a "natural disaster," but the term is misleading when viewed from a sociological perspective. Yes, it was one of the worst weather storms to hit the United States. But Katrina, sociologically speaking, was a perfect storm of wilding. It concentrated all the types of wilding in a single epic event. Political wilders failed to prevent the flooding in the first place. Corporate wilders made a killing off the mayhem following the storm. Individual wilders—from police to ordinary citizens—used the tragedy to get some additional pocket change and conveniences.

Katrina opened a window that had long been shut, one that allowed ordinary Americans to see the core of societal wilding rotting the fabric of our nation. Fortunately, it also has pointed the way to how we might move in a new direction and curb the wilding epidemic. In this chapter, we reflect on Katrina as a tragic monument to the different varieties of wilding in America and how Katrina reflects the old Sicilian adage "A fish rots from the head first."

Individual Wilding

Stories of personal wilding rocked America from the first day of flooding in New Orleans. We heard of snipers shooting at medevac helicopters as they tried to rescue critically ill patients from hospitals. We saw footage of looters breaking into stores and carrying out television sets and cartons of liquor. We heard shocking reports of rape, child molestation, torture, and murder inside the New Orleans Superdome, as thousands of abandoned residents tried to survive in barbaric conditions.

A month after the storm, new reports suggested that many of these stories were false. A new picture, of a large majority of the abandoned poor coming together to help and often save each other, began to emerge. All this, as I show later, suggests that the original reports of wilding on the streets reflected mainly media wilding and the national ingrained habit of "blaming the victim."

Nonetheless, some residents did exploit the chaotic, desperate situation to cherry-pick DVDs, televisions, computers, and other items from deserted stores or offices. A major target was a New Orleans Wal-Mart, where police joined residents in a frenzy of looting, carting off not only essential food and water but also computers and DVD players. The gun section of the Wal-Mart was cleaned out. There were also credible reports of a nursing home bus being carjacked, of liquor stores being broken into, and of car batteries and stereos being stolen.[4]

Some credible eyewitness reports of wilding in the Superdome came from vacationing British students who took shelter there. Jamie Trout, 22, kept a diary, writing, "It was something like Lord of the Flies—one minute everything calm, the next it descends into chaos." In one entry, he reports that "a man has been arrested for raping a seven year old in the toilet, this place is hell, I feel sick." Seeing guns, crack cocaine, and threats of violence, the students became so terrified that they formed a cordon with the young women inside and the young men on the outside, using chairs as a protective ring. Zoe Smith, 21, said, "We were absolutely terrified, the situation had descended into chaos."[5]

A month after Katrina, Judy Benetiz, director of the Louisiana Foundation against Sexual Assault, reported that individual women, who had been too afraid earlier, were coming to medical centers to report being raped. At this writing, the numbers and details have not been officially confirmed, and tales of the rapes of two young girls in the Superdome's women's restroom have been officially repudiated. But Benetiz says that individual women are slowly coming forward to report being raped or seeing rapes. Other witnesses filed reports with the police and media. Charmaine Neville, a New Orleans singer and songwriter, told WAFB-TV that she had reported to New Orleans police that "a lot of us women had been raped down there by guys who had come . . . into the neighborhood where we were."[6]

Regarding snipers, one man, Wendell Bailey, 20, was indicted on October 8 by a federal grand jury on the charge of firing out of his New Orleans apartment window at a military rescue helicopter during the storm. Police found two revolvers and a box of ammunition under his bed. No motive for the sniping was established; it was apparently a form of expressive wilding for pleasure or revenge.[7]

Elsewhere in the city, Pasado's Safe Haven, a Washington State animal rescue league that had saved more than 700 abandoned animals in New Orleans, offered a $10,000 reward to find those who had shot 14 dogs left by their owners. The dogs had been shot in the stomach in order to guarantee a painful, prolonged death.[8]

It was not only New Orleans residents who took to personal wilding. In Lilburn, Georgia, a week after the storm, a Salvation Army shop collecting donations for hurricane victims was looted of clothing and televisions. Store manager John Taylor said that the appliances had been filched from a dock behind the store. The Salvation Army had to buy a trailer in which its staff could lock up the donations.[9]

Three Texan truck drivers—with contracts from federal agencies to bring ice and water to New Orleans survivors—stopped just after the storm in the parking lot of a Family Dollar store just south of the city to loot the place. Although deputies were on duty, the truckers managed to go in and fill up and haul off many shopping carts "with everything from Barbie dolls to kitchen appliances to ladies' lingerie."[10]

Just after the storm, two Californians, Tino Lee and Gina Liz Nicholas, posed as Red Cross volunteers in Burbank, California, asking for donations.

On September 17, Burbank police arrested them and charged them with impersonating Red Cross officials and seeking to scam donors. U.S. District Attorney Debra Wong Yang said they had been using a "national tragedy . . . to line their pockets with money intended for victims."[11]

Beyond such street wilding, Katrina spawned a new breed of online or virtual looters, scam artists who had set up phony charitable Web sites within hours of the storm. With such names as katrinahelp.com and katrinafamilies.com, the online looters preyed on the sympathies of people who wanted to help the victims. Within three weeks of Katrina, more than 2,500 sites registered Katrina domain names. According to an Internet Storm Center, in Bethesda, Maryland, many had cyberlooting in mind.[12] On September 2, as the storm was going on, Florida attorney general Charlie Crist sued Robert Moneyhan, an enterprising super-cyberlooter who was webmaster for katrinahelp.com, katrinadonations.com, katrinarelief fund.com, and katrinarelief.com. Crist said the donations for all these funds were going not to survivors of the storm but into Moneyhan's own pocket.[13]

Another brazen cyberlooter was Gary Kraser. On his site, AirKatrina.com, he claimed to be piloting flights to rescue children and critically ill patients. On August 30, he fabricated that "I am shaking as I write this . . . I am crying as I read this. . . . I saw dogs wrapped in electrical wires alive and sparks flying from their bodies being electrocuted, as well as some people dead already. . . . I'm crying and hugging my dog now." In another entry on August 31, he wrote, "I don't think the little baby would have survived. She is undergoing transplant surgery at this moment as I am writing." Kraser said that "every dollar, every nickel" would go directly to help these rescue flights, and he received about $40,000 in two days, which he pocketed himself. Kraser was arrested on October 3 and charged with four counts of wire fraud.[14]

Corporate Wilding

On September 27, 2005, New Jersey became the first state to sue oil companies for price gouging in the wake of Katrina. A few weeks earlier, New Jersey drivers had reported sudden spikes of oil prices up to $3.16 a gallon, the highest ever in the state. New Jersey sued Hess, Sunoco, and Motiva Shell, as well as several gas stations, with violating its motor fuels and consumer fraud laws. New Jersey attorney general Peter C. Harvey said the oil companies were involved in "artificial inflation and economic exploitation." He added that there were other "unconscionable practices" that involved charging consumers' credit cards for more gas than they had received and filling tanks with low-octane gas while charging high-octane prices, but the price gouging was the corporate wilding that captured consumers' attention.[15]

All over the country, thousands of motorists called better business bureaus and special government hotlines to report price gouging, often in emergency situations just after the storm. In Alabama alone, a special hotline for price gouging got 890 calls in the few days immediately following the storm, complaining of unjustified price spikes. The Mississippi attorney general's office received more than 7,000 such calls on its own hotline. This led to attorney generals from more than 30 states conferring on September 1 to coordinate a national antigouging effort.[16]

Tennessee was among the first of several states to file suits against gas station owners, such as Tip Top Mart of Chattanooga, which had allegedly charged more than $5 a gallon after the storm. These practices understandably led many consumers to see gas station owners as the main culprits. But investigators in states such as Florida believe that it was the oil companies and suppliers that artificially had hiked the prices, leaving many stations no choice but to raise their own prices at the pump.[17]

New Mexico governor Bill Richardson called a special session of his state legislature after the storm to deal with price gouging by the oil companies. In an interview with Richardson, journalist Juan Gonzales noted that, right after the storm hit, Shell had put a notice on its Web site warning consumers of price gouging and asking them to report any stations that they suspected of doing it. But Shell, as Gonzales noted, with the highest profits of any corporation in the world, raised its prices to wholesalers six times in the 10 days following the hurricane. In the third quarter of 2005, following the storm, Exxon, the biggest U.S. oil company, reported one of the highest corporate quarterly profits in American history of $10 billion, representing a per-minute profit of $74,789 during the quarter. Royal Dutch Shell reported its own record profit of almost $9 billion, and all S&P 500 U.S. oil and gas companies reported an astonishing 62 percent rise in quarterly profits totaling $25.9 billion, leading a corporate-friendly Republican Congress to summon the heads of the five largest oil giants and interrogate them about oil profiteering.[18] Richardson, a former energy secretary in the Clinton administration, noted that "there's an unexplained trend between the price of gasoline at the pump and the price of crude. In other words, wholesale prices have nearly tripled. So the increase in prices at the pump and gasoline, what consumers are paying, is disproportionately high." He said that the "increase is so high" that he and other governors were asking for a more formal investigation by the president and Congress into corporate oil price gouging.[19]

While the oil companies were major wilders, there were wilding plums for a huge range of other giant companies, especially those involved in reconstruction efforts and with useful political connections. Within a month of the storm, the *New York Times* found that 80 percent of the $1.5 billion in relief and rebuilding contracts had been awarded in no-bid or very limited bidding arrangements, mainly to huge, politically connected corporations such as Halliburton and Bechtel. These firms, which have been investigated for fraudulent overbilling and mismanagement of similar projects in Iraq, were represented by the likes of Joe Allbaugh, who wore three hats: President Bush's former campaign manager, former head of the Federal Emergency Management Agency (FEMA), and head of a lobbying organization for giant corporations seeking big profits from the New Orleans disaster (although Allbaugh denies representing them for federal contracting purposes). Representative Bennie Thompson (D) of Mississippi said that this "is just more of the good-old-boy system, taking care of its political allies." Al Skinner, the inspector general of the Homeland Security Department, said this of the sordid cronyism and bidding process his staff was investigating, "When you do something like this, you do increase the vulnerability for fraud, plain waste, abuse and mismanagement." Skinner's investigation didn't stop Bechtel from instantly raking in a $100-million contract; or Halliburton's subsidiary, Kellogg Brown & Root from getting a quick $60 million; and from another $568 million going to Ashbritt Environmental, a former client of the lobbying firm of Mississippi's governor and former Republican National Committee chair, Haley Barbour.[20] Many smaller Gulf Coast companies complained of the favoritism received by the big companies outside the region with Washington connections. In the first wave of contracts, valued at about $2 billion, only 3.8 percent went to Alabama firms, 2.8 percent to Louisiana firms, and 1.8 percent to Mississippi businesses. With more than 90 percent of reconstruction work going to companies outside the region, profits would not be reinvested in the Gulf to give residents long-term jobs or sustain local businesses. The *Washington Post* reported that, according to local political and business leaders, "the region's economy will be stymied if funds flow primarily into the pockets of large, out-of-state corporations . . . the government has tilted the playing field against the companies that most desperately need the work." All the outrage over blatant corporate cronyism led R. David Paulison, acting director of FEMA, to announce that $400 million of contracts initially awarded without competition would be renegotiated competitively, although as of mid-November 2005, FEMA had failed to do so for at least three of its largest no-bid contracts to Bechtel, Shaw, and Fluor for housing and construction, without any spending limits, although federal investigators were newly recommending spending caps.[21]

Political Wilding

Political wilding literally created the New Orleans disaster, with former and current administrations failing to fund reconstruction of the levees that would have prevented flooding by a massive hurricane, as well as creating crony appointments incapable of responding to the disaster that they knew was coming. Political wilding after the storm delayed and bungled the governmental response, leading to the tragic loss of life and property that beset millions of mainly black and poor residents. The wilding of an emerging system of "disaster capitalism" allowed the government and its corporate allies to eliminate worker and environmental protections and make astounding profits, all in the name of compassionate conservatism and rebuilding America. The sordid actions of government, to enrich politicians and corporations at the expense of needy citizens, highlights American wilding as an epidemic starting at the top leadership of the nation, in the White House and on Capitol Hill.

On September 1, 2005, President Bush said on *Good Morning America*, "I don't think anyone anticipated breach of the levees." But a FEMA report before September 11, 2001, explicitly named a hurricane disaster in New Orleans as one of the three most likely catastrophes in the United States, along with a San Francisco earthquake and a terrorist attack on New York City. In 2002, FEMA director Joe Allbaugh, a close Bush confidant, ordered a simulation of a New Orleans hurricane that envisioned "that some part of the levee would fail. . . . The water will flow through the city." Local emergency officials did their own studies. Emergency coordinator Walter Maestri in Jefferson Parish, in New Orleans, announced in September 2002 that a widely publicized simulation of a massive storm led them to "change the name of that storm from Delaney to K-Y-A-G-B— kiss your ass goodbye—because anybody who was here as that category five storm came across was gone."[22]

Federal and local officials have known at least since 1995, when a hard rain flooded New Orleans and killed six people, that the levees had to be strengthened. In 1995, Congress funded the Southeast Louisiana Urban Flood Control Project (SELA) to help rebuild the levees, and it allocated $430 million over the next decade to the project. As early as October 2001, though, the New Orleans *Times-Picayune* reported that "federal officials are postponing new projects . . . of SELA," endangering the city. Modest spending on the program continued until 2003, when the Bush administration cut off most of its funding. In June 2004, with the levees dangerously weakening, the Army Corps of Engineers project manager, Al Naomi, pleaded for $2 million more from Washington, telling the *Times-Picayune* that "the levees are sinking. Everything is sinking, and if we don't get the money fast enough to raise them," he said prophetically, disaster loomed. "The problem that we have isn't that the levee is low but that the federal funds have dried up so that we can't raise them."[23] The Army Corps of Engineers, responsible for a multiyear project to fix the levees, saw its budget cut for the New Orleans Hurricane project repeatedly by the Bush administration:

> Fiscal year 2004: Army Corps request: $11 million; Bush budget: $3 million
>
> Fiscal year 2005: Army Corps request: $22.5 million; Bush budget: $3.5 million[24]

For fiscal year 2006, Bush proposed $3 million, a precipitous cut after the intense Florida hurricane season and when the Corps of Engineers, New Orleans officials, and others were clamoring for funding for a $15-million project for Lake Pontchartrain, the Corps of Engineers was seeking $35 million for new levee construction, and further studies were recommending how to rebuild the levees to protect against the worst hurricanes. A study released eight weeks after the storm by three different teams of independent engineers revealed that design failures by the Corps of Engineers—with the concrete pilings not dug deep enough to withstand even a Category 3 storm surge—were responsible for major levee breaches during Katrina. The catastrophe in New Orleans, that the local New Orleans media and citizens had warned about so many times, would have been prevented had the design flaws been fixed.[25]

Deceiving the public about the administration's own knowledge of the risk to New Orleans and establishing budget priorities to offer huge tax relief to President Bush's rich supporters and slash money for urgent domestic priorities, including protection of New Orleans, were acts of blatant political wilding. These actions helped contribute to what journalist Mike Davis called "the murder of New Orleans."[26]

Beyond failing to prevent the flooding by rebuilding the levees, political wilding immediately surfaced in the delayed, bungled federal response to the disaster, even as deadly, toxic water submerged the city, especially the Lower Ninth Ward neighborhood where mostly black, poor people lived. The larger wilding question, to which we return later, is whether the victims' race and class made them more expendable in the eyes of the Bush Administration. There is virtual unanimity that Homeland Security and FEMA shockingly failed to act to save them, contributing to the death and suffering of hundreds of thousands. Even President Bush tacitly acknowledged the catastrophic failure when he accepted the quick resignation of FEMA director Michael Brown and promised his own internal investigation of what went wrong.

Though people were dying in New Orleans, Bush had initially flown to the Gulf Coast and told Brown, "Brownie, you're doing a heck of a job." But Brown became notorious when he announced on television during the storm that he had no idea that thousands of survivors were holed up in the New Orleans Convention Center without food, water, or police protection. The desperate plight of the people at the Convention Center had been aired for days on CNN, and the fact that Brown had no clue of their existence when nearly everyone else in the United States had seen them there exposed his and FEMA's complete incompetence. Brown compounded the problem by telling national television that he had directed FEMA to send "all available resources to get to that convention center to make sure that they have the food and water and medical care that they need." At the Convention Center itself, while Brown dithered, a CNN producer told viewers, "It was chaos. There was nobody there, nobody in charge. And there was nobody giving even water. The children, you should see them, they're all just in tears. There are sick people. We saw . . . people who are dying in front of you." Also on the scene as Brown spoke was evacuee Raymond Cooper, who said, "Sir, you've got about 3,000 people here in this—in the Convention Center right now. They're hungry. Don't have any food."[27]

What CNN called "The Big Disconnect"—between what the government was saying and what was happening on the ground—illustrated political wilding of disinformation, incompetence, and abandonment. Brown said, "I have just learned today . . . that we are in the process of evacuating hospitals, that those are going very well," while CNN's medical correspondent, Dr. Sanjay Gupta, was saying, "It's gruesome . . . when patients die in the hospital, there is no place to put them, so they're in the stairwells. It is one of the most unbelievable situations I've seen as a doctor, certainly as a journalist as well. There is no electricity. There is no water. There's over 200 patients still here remaining."[28]

On civil unrest and security, it was the same disconnect, with officials either clueless or misinforming the public about the disintegrating conditions in New Orleans, conditions for which they were responsible. Brown said, "I've had no reports of unrest," while CNN's Chris Lawrence was reporting, "From here and from talking to the police officers, they're losing control of the city. . . . The police officers came by and told us in very, very strong terms it wasn't safe to be out on the street." Brown said about the overall federal response, "Considering the dire circumstances that we have in New Orleans, virtually a city that has been destroyed, things are going relatively well," and Homeland Security director Michael Chertoff said, "Now, of course, a critical element of what we're doing is the process of evacuation and securing New Orleans and other areas that are afflicted. And here the Department of Defense has performed magnificently, as has the National Guard, in bringing enormous resources and capabilities to bear in the areas that are suffering." As they were talking, crowds at the Convention Center chanted, "We want help," and New Orleans mayor Ray Nagin bluntly dismissed Brown and Chertoff: "They don't have a clue what's going on down there."[29]

The horrific rescue failures partly reflected cronyism, a form of political wilding rampant in the Bush administration. The appointment of political hacks as a favor for past contributions is hardly new, but Bush brought it to new heights, putting loyalists in critical positions in security, public safety, health, and other life-and-death departments who had no past relevant work experience. It is less difficult to understand FEMA's catastrophic bungling—which caused many deaths and irreversible urban destruction—when you see that Michael Brown became director of FEMA after serving for 11 years as director of the International Arabian Horse Association. He also allegedly made up parts of his résumé about overseeing emergency services in a small Oklahoma town; another city official said Brown had been an "intern."[30] Brown became FEMA director without any emergency expertise but through his close association with Joseph Allbaugh, Bush's campaign manager and former FEMA director, who later helped coordinate corporate interests in the reconstruction. Ironically, during the flooding, Allbaugh went down to New Orleans well before Brown, a commentary on the scale of both corporate wilding and the hapless bureaucratic wilding of FEMA and Homeland Security.

A closely related form of political wilding, even more important than the bungled rescue efforts, is what author Naomi Klein calls "Disaster Capitalism." It is the exploitation of catastrophes, whether wars or hurricanes, to purge their victims from choice pieces of real estate, squeeze profits out of desperate cities or countries, and reconstruct a city, region, or entire country as a corporate robber baron paradise. In the name of compassionate conservatism and social reconstruction, politicians will ram through a set of low-wage, environmentally unregulated, socially miserly, and racist policies that constitute political and economic wilding on a grand scale. It has led some analysts to conclude that New

Orleans will end up being ethnically cleansed, a city whitened and gentrified.[31]

Klein notes that reconstruction has become a huge global industry, led by Washington and a host of giant global engineering and energy companies, big nongovernmental organizations (NGOs), and international banks. According to Shalmali Guttal, a Bangalore researcher, "Now we have sophisticated colonialism and they call it reconstruction. . . . It's not reconstruction at all—it's about reshaping everything." Klein argues, "If anything, the stories of corruption and incompetence serve to mask this deeper scandal: the rise of a predatory form of disaster capitalism that uses the desperation and fear created by catastrophe to engage in radical, social and economic engineering. And, on this front," she notes, "the reconstruction industry works so quickly and efficiently that the privatizations and land grabs are usually locked in before the local population knows what hits them."[32]

Klein wrote this before Katrina, about the "disaster capitalism" emerging after the deadly Southeast Asian tsunami in 2004. But it applied perfectly to New Orleans after the storm, when she interviewed Mark Drennen, the city's leading corporate lobbyist. "Drennen was in an expansive mood," she writes, "pumped up by signs from Washington that the corporations he represents—everything from Chevron to Liberty Bank to Coca-Cola—were about to receive a package of tax breaks, subsidies and relaxed regulations so generous it would make the job of a lobbyist virtually obsolete."[33] Within a month of Katrina, Congress had already promised $62 billion for reconstruction, billions of which would soon be allocated in no-bid contracts to the best-connected giant corporations of "disaster capitalism," including Fluor Corporation, Shaws, Allbritt, and, as noted earlier, Halliburton and Bechtel.

While the huge money going to these corporations has been widely reported, the ultraconservative political vision that aims to transform the entire economy and social structure of the city has been less publicized. The Bush administration has declared the emergency—based on the rhetoric of compassion and speedy relief—grounds for eliminating many of the most important worker, social welfare, and environmental protections that sustain U.S. civil society. For years, conservatives have sought to repeal the 1931 Davis-Bacon Act, a labor law requiring that federal contractors pay the "prevailing wage" in the region, a vitally important federal guarantor of good wages. In the last decade, Republicans have tried nine times to repeal Davis-Bacon, but it was only with Katrina that they succeeded. Bush declared a "national emergency," allowing him to suspend the law and permit giant contractors to pay poor Gulf Coast or immigrant Mexican construction workers, some of them storm victims, a minimum wage that was about half the prevailing wage. Richard M. Rogers, a Massachusetts trade union official, said, "It is unconscionable that President Bush would use a national tragedy to promote his antiworker agenda."[34] Eight weeks after the storm, in the wake of a huge storm of outrage from labor and the public, President Bush reversed his position and promised to respect Davis-Bacon. But the corporate bonanza would continue.

The Bush administration used the "national emergency" provisions to waive the rule that contractors adhere to affirmative action and to permit the Environment Protection Agency (EPA) to suspend any regulation in the Clean Air Act that might impede relief. The president went further, proposing to make this waiver operable in the future whenever the agency decides that "emergency conditions" exist. Bush and congressional Republicans see Katrina as a beautiful opportunity to remake society, with Senator Rick Santorum of Pennsylvania, an outspoken conservative, saying about the poor of New Orleans, "The conditions that people were living in I would argue were a result of liberal policies. And now," Santorum continued, "we've got some alternative ideas." What are these alternative ideas? Bush calls it a "Gulf Opportunity Zone." It would give companies freedom to ignore worker and environmental regulations as incentive for rebuilding, while cutting social programs such as Medicaid, the federal program for medical assistance to the poor.[35] This led to the surreal situation of Bush refusing to offer hurricane victims assistance under Medicaid, in the name of giving speedy relief (delivered by the subsidized disaster corporations) to these same people.

The broader variations of disaster capitalism were outlined in a report of the House Republican Study Committee, a group of conservative House members who proposed 32 "Pro–Free-Market Ideas for Responding to Hurricane Katrina and High Gas Prices." These include private school vouchers, drilling in the Arctic, automatically repealing environmental regulations and Davis-Bacon in disaster zones, creating a flat tax in the affected region, and applying broader tax incentives and subsidies that promote corporate investment in special competitiveness or development zones.[36]

Ethnic cleansing, a term used by some of the evacuees themselves, could be the ultimate political wilding, involving a change in the race and class demographics of the city that would purge thousands of African-American residents. People began returning to New Orleans after Hurricane Rita, the second huge hurricane following Katrina, but most were white, in a city that before Katrina had been two-thirds black. Many saw this as pure happenstance, reflecting the geographic reality that most African-Americans had lived in the lowest-lying poor neighborhoods, which the storm had lashed mercilessly. But many African-Americans who had lived in these neighborhoods were physically barred by police from returning. Three months after the storm, on December 1, New Orleans officially reopened all parts of the Ninth Ward to its residents, but Mayor Ray Nagin indicated this was still a "look and leave" policy, with residents able to go and look at their homes only between 8 A.M. and 4 P.M.[37]

Civic leaders now talk about building new housing over time to integrate the French Quarter, Garden District, and other mainly white neighborhoods in the high-lying, affluent areas of the city. But there are already surprisingly high numbers of vacant apartments in these neighborhoods: more than 11,600 vacant apartments exist in neighborhoods that remained mainly dry, and 23,270 if you include Jefferson Parish. These vacancies could immediately house almost 70,000 poor evacuees, who could pay for them with rental vouchers and Section 8 provisions that would suspend rent until they could find jobs. Representative Sheila Jackson Lee of Texas (D) said she would sponsor legislation to provide rental vouchers for this end. But she came up smack against the ambivalence of many whites about integrating their neighborhoods, as well as President Bush's desire for an "ownership society," which prefers incentives for home ownership in some distant future rather than adding more rental opportunities now.[38] Some poor African-American evacuees who tried to get back into New Orleans were blocked entry, others found their public housing projects shut indefinitely, and the New Orleans Housing Authority "informed the landlords of people assisted by federal rent vouchers that government rent subsidies for impacted units have been suspended indefinitely."[39] A mass shortage of affordable housing had forced many evacuees to relocate in FEMA's trailer campuses set up far from New Orleans or around the nation wherever other housing or jobs are available.[40] Three months after the storm, a majority of the poor neighborhoods remained empty, with evacuees and affordable housing advocates claiming that many poor residents were being "locked out" by government housing and relocation policies. Mass relocation could dramatically whiten New Orleans, draining the poor African-American population from the city along with the flood waters. To the extent that this is a product of deliberate policy, it constitutes the ultimate political wilding.

The fears of ethnic cleansing among the New Orleans poor, especially in the Ninth Ward, mushroomed after the release on January 11, 2006, of the first report by Mayor Nagin's "Bring New Orleans Back" Commission, which had been charged with creating a master redevelopment plan. The report envisages a much smaller city of about 200,000 compared with the 500,000 pre-Katrina population, and gives authorities the right to use eminent domain to seize property in neighborhoods that are viewed as not "sustainable." Sustainability is decided by officials based partly on the return rate of evacuees, a process that the officials themselves had slowed or stopped in poor neighborhoods. The commission decided to put a four-month moratorium on any redevelopment in badly flooded neighborhoods, such as the Ninth Ward, while more affluent neighborhoods were allowed to begin rebuilding immediately. Former New Orleans mayor and current Urban League chair, Marc Morial, a dissenting member of the commission, joined angry Ninth Ward residents in denouncing this as a discriminatory measure that would lead to the abandonment or appropriation of poor areas deemed "unsustainable."[41]

When *Newsweek* interviewed Morial, he said that the commission's master plan did not honor or respect the poor and black evacuees. It was discriminatory in intent, "[b]y having a building moratorium and giving the victims the obligation to prove the viability of their neighborhoods. What I saw was a massive plan that redlined neighborhoods (for demolition), wrapped around a major land grab. The idea was: if we the commission don't think the neighborhoods are viable, we'll come in and take your property and turn it over to a real estate developer."[42]

Societal Wilding

A picture is worth a thousand words. And the pictures that we Americans kept viewing on our TV screens during the Katrina crisis seared our brains: desperate people walking down the interstate from New Orleans like refugees from a third world country with only their shirts on their back; dead bodies floating in the toxic water of the flooded city; armed bands roaming and looting deserted streets; people begging for police protection at the Superdome and crying out for food and water at the Convention Center.

The faces were black and poor. We had not seen these faces—featured on national TV—for years. The shame of black, urban poverty is a harsh truth of big-city life all over the United States. But most Americans had forgotten about the urban poor, something that is not an accident, but a design of the politicians and the media.

Katrina exposed that the emperor had no clothes. After years of discussion of the magic of the free market—how it lifts all boats—Katrina woke Americans up to the wilding at the center of our society. We remain a society segregated by race and class, with 40 million poor people and millions more teetering on the edge. The problem has intensified by virtue of deliberate policies carried out by ruling elites who had promised an SUV in every garage and a return to traditional moral values.

Senator Barack Obama of Illinois (D) observed, "I hope we realize that the people of New Orleans weren't just abandoned during the hurricane. They were abandoned long ago—to murder and mayhem in the streets, to substandard schools, to dilapidated housing, to inadequate health care, to a pervasive sense of hopelessness."[43]

What Obama didn't say was that both political parties had abandoned the poor over the last several decades in order to serve their corporate patrons—and that this abandoment is the dominant systemic wilding of our current order. During the New Deal, Franklin Roosevelt challenged the failed corporate regime of the 1920s, mobilizing workers, family farmers, and the poor to recapture government from corporations and helping to create jobs and social welfare for all. But by 1980, in the name of compassionate conservatism, the New Right elected President Reagan with the intent of dismantling the New Deal and restoring government to corporate ownership.[44]

The new corporate regime systemically set about smashing unions, weakening environmental rules, cutting social spending, ending welfare, and siphoning off billions of dollars to "corporate welfare," while dramatically cutting the taxes of the rich. This deliberate "reverse Robin Hood" policy has had predictable effects nakedly exposed in Katrina. Poverty in America is now increasing. The gap between rich and poor is skyrocketing. The plight of urban African-Americans is worsening. All of this was happening before Katrina but went largely unseen, as Americans became more geographically and economically separated by race and class.[45]

The promise of Katrina is that it opened, at least for a short period, a new window to see through the blinders that have been carefully constructed by ruling elites. The immediacy of the tragedy, the tortured faces of the urban poor, the abandonment and destruction of "the least among us" have the potential to dramatically change the conversation in America. It is no longer as easy to deny the terror of poverty or America's current segregation by race and class, a new American apartheid. As *Newsweek*'s Jonathan Alter writes, Katrina created a change: "For the moment at least, Americans are ready to fix their restless gaze on enduring problems of poverty, race and class that have escaped their attention . . . this disaster may offer a chance to start a skirmish, or at least make Washington think harder why part of the richest country on earth looks like the Third World." Sociologist Andrew Cherlin said of Katrina that "this was a case where the poor were clearly not at fault. It was a reminder that we have a moral obligation to provide every American with a decent life."[46]

But we still lack political leaders and media analysts capable of explaining why this systemic wilding has occurred and how it can change. The Bush administration and Republican congressional leaders have added insult to injury by using the storm to push through the punitive "disaster capitalism" that will intensify the problems of the poor and perhaps ethnically cleanse New Orleans. Indeed, one of the most chilling forms of wilding during the reconstruction was the decision by Congress to pay for rebuilding by dramatically cutting social programs—in the Gulf Coast and around the nation. We were left with the absurdity of cutting antipoverty programs—for education, health care, and social welfare—in the name of helping the poor.

Even white, affluent residents are feeling abandoned, wondering angrily whether any kind of viable city will be rebuilt. On the day before Thanksgiving, November 23, 2005, 12 weeks after the storm, John Biguenet, a novelist and New Orleans resident, wrote that that he does not have much to feel thankful about. "On my way every day to where we used to live," he laments,

> I drive through a city I love that lies in ruins. The park that lines one of the boulevards I follow home is now a solid wall of debris 20 feet high. On the other side of the street, desolate houses destroyed by the flood gape back with shattered windows, open doors and ragged holes in rooftops kicked out by families trapped in their attics when the water rose . . . everything is covered in a pall of gray dust, as if all the color of this once vibrant city has been leached out.

Biguenet added that only "fifteen percent or so of residents have returned. Most people can't come home . . . half the houses in New Orleans are still not reconnected to the city sewer system and as many still lack national gas for heating and cooking, 40% have no electricity and a quarter of the city is without drinkable water." Beyond the wilding of corporate reconstruction lies the wilding of complete abandonment of New Orleans, and it is still unclear which will triumph.[47]

Only new social movements will bring sane analysis and solutions to the wilding epidemic. Memories of Katrina may yet catalyze them and build support among the public. The role of sociologists is to help build awareness of race and class wilding systems, and to condemn them in forthright terms while offering a new direction.

Katrina's Lessons

While Katrina was a perfect wilding storm, it also demonstrated why there is hope. It showed that while wilding has taken over Washington and our nation's elites, it has not yet swallowed up the rest of our society. Remember first, that much of the looting and other personal wilding originally reported by the media during the storm proved to be false. While it is true that many residents broke into grocery stories, Wal-Marts, or pharmacies, the majority did it to get the food, water, and medicine to help their families and neighbors survive. Rather than participating in a wilding frenzy, most residents exhibited remarkable solidarity, risking their own homes and lives to help others survive.

A month after the storm, the new story was how officials and the media got it terribly wrong about looting. Police Chief Eddie Compass had told Oprah Winfrey on her show about infants being raped, and Mayor C. Ray Nagin also told her that people have been "in that frickin' Superdome for five days watching dead bodies, watching hooligans killing people, raping people." Often without careful documentation or attribution, the mass media carried sensationalist stories of hundreds of bodies piling up in the Superdome, mass rapes being committed, people getting their throats slit, and armed gangs taking over the city. Virtually all these stories were untrue.[48]

At the Convention Center, authorities found four bodies, not the scores of corpses reported to be piling up there. At the Superdome, which was housing 20,000 people, only six bodies were found—four dead of natural causes, one by suicide, and one of a drug overdose. Nobody was murdered at the Superdome and one at the Convention Center. It turned out that the desperate evacuees had been remarkably restrained after being left for five days without food, water, showers, air conditioning, or security in the Superdome and Convention Center, many going out of their way to help the ill or elderly to survive.[49]

But before showing why the true story offers hope, let us be clear about the wilding effects of authorities and media getting it so wrong. From the start, many pundits had already cast blanket damnation on the poor, beginning a wave of bigotry and an unfolding media wilding of vast proportions. Eminent conservative journalist George Will played the "blame the victim" game when he wrote in a column about Katrina, poverty, and chaos in New Orleans that "it is a safe surmise that more than 80 percent of African American births in inner-city New Orleans—as in some other inner cities—were to women without husbands. That translates into a large and constantly renewed cohort," wrote Will, "of lightly parented adult males, and that translates into chaos in neighborhoods and schools, come rain or come shine." Will lectured the poor in New Orleans and everyone else that there are three "rules" to avoid poverty: "Graduate from high school, don't have a baby until you are married, don't marry while you are a teenager. Among people who obey those rules poverty is minimal."[50]

In other words, if the poor were violent during Katrina or had trouble getting out of the city, it was their own failure to follow "the rules" that explains their sorry fate.

Many bloggers were more explicit. Conservative pundit Karen H. Pittman wrote just after Katrina that "I have an inherent antipathy towards that certain sub-species of human animal that is now commandeering the streets of that fetid city, truly now a razed City of the Dead." She said she lacked the words to express "just how thoroughly revolted I am by these mack daddies and gangstars and brazen bitches-with-FATitudes (in-these-lowlife-latitudes) when I hear them squawking on-camera about how 'aint nobody did nuthin' fa us'—when they were told to leave."[51]

While such contempt for the poor came mostly from conservative pundits and bloggers, the mainstream press created media wilding by reporting false, sensationalist stories without adequate verification. Although they later recanted, the original stories tragically evoked the media wilding discussed in the first chapter of this book during the 1991 New York City Central Park rape, which led to mistaken convictions of rape by inner-city youth and fed into many racist stereotypes. Katrina media wilding had its own ripple effects. Based on the fear of evacuees fed by press reports, or by racism according to some eyewitnesses, police in the neighboring suburb of Gretna pointed guns and fired a warning shot at Katrina survivors on the Mississippi River Bridge trying to walk out of New Orleans to Gretna.[52] On another front, the Red Cross was not permitted to deliver aid into the city because the city had been deemed as "too dangerous" by the National Guard, which was suffering from the same media-fed misperceptions. And Louisiana governor Kathleen Blanco, who finally ordered in the National Guard, had proclaimed, "Three hundred of the Arkansas National Guard have landed in the city of New Orleans. These troops are fresh back from Iraq, well trained, experienced, battle-tested and under my orders to restore order in the streets. They have M-16s and they are locked and loaded. These troops know how to shoot and kill and they are more than willing to do so if necessary and I expect they will." Pre-existing racist stereotypes as well as media wilding brought out a siege mentality, leading top officials to wage war on the storm's victims.[53]

Because so many of the Louisiana National Guard were bogged down in Iraq, Governor Blanco had to turn to other National Guards, such as those from Arkansas, to go into the city. They were joined by private security firms, such as Blackwater USA, that also had experience in Iraq. They functioned as urban vigilantes, walking the streets with cocked M-16s and commandeering apartment buildings where they planted American flags and appeared ready to wage a new war against the evacuees themselves.[54]

Media wilding contributed to the growing militarization of the government's response, led by President Bush, who announced a new plan to change a century-old law that prevented active duty military from intervening in domestic affairs. Bush now proclaimed that we needed battle-tested active military for active deployment at home as well as around the world, not only to address hurricane situations but to confront crises, such as a potential avian bird flu pandemic.[55] Unfettered militarization of domestic security can be seen as yet another expression of political wilding, with seeds that had been sown well before Katrina, but have been fed dangerously by the storm.

Despite all their misfortunes, evidence continues to mount that the storm's victims were largely restrained and civil, and often heroic in helping their neighbors. They are among those millions of citizens who, as I argued in the first chapter, are not yet infected by the wilding culture. Their desperate plight—as well as their proven ability to endure incredible calamity without resorting to mass wilding—bodes well for the future of the country. These ordinary Americans will have to help lead not only the rebuilding of New Orleans but also a change of course in the nation.

What this new direction might look like is something I consider in the next chapter. But we should note here that millions of other Americans, in their own responses to Katrina, demonstrated the generosity of spirit that can help solve our current crisis. In the first week of the hurricane, only weeks after many had contributed funds to the Asian tsunami relief funds, millions of the same and new ordinary folk dug into their pockets to give more, while also offering up homes and churches for housing the evacuees. As I show in the next chapter, such altruistic spirit and behavior, while not sufficient to stem the wilding epidemic, is, along with a new social and political agenda, the foundation of hope.

Beyond Wilding

Resurrecting Civil Society

An injury to one is the concern of all.

—Knights of Labor motto

Wilding has taken a devastating toll on America, but it has not permanently incapacitated it. Societies, like individuals, have a powerful natural resistance and a remarkable capacity to regenerate themselves. While the Ik society has been destroyed, America, always resilient, has far greater economic and cultural resources to revitalize itself. To succeed however, it will have to focus all its efforts on the task, which involves shoring up the ideal of a "civil society" at its very foundations.

Creating and supporting a civil society is the underlying antidote to the wilding virus. Civil society involves a culture of love, morality, and trust that leads people to care for one another and for the larger community. A civil society's institutions nurture civic responsibility by providing incentives for people to act not just in their own interest but for the common good. Governments must provide a supportive framework, but a robust civil society cannot be legislated. It must arise from the cooperation and moral sensibilities of ordinary people who understand that their own fulfillment requires thriving communities and an intact society.

Although there is no magic formula and no perfect model, civil society is the strongest and most suitable medicine for the wilding epidemic. Americans now must urgently recognize that they need to dedicate themselves unwaveringly to reconstructing their society.

The Case for Hope

More than 150 years ago, Alexis de Tocqueville worried that America was vulnerable to an individualism that "saps the virtues of public life" and "in the long run" might "attack and destroy" society itself. Tocqueville described it as an individualism "which disposes each member of the community to sever himself from the mass of his fellows" and to "feel no longer bound by a common interest." Americans must always be on guard, Tocqueville advised, against the deterioration of their individualistic culture into "a passionate and exaggerated love of self, which leads a man to connect everything with himself, and to prefer himself to everything else in the world."[1]

Tocqueville did not disapprove of the healthy self-interest that energized Americans, but he saw the thin line that separates American individualism from wilding. Without strongly developed moral codes, the restless pursuit of self-interest inherent in a market economy could at any time degrade into an egoistic menace that might destroy society. But Tocqueville, a sober observer, was also extraordinarily optimistic about the American experiment. Counteracting the wilding virus was another side of America, the strength of its civil society. One manifestation of this was the personal generosity and helpfulness that he observed in all his American travels. "Although private interest directs the greater part of human actions in the United States," Tocqueville wrote, "it does not regulate them all. I must say that I have often seen Americans make great and real sacrifices to the public welfare; and I have remarked a hundred instances in which they hardly ever failed to lend faithful support to each other." Because an American is neither master nor slave to his fellow creature, "his heart readily leans to the side of kindness."[2]

Tocqueville recognized that the kinder and gentler side of American life was grounded in the political rights and free institutions that "remind every citizen, and in a thousand ways, that he lives in society." Tocqueville marveled at Americans' propensity to "constantly form associations" of a thousand kinds in which they "voluntarily learn to help each other." Americans were constantly connecting and spontaneously creating the bonds of friendship, trust, and cooperation that lie at the heart of civil society.[3]

In the century and a half since Tocqueville's visit, the wilding epidemic has spread throughout America, but it has not totally destroyed the civil society that made such an impression on him. Much evidence suggests that Americans retain some of the openness, generosity, and moral idealism that, in Tocqueville's view, differentiated them from Europeans. Likewise, the free institutions and "propensity to associate" have not vanished. It is the sturdiness of this base, its survival in the face of the wilding onslaught, that offers grounds for optimism and a direction for the future.

While Katrina has been seen as a cauldron of wilding, it is also a symbol of the love and altruism that remain strong in our culture and people. In 2005, Americans dug into their pockets to donate billions of dollars to Katrina victims, only months after they had given record amounts to the victims of the tsunami in Southeast Asia. By the fall of 2005, the United Way reported donations of over $4 billion in charity in response mainly to Katrina, and thousands of other charitable organizations have collected, in total, more than $10 billion in relief funds, much of it from Americans who were struggling to make it through the week on their own diminishing wages.

But donations to charity were only a small part of the evidence of the survival of an "other America" not yet poisoned by the wilding epidemic. In New Orleans itself, much of what has been portrayed as wilding by the abandoned residents was actually an outpouring of collective efforts to feed and care for each other. When stores were raided, it was usually to get food and medicines for neighbors and friends who needed it and couldn't get it for themselves.

Many others still in the city were heroic in their rescue efforts, risking their own lives to save others. As two observers in New Orleans put it, the real "heroes and sheroes" of Katrina were

> [t]he maintenance workers who used a forklift to carry the sick and disabled . . . Nurses who took over for mechanical ventilators and spent many hours on end manually forcing air into the lungs of unconscious patients to keep them alive. Doormen who rescued folks stuck in elevators. Refinery workers who broke into boat yards, "stealing" boats to rescue their neighbors clinging to their roofs in flood waters. Mechanics who helped hotwire any car that could be found to ferry people out of the city. And the food service workers who scoured the commercial kitchens, improvising communal meals for hundreds of those stranded.[4]

It didn't take Katrina to bring out the "other America," for Americans have been altruistic and loving to their fellow citizens for decades. Each year in Boston, more than 50,000 people join the Walk for Hunger. The marchers hike for 20 miles, often in inclement weather, to raise money for Project Bread, a group that helps provide meals for the homeless and hungry. Each participant takes time to approach sponsors, who agree to donate a certain amount of money for each mile that the walker completes. As one curbside viewer said, "You've got the elderly walking, you've got kids walking, you've got families walking. To me, it's the most beautiful sight to see all the people walking." Such walks are only one in a cornucopia of charitable endeavors that regularly take place in cities and towns across the United States.

At the very time that taxpayers are revolting and turning off the public spigot, volunteers are stepping in to help stop the shortfall that their own votes have precipitated. In many towns across the country, playground construction is done mainly by volunteers, in the spirit of traditional community barn-raising. In Plymouth, Massachusetts, the town library stays open only because of the generosity of more than 50 volunteers; in nearby Raynham, the school libraries are run entirely by volunteers. Community booster groups rally to raise money to paint public buildings, keep school sports programs going, and plant trees and maintain the city parks.[5]

Such anecdotes are backed up by hard statistics documenting the generous side of America. About 7 out of every 10 households contribute to charity, donating an average of almost 2 percent of household income, a figure almost four times greater than that in Canada and England (a comparison that should take into account the national health plans and large social welfare programs that taxpayers in the latter countries support, thereby reducing the need for charity). About 45 percent of Americans over the age of 18 sacrifice their own time to volunteer, averaging about four hours a week and totaling almost 20 billion hours of volunteer time nationwide.[6]

How can the wilding epidemic spread at the same time that moral commitments and compassionate behavior persist at these levels? As I argued in Chapter 1, America is simultaneously host to a wilding culture and a civil culture, with sectors of the elites increasingly immersed in wilding and a vast number of ordinary Americans uneasily straddling the two cultures. Most Americans' lives are a struggle to reconcile wilding impulses with a nagging conscience that refuses to die. Many succumb to wilding pressures at the office but rediscover their humanity with family or friends. Conversely, some become wilders in their personal lives but express their conscience in admirable careers dedicated to constructive professional or business enterprise, public service, or social change.

The stubborn persistence of civil society and moral commitment provides a fertile seedbed for social reconstruction. The way to stop the wilding epidemic is to bolster all the empathic and moral sensibilities that Americans already display. Although these need to be fortified and mobilized with new visions, the project is more akin to catalyzing the surviving immune system of a weakened patient than transplanting a new immune system to a patient whose own defenses have been destroyed.

But solving the problem will take serious cultural and institutional change. As I have argued, wilding grows out of an American individualism that is deeply rooted. The country's leadership and major institutions increasingly fuel Americans' wilding side and provide serious disincentives to their less egoistic inclinations. We need to cultivate the culture, economics, and politics of a civil society, where the rules of success encourage attention to morality and the common good. More precisely, we must rewrite the rules of the game so that those who neglect the collective interest will not prosper and those who take it into account will realize their just rewards.

Rethinking the American Dream: A New Communitarianism?

The American Dream has not always been a cultural template for wilding. As we consider rewriting the Dream for a better future, we have the consolation that we can look to our history for guidance. Through most of America's past, the purely materialistic and individualistic side of the Dream has tended to be balanced by a moral and community-oriented side, preventing the Dream from transmuting into a wilding recipe. Moreover, the Dream has been inclusive, defining a set of common purposes to which all Americans could aspire. These historical features of the Dream need to be recaptured in order to fortify civil society and purge the wilding epidemic.

The individualistic dream dominating the present has its roots in the mythology of the self-made man and, as historian James Combs argues, "stems from the ideology of capitalism and the myth of unlimited abundance." The nineteenth-century novelist Horatio Alger immortalized the materialist Dream in his rags-to-riches fables. In its current form, it celebrates American heroes such as basketball superstar Michael Jordan, who rose to fabulous success through his extraordinary individual talent and hard work.[7]

The materialistic dimensions of the Dream have become so dominant that most Americans have forgotten that there was once another side to the Dream. America has traditionally defined itself in terms of a set of high moral ideals, including democracy, equality, and tolerance. Values growing out of the religious and political foundations of the country, including the Puritan zeal for community and the American Revolution's idealization of civil democracy, helped shape another dream, one that mythologized family, community, and civic responsibility. Throughout most of American history, the materialistic Dream prevailed, but the dream that elevated community values provided a warning that success should not be achieved at any price. America idealized its rural and small-town communities where, to a greater or lesser degree, as Combs notes, "religion, family, and democratic good feelings tempered the quest for power and money." Small-town community is still part of American mythology, which helps explain why President Clinton proudly publicized his roots in the town of Hope, Arkansas, and President Bush Jr. speaks nostalgically of his boyhood in a tiny Texan town.[8]

The two dreams define a creative tension in American history. While at some times in our history the materialistic Dream prevailed, in the 1930s, the Great Depression mobilized Americans to rally together and fashion a collective lifeline to ride out the economic storm. President Franklin Delano Roosevelt reinvigorated the dream of moral community, using the government to affirm that in a time of desperate need, Americans would take care of each other. Three decades later, in the 1960s, a whole generation of youth plunged into social activism and communal experiments, seeking a morally attractive alternative to the materialist Dream of their 1950s childhoods.

The failure of the aspirations of the 1960s has led, in the decades since then, to perhaps the most self-centered Dream in American history. To purge the wilding epidemic, Americans in the twenty-first century will have to rediscover and refashion a version of the moral, communitarian dream in order to temper the current fever of individualistic materialism and resurrect civil society.

The moral vision will have to be creative because of the new threats that unchecked materialism now pose. It will have to encompass an ecological morality, for we now know that the untrammeled materialist Dream is incompatible with planetary survival, being a form of wilding directed against nature itself. Global warming—the catastrophic heating up of the Earth through promiscuous use of fossil fuels—is only the most frightening of the legacies of such environmental wilding. If Americans cannot learn to live within the limits dictated by the environment, we will be engaged not only in crimes against nature but also in a form of wilding against future generations who will bear the ultimate consequences.

Americans find it hard to accept any limits on materialism, for the dominant Dream has equated freedom and fulfillment with the right to become as rich or famous as luck, talent, or hard work permits. To suggest that Bill Gates should not have been allowed to make or keep the $51 billion he now has strikes us as un-American. But a civil society must respect not only ecological limits but also those dictated by the traditional American morality of fair play and egalitarianism. Uncapping all limits in the recent orgy of greed and deregulation has polarized the country, creating an unprecedented and morally unbearable division between rich and poor.[9]

Civil society is a society of inclusion, and the new Dream will have to script new trade-offs between individual freedom and the survival of the community. This ultimately requires reviving a moral dream of community; not the utopian vision of communes that failed in the 1960s, but something that is simultaneously more modest and more ambitious: a reawakening of the American sense of community that can mobilize the country to unify and preserve itself in an era of unprecedented division.

The Social Market: Sociological Sense and Dollars and Cents

As Americans have struggled to choose between the materialist dream and the moral dream, they have had to wrestle with the tensions between the free market and community. The market system is an excellent vehicle for delivering the promises of the materialist dream, at least for the wealthy, but it is far less effective in preserving the moral fiber of society. In periods when the moral dream has come more strongly to the fore, as in the 1930s and 1960s, Americans have pioneered economic models, such as the New Deal and the Great Society, that have departed from free-market scripture.

Europeans have spent an entire century building an alternative with a social conscience to the free market. The Swedes, Danes, Austrians, and Germans recognize that they are not playing Adam Smith's game. "We are not operating a marketplace economy," admits German industrialist Helmut Giesecke, but rather a "social marketplace economy [that] guarantees food, shelter, schooling, and medical attention to every person, not as welfare but as human rights." Government, labor, and business work together to reconcile prosperity with social justice. German business has supported this program, according to Giesecke, because "this social network really works," leading to a well-educated, healthy, and motivated workforce whose productivity keeps increasing.[10]

Perhaps ultimately the Germans support the social infrastructure because they know firsthand the horrific consequences when society totally breaks down. They have experienced a Germany gone completely wild, and many recognize that it could happen again. The greater internal homogeneity of Germany, Austria, Sweden, and other European "social market" societies also allows them to feel a greater connection to others and to savor the sense of family. Even as European cultures grow more individualistic and consumerist in the context of globalization, their social marketplace economies may prevent a descent into wilding.

The development of an American social market could be one of the most potent remedies for the wilding epidemic. It would provide a way to reconcile economic growth and justice, and to help solve America's social problems by building on its own deepest value: democracy.

The European model is a universal welfare state, in which the government shelters groups unprotected by the market, responds to the medical, housing, and social needs of the population that the market neglects, and comprehensively regulates business to ensure social responsibility. But the record of American history, as well as its current fiscal crisis, argues against the likelihood that Americans, barring another Great Depression, will look solely to the state, though there is a crucial role for government to play in stopping the wilding epidemic.

The key to a social market system is new institutions, both public and private, that rectify the tendency of our current market economy to write social costs and benefits out of the equation. The American market responds mainly to the desires of the individual actor—whether a person or corporation—and is largely indifferent to the spillover effects that transactions may have on the rest of society. When a factory decides to pollute, the social cost of bad air and ensuing discomfort or respiratory disease is what economists call an "externality": a real cost, but one that the factory owner can ignore, because society, rather than the factory, pays the ultimate bill. In the pure free-market model, there is neither an economic incentive for the individual to help society nor a market disincentive to be antisocial; the market simply does not discriminate, operating with so-called benign neglect. As such neglect accumulates, with the market turning a blind eye to the millions of externalities that affect society every day, benign neglect becomes catastrophic social blindness, and civil society is placed in jeopardy.

A social market corrects such social blindness by writing social costs and benefits back into the equation. It is a market that seeks to internalize the externalities, thus becoming socially responsible by giving social stakeholders a voice in corporate decisions and by devising strategies to guarantee that economic wilders pay the cost of their sociopathic behavior (and conversely, that the good citizen will receive his or her just rewards). One approach, appealing to Americans wary of government and committed to democracy, involves redesigning economic institutions to be better equipped to exercise social responsibility on their own initiative. An important example is new corporate ownership and participation arrangements, in which workers and local citizens gain a voice and can speak up for the needs of the larger community. The Germans, although relying primarily on government, have also invented a "co-determination" system, which requires that every industrial enterprise with more than 500 workers select half its governing board of trustees from among its own employees. This has been successful for more than 40 years, contributing not only to the German economic boom but also to a civil industrial society in which ordinary workers have been able to ensure that their health and safety are protected, their grievances addressed, and their jobs protected by investment strategies that prioritize domestic employment as well as overseas profit. Co-determination is a version of economic democracy that works.

Sociologist Severyn Bruyn describes the many down-to-earth ways, some already highly developed in America, to fashion a social market that works to dissuade economic wilding and preserve civil society without resorting to big government. Numerous forms of worker ownership and participation, including cooperatives and Employee Stock Ownership Plans (ESOPs), in which employees own a piece or all of their companies, can help compel companies to treat their employees fairly and practice workplace democracy. The cooperative, as its name implies, has the potential to turn the workplace itself into a civil society because everyone within it has equal rights, and self-interest is more closely wedded to the collective interest than in a conventional firm. Another innovation involves corporate social charters that bind businesses to designated social missions, as in the case of community credit unions that are structured to reinvest in the community and offer low-interest loans to poorer residents. Land trusts—modern versions of the early British and colonial American concept of the commons—can remove property from the commercial market and legally ensure that it is used to serve community needs. A new field of social accounting can help take stock of the social costs and benefits of corporate decisions. Social capital, such as the trillions of dollars in American pension funds, one of the largest and still-growing pots of money in the world, can be used to invest in affordable housing and community economic development. The new practice of social investing could be the first step in turning the stock market into what sociologist Ritchie Lowry calls "good money," where investors seek a profit but also a social return on their money. "Social screens"—report cards on companies compiled by outside analysts—now tell investors which corporations are economic wilders. Companies that want to attract the funds of millions of social investors have to demonstrate not only what they are doing for the bottom line but also what they are doing for their communities.[11]

America has not yet built a main highway toward this version of the social market, but it is already carving out many smaller roads in that direction. There are now more than 10,000 American ESOPs, including huge companies such as United Airlines, Avis, and Weirton Steel, and evidence indicates that they are more responsive to their employees and their customers. Studies show that worker-owners are more productive and deliver higher quality, with Avis now number one in ratings of customer satisfaction. Hundreds of ESOPs and cooperatives, including large worker-owned factories, practice sophisticated forms of workplace democracy. They are proving effective in job creation and retention, and they are responsible for saving hundreds of jobs during the epidemic of factory closings in the last decade. According to polls, including one by Peter Hart, economic democracy makes sense to most Americans; approximately 70 percent say that they would welcome the opportunity to work in an employee-owned company.[12]

A New New Deal

As soon as you start talking about any kind of new role for government, many Americans roll their eyes. After all, wasn't America founded on the principle of limited government? Hasn't America prospered by rejecting the European ideas of the welfare state and relying instead on individual initiative? The Republican Party is on a never-ending crusade to cut government (or "shrink the beast"). Bill Clinton, the only Democratic president since Reagan, sang the same tune, vowing to "end welfare" and shrink the state.

But when the raging winds of Katrina blew across the Gulf Coast and destroyed much of New Orleans, even the Bush administration insisted that government had to step up to the plate. Bush traveled six times in two months back to New Orleans to promise that he would never let the city die. An antigovernment Republican president suddenly was talking about the sacred connection between an active government and a healthy community. Who would have thought that Bush would mimic Franklin D. Roosevelt, another president who promised to use the federal government to rebuild American communities in hard times? Whether it's a hurricane or a depression, when communities come under stress, everyone suddenly becomes aware that government and community are intertwined.

Roosevelt's New Deal saved Americans from the wilding extremes of hyperindividualism and the Depression created by the 1920s. We may be near a new such awakening today. Katrina was just one of many new crises that are leaving ordinary working Americans feeling like they have been left out in the cold to fend for themselves—and that they could use a little help from government to rebuild their communities. As Americans see their wages stagnating and their jobs shipped overseas, their roads and bridges eroding, their public schools failing their kids, and their neighborhoods straining under poverty and crime, more than two-thirds tell pollsters that they believe that the nation is headed in the wrong direction.

The new direction they need—one essential to ending our current wilding epidemic—is a new New Deal. It will not be a clone of Europe's welfare state or Roosevelt's own New Deal. It is not a call for massive government or even "big government," but rather an activist government accountable to communities and ordinary citizens rather than big business. It will nourish the social market of socially oriented business, and it will offer all Americans a safety net.

The philosophy of the new New Deal is to wed the social market with a government committed to building an inclusive community. No American will be left behind in this community, and the very idea of inclusion will become central to the American creed and constitution. From the beginning, the nation has not lived up to the rhetoric of inclusion, segregating people by race, gender, and class. But inclusion has always been the defining ideal. The creed extends the same rights to all citizens, and the Bill of Rights has evolved to explicitly guarantee the same protection and rights to everyone, whatever their race, gender or class.

The new New Deal will help strengthen and build new prosperous communities for those communities historically left behind, particularly those who are black, female, and poor. They were most exposed to Katrina, and they are the most vulnerable to the global market. As this twenty-first-century New Deal seeks to protect them, it will also seek to nurture those who, as political scientist Robert Putnam puts it, are now "bowling alone," without any community at all. But all Americans, even the affluent, will need protection from the environmental and social hurricanes to come. The role of government in the coming age is to bring diverse people and classes together to meet their common needs, building social infrastructure and social insurance as a big umbrella sheltering all of us against twenty-first-century environmental hazards and globalization's violent social storms.

The new New Deal sees government as just one of many ways in which ordinary citizens in a democratic society can come together to care about and protect one another. Government exists to help civil society sustain itself, subject to the limits that communities place upon it. Government is an instrument of the people. But this should not blind Americans—who have been told for so long that government is evil—to the essential role of government in protecting people and building community. Today, there are a few key new roles for government in building community. One is to remedy the crisis of job loss and insecurity, so closely linked to corporate globalization, by putting appropriate regulations on the destabilizing floods of global finance and helping put displaced workers back to work on national projects, such as energy independence. Communities can't survive without jobs, and government can supply critical financing to help vital, new, environmentally friendly industries save cities and the planet itself. Another key government role is extending health care to every American. Americans see how vital Medicare is for their parents and grandparents, and recognize that, with 45 million Americans now without health insurance, it is just as important for their children and themselves. A third is to ensure a "living wage," so that no American working full-time is mired in poverty. A fourth is to ensure global collective security with foreign policy that does not create more wars, respects civil liberties at home and abroad, and encourages diplomatic cooperation and equality among all nations.

But will Americans support this new activist role for government? On big public issues of jobs, poverty, and community, a majority of ordinary Americans, who tend to label themselves as philosophically conservative, support strong government programs on education, health care, and social security to bring us together. Both liberals and conservatives yearn for some form of community as an antidote to the wilding crisis, and they are willing to fight politicians who do not see government as essential to the solution. When, in the name of individual initiative and the free market, Bush tried to privatize Social Security and cut back Medicare, he got clobbered politically. Despite 30 years of conservative efforts to demonize government, most Americans see that they can't survive globalization or a severe health crisis in the family or another giant hurricane on their own. Common sense in hard times is bringing Americans together, a first step toward rebuilding community, reactivating government, and ending the wilding crisis.

The new New Deal is a moral as well as economic agenda. The core moral themes are inclusion, accountability, and community. Progressives will win—and stop the wilding crisis—only when Americans see the "moral values" driving the new New Deal. Its policies are all designed to alleviate suffering caused by moral neglect and cancerous individualism. Its goal is to build the foundations of a community that shelters and protects all Americans. This is the only moral politics that makes sense in an age of wilding.

A New Bill of Rights?
The Politics of Civil Society

America's romance with individualism and the free market has its virtues, but it has clouded Americans' understanding of what makes society tick. Civil society arises only when individuals develop strong obligations to the larger "us" that can override the perennial, very human preoccupation with the self. Such larger commitments bloom only under special conditions: when the community shows that it cares so deeply for each of its members that each member fully understands his or her debt to society and seeks to pay it back in full.

The Japanese and Europeans, in their very different ways, seem to appreciate this deal, or contract, that preserves civil society. Japanese corporations have historically enveloped the Japanese worker in a cocoon of secure employment, health benefits, housing, and other social necessities that make it almost impossible for most workers to imagine life outside the group. Through their expansive welfare states, the Europeans deliver their own bushel of benefits and entitlements that citizens recognize as indispensable to personal survival and happiness. Both systems possess their own serious problems and are partially eroding in the face of global economic pressures, but they continue to succeed in creating an allegiance to the larger community that fosters an immunity to the wilding epidemic.

Each civil society has to find its own way of inspiring its members' devotion, but all must deliver those rock-bottom necessities essential to the pursuit of life, liberty, and happiness. These include some level of personal safety, food, shelter, and a livelihood. Social orphans deprived of these essentials are unable to fulfill any larger obligation to society, for their existence is entirely consumed by the brutish struggle for personal survival.

The concept of such social necessities leads to the idea of social citizenship, an extension of the familiar but narrower notion of political citizenship. The rights to health care, housing, and a job can be seen as social rights, parallel to our political rights to the franchise and to free speech, which are enshrined in our Constitution. Political rights apply to all citizens automatically because they are the precondition of democracy as a system. Similarly, social rights should be extended automatically to everyone, for these rights are the precondition of civil society's survival.

The Japanese deliver such social rights through a paternalistic, corporate, largely private extended family, whereas the Europeans do it through the welfare state. America will have to find its own way. Ideally, the emerging institutions of the social market will eventually provide a local, democratic, and nonstatist solution. One possibility is an American version of the success achieved by Mondragon, a remarkable complex of more than 100 industrial cooperatives in the Basque region of Spain. Over the past 40 years, Mondragon has succeeded in guaranteeing job security, housing, health care, and education to its members, with scarcely any help from the state. Workers have created cooperative schools, hospitals, insurance companies, and banks that offer robust social security from birth to death. The Mondragon complex, which is the largest manufacturer of durable goods in Spain and employs thousands of worker-owners, has never permanently laid off a worker, reproducing the equivalent of the Japanese system of lifetime employment, while also inventing new cooperatives in one of the most impressive programs of job creation in the world.

Whether an American social market could evolve in such a direction is purely speculative, but clearly there are ways to provide social rights that are realistic, democratic, and do not require a big and overly intrusive government. America is the only major industrialized country not to offer health care as a social right to all its citizens. In Germany and other European countries, the federal government is involved in collecting taxes to support national health care, but it allows provincial councils and local communities to administer their own programs.

Although government is not the preferred agent in our society, it has a leading role to play in areas such as education, health care, and social welfare, where human need rather than profit is the only acceptable moral compass. Government is also the guarantor of last resort. When people are homeless, starving, or jobless, civil society has failed, and a wilding virus is activated. Remedies to these problems are not silly idealism or bleeding-heart liberalism, but a conservative and prudent defense of the social order that requires public action.

For this reason, legal scholars, such as Columbia University law professor Louis Henkin, are pointing to "genetic defects" in our Bill of Rights that constitutionally guarantee political but not social citizenship rights.[13] Even these political rights are now in severe danger. The war on terrorism is threatening free speech, privacy, due process, and a host of other basic protections in the Bill of Rights that prevent the government from destroying our liberty. These are "negative" rights—in the sense that they tell government what it can *not* do to infringe on our freedom, but they are at the very center of our constitutional order and are now at serious risk. In Chapter 8, I detailed the alarming trends toward a Big Brother society that would erode our most fundamental constitutional rights and could take us toward an Orwellian society, cloaked in the rhetoric of democracy, in appeals to the rule of law even as it is being subverted, and in the rituals of flawed elections. At the end of this chapter, I make clear how students and others must act now to prevent the kind of egregious political wilding in the name of the war on terrorism that could end liberty as we know it.

The first challenge, then, is to preserve the purely political or "negative" rights built into our Constitution. Every American citizen has a major responsibility to prevent the war on terrorism from becoming a license for unchecked governmental and presidential power. Another terrorist attack similar to 9/11 on the United States might lead President Bush or future presidents to suspend permanently our rights in the name of protecting us, undermining the Bill of Rights and the requirement that even the president must obey the law. Protecting the "negative" rights in the Constitution is only a first but necessary step toward building the foundation of true democracy and community: a matrix of negative and positive—or political and social—rights. But if we are not able to protect our existing rights, and are scared by our leaders into turning Big Brother authority over to them, we will have no possibility to enjoy any rights at all. The United States would then move toward a *1984* Orwellian society, in which the president becomes a virtual dictator.

But as we struggle to save our political or "negative" rights ensured in the Constitution, we must simultaneously expand our vision to build new "positive" or social citizenship rights in the United States. Chief Justice William Rehnquist, in a 1989 Supreme Court decision, argued that the Constitution confers "no affirmative right to governmental aid, even when such aid may be necessary to secure life." This led constitutional attorney Paul Savoy, former dean of the John F. Kennedy University School of Law, to point out that "our civil rights and civil liberties are rights in the negative sense" and "do not include affirmative obligations on government. We do not have a constitutional right to have the state provide us with health care, or give us shelter if we are homeless, or prevent a child from being beaten or from starving to death." A coalition of unions, environmentalists, and community groups has responded by calling for a second Bill of Rights that would entitle all citizens to the elementary social rights of shelter, food, and health care.[14]

Such social rights have already been embraced by most nations of the world and by the United Nations. The 1948 U.N. Universal Declaration of Human Rights explicitly embraces the right of all people to employment, shelter, education, and health care. The International Labor Organization, a U.N. agency, spells out the rights of all workers to associate freely in unions of their choice and to earn a living wage. There are also U.N. agreements on the rights of women, children, and the environment. Unfortunately, many of these rights are not enforced—and the U.N. has no mechanism to do so. To combat wilding in the global economy, it is essential that the U.S. government, a signatory of many of the U.N. human rights documents, move aggressively to support international means of enforcing social rights both abroad and at home.[15]

Social rights are not a free ride for the population, for with them come demanding social obligations. Citizenship is an intimate dance of rights and obligations, and social citizens will need to enthusiastically embrace the moral obligations that come with their new entitlements. This means not only willingly paying the taxes required to keep civil society healthy, but also devoting time and effort to community-building at work, in the neighborhood, and in the country at large.

The problem with the left is that it demands rights without spelling out the obligations that have to accompany them; the problem with the right is that it expects obligations to be fulfilled without ceding social rights in return. Both positions are absurd because rights and obligations are flip sides of civil society's coin of the realm. We need a new politics that marries the left's moral passion for rights with the right's sober recognition of duty.

Defending Our Lives: Getting from Here to There

But what do we do now? Americans are pragmatic people who want down-to-earth answers. Although there is no recipe or magic formula, we can act now to stop the wilding epidemic. If we want to survive with our humanity intact, we have no alternative.

Since wilding can destroy society, we are all fighting to stay alive. Obviously, if we each felt we had a desperate illness, we would mobilize ourselves to act immediately to save ourselves. But since wilding is a societal crisis, not a biological illness, individuals can feel a deceptive immunity. It is possible to feel healthy, have fun, and enjoy life as society begins to come undone.

But as the epidemic spreads, everyone will increasingly feel at risk. The personal meaning of the wilding crisis is that we each have to spend more and more time simply defending our lives, our property, our livelihood, our health, our physical safety, and our egos. This imposes a terrible burden on the individual, and it can easily fuel the "me" mentality at the heart of the problem, but it also unlocks the riddle of what to do. Not only will the illusion of immunity diminish, but also will the wisdom of dealing with the underlying disease, not just the symptoms, become more apparent.

One can start defending one's life, as Albert Brooks's 1990s film comedy of that title suggests, either wisely or foolishly. The shortsighted approach involves trying to save oneself by abandoning everyone else, like the suburbanites who cocoon themselves within homes wired with the latest security technology and who refuse to pay taxes to support the center city. Robert Reich suggests that such a "politics of secession" is sweeping upper-middle-class America.[16] If so, it is a blind and morally unsustainable choice, for it creates short-term symptomatic relief while worsening the disease.

Because the disease is social, so, too, must be the cure. As the social infrastructure begins to ulcerate and bleed, the rational long-term way to defend one's life is to help repair the damaged societal tissue, whether it be potholes in the road, hungry people sleeping on grates, or sociopathic competitiveness at the office. Doing the right thing then, is defending one's life by cooperating to build up community strength and bolster personal and collective resistance to wilding. This requires no saintly sacrifice for the common good but rather a tough-minded and clear-eyed assessment of where the threat lies. When facing a wilding threat, the first question to ask is "What in my social environment or me is creating this threat?" Once that question is answered, the next one is "What can I do about it?" Some cases of wilding will require purely personal change: falling back on all one's psychological and moral strength, as well as love and support from family, friends, or mentors, to counter wilding impulses within oneself or susceptibility to wilding influences in the environment. Most cases will also require acting for some form of social change to extirpate the external poison, whether at work, in the neighborhood, or in the White House; this is typically achievable only with the help of others.

Fortunately, the wisdom of social action is obvious in a huge variety of circumstances, and Americans are already responding, especially when their own health is involved. When children in Woburn, Massachusetts, were getting sick because of toxic chemicals, parents got together to clean up the toxic dump and hold the wilding factory accountable. Americans are recognizing that staying healthy has become a political action project requiring a massive environmental cleanup, and they are not waiting for lackadaisical governments to take the lead. "People are recognizing they can in fact control their environment," Hal Hiemstra, a Washington environmental activist notes. "They're starting to say, 'we've had it.'" The *Boston Globe* reports that "an environmental wake-up call [is] being sounded nationwide by communities alarmed by the federal government's inertia and inspired by their own sense of power to reshape the landscape." These activists are not only defending their lives but, the *Globe* observes, "are local heroes on planetary matters."[17]

Heroes of a different sort are the residents of suburban communities around Minneapolis, who swam against the tide and rejected the politics of secession, the suburban wilding that helped push Bridgeport, Connecticut, into Chapter 11 bankruptcy and left New York City and hundreds of other cities teetering on the brink. The Minnesota suburbs joined with Minneapolis to form a regional pact "whereby any community enjoying 40 percent more than the average growth of the region in any given year would have to share with the other signers of the pact." Such apparent sacrifice for the larger good is just plain common sense, because if the city center failed, it would bring the surrounding communities down with it. The great irony, as John Shannon of the Urban Institute notes, "is that Minneapolis is now enjoying boom times and must pay out to the suburbs." A modern Aesop's fable, it shows how cooperation for the common good is, indeed, a form of enlightened self-interest.[18]

We can begin to cure the wilding sickness by doing more of what we have always done well and doing it better: taking responsibility for our lives through civic participation. Tocqueville was amazed at the richness of America's democracy; its dense web of voluntary associations and democratic town meetings made it unique. "The free institutions which the inhabitants of the United States possess, and the political rights of which they make so much use," Tocqueville explained, "remind every citizen, and in a thousand ways, that he lives in society." In other words, democracy, and more democracy, is the best antidote for wilding and the most nourishing food for the social infrastructure.[19]

Americans have become apathetic and indifferent to national politics, but we still retain our propensity to join together in what Tocqueville called "an immense assemblage of associations." One researcher suggests that there are now more than 500,000 self-help groups in the United States, with more than 15 million members; many, whether they be alcoholics, abused children, battered spouses, or co-dependents, are casualties of the wilding epidemic who, by joining with others, are taking enlightened first steps toward not only recovering personally but also rebuilding civil society. The same can be said of the millions of others involved in volunteer efforts and political activism at local or higher levels.[20]

Millions of Americans recognize that giving back can be both fun and morally compelling, and they are serving their communities in movements to help the homeless, feed the hungry, care for AIDS patients, tutor the illiterate, protect the environment, and help organize America's workers and poor people. Many recognize that in addition to individual volunteers, we need sustained social movements that can provide the voice and muscle for ordinary citizens against the power of giant, greedy corporations and unresponsive government. This will require, most of all, the resurrection of a labor movement that speaks for social justice and economic democracy.

On Boston College's campus, many students who have engaged in community service work have begun to realize that service is not enough. While it helps individuals in trouble, it does not solve the societal problems that put people in difficulty in the first place. Students who work in soup kitchens begin to ask why there are so many hungry people, and those working in battered women's shelters ask why there is so much domestic violence. This leads them to recognize that it will take collective action—that is, social movements aimed at changing institutions—to truly solve the underlying causes of the problems that plague the people they want to help.

Young people have a special role in combating the wilding epidemic, and those privileged enough to study in colleges and universities have a special responsibility to help change our society through education and social action. They have developed some skills of critical thinking. They have access to the Internet, a key tool to educate themselves and their peers, and a vital springboard for social activism. And they are on a college campus, historically one of the best places to come together with their peers and help change the world.

On my own campus, over the last seven years, a network of activists called the Global Justice Project (GJP) has been an inspiring example. It is made up of students who have decided that they want to make a difference. Some want to protect civil liberties and protest the PATRIOT Act; some want to promote fair-trade coffee; some want to make the campus safer for female students at night; some want to end sweatshops or help organize immigrant workers in nearby hotels; some want to work against global warming and for a sustainable environment; some are passionate about peace in the world and organize activism against the war in Iraq or the carnage in Sudan; some are sick about the role of big money in politics and are working for campaign finance reform. These students are passionate about education and sponsor talks, films, and panels on campus. But they are much more concerned with changing the world than just talking about it.

Over recent years, I have noticed three things about this group. One is that many of the students came to GJP after doing service projects, such as helping battered women, serving food in soup kitchens, or rebuilding houses in Appalachia or Nicaragua. Service is very popular both on a Jesuit campus, such as Boston College, and on campuses all across the country. Some students do it to pad their resumes, but most are very idealistic. As students develop direct personal contact with poor people and communities, they get very emotionally involved and begin to wonder why such good people are living such hard lives. Many realize that their service activities, though wonderful one-on-one experiences, are something like putting a bandage on deeper wounds. They will not solve the societal problems that have caused poverty in the first place, until they start changing the larger economic and political system. This leads them to GJP, which is focused on understanding and changing society itself.

A second observation is that GJP's structure is much like a network—indeed, much like the Internet on which they rely to publicize their activities and coordinate different protests and educational campaigns. Students passionate about fair-trade coffee form a small group and start negotiating with corporate and university officials on campus; the larger GJP group offers its support for bigger actions to force corporate and university officials to listen and comply. Students who feel deeply about torture or militarism or constitutional rights organize peace vigils, protests against the PATRIOT Act or against spying and wiretapping by the government, and information campaigns on campus, and they come to the fair-trade subgroup and others in the broader network to get support for their peace work. And so it goes. The GJP pools the efforts of small groups in order to build a large network that has clout; each group lends support to other groups to build leverage for power-packed large actions that each small group could not produce on its own.

Third, GJP offers a community to activists who might burn out without a lot of support. It's hard to find time and energy for activism when you are studying for midterms or feeling isolated. But the GJP network brings students together in small and large groups to eat, talk, and make new friends. The students want to bring justice and community to the larger society, but they can't succeed without creating community among themselves. They play music together, eat together, go to protests together, and talk late into the night. Many become close friends, live together, and support each other through personal or emotional problems. Building community is both a means and end, and both are essential antidotes to the wilding epidemic.

Antisweatshop activists on campus have joined forces with the labor movement to end corporate wilding here and around the world. The labor movement, while demonized by many U.S. business leaders, is becoming a genuine voice for the community at large. Recall that "solidarity forever" has always been the rallying cry of the labor movement and that as corporations threaten community at home and abroad, the very concept of "union" tells us what we need: people coming together to defend human values against greed and exploitation. Peace activists on campus are seeking to build the same sense of solidarity as labor activists among all peoples of the world, rejecting the idea that the United States has the right as the world's only superpower to invade weaker countries or dictate to the whole world. The new peace activists, rejecting any concept of American empire, are committed to a view of the world as a community of equals. The effort to end the wilding of militarism and create a new global culture of peace has become completely intertwined with the struggle for justice, creating the vision of "peace and justice" that guides the philosophy of more and more students on my campus and universities across America and around the world.

Other social movements are also vital for people seeking to end the wilding crisis. I discussed in Chapter 4 the post-Seattle global justice movement that is bringing together students, workers, environmentalists, feminists, and civil rights groups from around the world to forge a new world community based on human rights rather than money. Each of these movements has its own agenda essential to combating aspects of the wilding crisis; as they learn to work together for peace and justice at home and abroad, they offer the best chance to make a difference that we have seen in a long time. Anyone concerned with the wilding crisis should learn about these different movements and join them. For in these movements lies the chance not only of changing the world but of creating a new form of community for oneself.

Americans' indifference to national politics less reflects pure selfishness or apathy than despair about leaders and the absence of real choices. America desperately needs a new generation of political leaders who will tell the truth about the wilding crisis and articulate a new moral vision. But because no such leaders are now in view, the burden of change falls on the rest of us, where it ultimately belongs.

Notes

Chapter 1

1. APBNews.com, 2000. "Central Park Groping Victims Rise to 24." *APB-News.com*, June 14, pp. 1–2. Retrieved from www.APBNews.com on June 14, 2000; ABCnews.com, 2000. "New Reward in Park Attacks." *ABCnews.com*, June 17. Retrieved from http://abcnews.go.com/sections/us/DailyNews/central park000617.html on June 18, 2000; Cloud, John, 2001. "The Bad Sunday in the Park." *Time.com* January 2006. Retrieved from www.Time.com on February 7, 2001.
2. APBnews.com. "Central Park Groping Victims Rise to 24."
3. Cloud. "The Bad Sunday in the Park."
4. "Move to Kill Victim Described by Defendant in Jogger Rape." 1989. *New York Times*, November 2, p. 1.
5. "Testimony Has Youths Joyous after Assault." 1989. *New York Times*, November 4, p. 1.
6. "Three Youths Jailed in Rape of Jogger." 1990. *Boston Globe*, September 12, p. 9.
7. "The Central Park Rape Sparks a War of Words." 1989. *Newsweek*, May 15, p. 40.
8. Williams, Patricia J., 2002. "Reasons for Doubt." *The Nation*, December 30, p. 10.
9. Ibid.
10. Graham, Renee, 1990. "Hoax Seen Playing on Fear, Racism." *Boston Globe*, January 11, p. 24.
11. Graham, Renee, 1990. "Fur Store, Quiet Street Are Now Macabre Meccas." *Boston Globe*, January 16, p. 20.
12. Turnbull, Colin, 1972. *The Mountain People*. New York: Simon & Schuster.
13. Ibid., p. 86.
14. Ibid., p. 153.
15. Ibid., back cover.
16. Ibid., p. 132.
17. Ibid., p. 132.
18. Ibid., p. 137.
19. I am indebted to Mike Miller for suggesting the terms *instrumental* and *expressive* wilding.

20. I am indebted to Mike Miller for his suggestion of "two Americas."

21. For an excellent book on the subject, see Taylor, John, 1989. *Circus of Ambition: The Culture of Wealth and Power in the Eighties*. New York: Warner Books.

22. Trump, Donald, with Tony Schwartz, 1987. *Trump: The Art of the Deal*. New York: Warner Books.

23. Lewis, Michael, 2001. "Jonathan Lebed's Extracurricular Activities." *New York Times Magazine*, February 25, pp. 26*ff*.

24. Callahan, David, 2001. "Here's to Bad Times." *New York Times*, February 5, p. A21.

25. Taylor, *Circus of Ambition*, p. 8.

26. Shames, Laurence, 1989. *The Hunger for More: Searching for Values in an Age of Greed*. New York: Times Books.

27. Miller, Mathew, and Peter Newcomb, eds., 2005. "The 400 Richest Americans." *Forbes*, September 22. Retrieved from http://www.forbes.com/richlist on January 2006.

28. Ibid. Regarding the income figures, see Collins, Chuck, and Felice Yeskel, 2005. *Economic Apartheid in America*. New York: New Press, p. 59.

29. Collins and Yeskel, *Economic Apartheid in America*, p. 57.

30. Economy in Crisis, 2004. "A Colossus with Weak Knees." Economy in Crisis, August 3. Retrieved from http://www.economyincrisis.org/article_20.html on January 2006.

31. Collins and Yeskel, *Economic Apartheid in America*, p. 43.

32. Reich, Robert B., 1991. "Secession of the Successful." *New York Times Magazine*, January 20, pp. 16–17, 42–45.

33. De Tocqueville, Alexis, 1985. *Democracy in America*. Vol. II. New York: Knopf (originally published 1840), pp. 137–138.

34. Durkheim, cited in Lukes, Steven, 1973. *Emile Durkheim: His Life and Work, a Historical and Critical Study*. New York: Penguin, p. 207.

35. Ibid.

36. Ibid.

37. Marx, Karl, cited in Tucker, Robert C., 1972. *The Marx-Engels Reader*. New York: Norton, p. 337.

38. Lukes, *Emile Durkheim*, p. 218.

Chapter 2

1. CNN.com. 2004. "Peterson Guilty of Murder." *CNN.com*, November 12. Retrieved from http://www.cnn.com/2004/LAW/11/12/peterson.verdict/ on January 2006.

2. Ryan, Harriet, 2004. "Financial Analyst Gary Nienhuis Said Scott Peterson's Fertilizer Business Was Struggling to Survive at the End of 2002." Court TV, August 2. Retrieved from http://www.courttv.com/trials/peterson/080204_ctv.html on January 2006.

3. Lavoie, Denise, 2005. "Mo. Radio Show Host Held in Wife's Death." Washingtonpost.com, November 7. Retrieved from http://www.washington post.com/wp-dyn/content/article/2005/11/07/Are005110700900.html on January 2006; Saltzman, Jonathan S., 2005. "Poison Murder Case Is Detailed." *Boston Globe*, November 22, pp. B1, B4.

4. Jewell, Mark, 2005. "Missouri Radio Host on Trial for Killing Wife for BMW." *Insurance Journal*, November 21. Retrieved from http://www.insurancejournal.com/magazines/midwest/2005/11/21/features/63066.htm on January 2006.

5. AP, 2000. "Wife of Slain NFL Player Indicted for Murder." October 17. Retrieved from http://cnews.tribune.com/news/story/0,1162, wbdc-sports-68648,00.html on February 2001.

6. AP, 1998. "East Texas Pharmacist Pleads Guilty to Wife's Murder." March 11. Retrieved from http://www.reporternews.com/texas/murd0311.html on Febrary 2001.

7. McGinniss, Joe, 1989. *Blind Faith*. New York: Signet, p. 420.

8. Ibid., p. 62.

9. Ibid., p. 86.

10. Ibid., p. 89.

11. Ibid., p. 87.

12. Ibid., p. 308.

13. Ibid., p. 414.

14. Ibid., p. 297.

15. Ibid., p. 436.

16. Bass, Alison, 1990. "Cold-Blooded Killers Rarely Stand Out from the Crowd." *Boston Globe*, January 15, p. 34.

17. Ibid.

18. Fox, James Alan, and Jack Levin, 1990. "Inside the Mind of Charles Stuart." *Boston Magazine*, April, pp. 66*ff*.

19. Bass, "Cold-Blooded Killers," p. 34.

20. Fox and Levin, "Inside the Mind of Charles Stuart."

21. Hamil, Pete, 1990. "Murder on Mulholland." *Esquire*, June, pp. 67–71.

22. Hughes, Kathleen, and David Jefferson, 1990. "Why Would Brothers Who Had Everything Murder Their Parents?" *Wall Street Journal*, March 20, p. A1.

23. "A Beverly Hills Paradise Lost." *Time*, March 26, 1990, pp. 64*ff*.

24. Ibid.

25. Ibid., p. 69.

26. Hughes and Jefferson, "Why Would Brothers?" p. A10.

27. "A Beverly Hills Paradise," p. 69.

28. Ibid., p. 72; Hughes and Jefferson, "Why Would Brothers?" p. A1.

29. Hughes and Jefferson, "Why Would Brothers?" p. A1.

30. "A Beverly Hills Paradise," p. 69.

31. Hughes and Jefferson, "Why Would Brothers?" p. 1.

32. Hussman, Lawrence, 1983. *Dreiser and His Fiction*. Philadelphia: University of Pennsylvania Press.

33. Sennott, Charles M., 1994. "Kin Have Misgivings about Death Penalty." *Boston Globe*, November 8, p. 10.

34. Adler, Jerry, 1994. "Innocents Lost." *Newsweek*, November 14, pp. 27*ff.* "Night That Turned Mom into a Killer." 1994. *National Enquirer*, November 14, pp. 28*ff.*

35. Sennott, Charles M., 1994. "Bid to Climb Social Ladder Seen in Smith's Fall to Despair." *Boston Globe*, November 8, pp. 1, 10.

Chapter 3

1. Barstow, David, and Sarah Kershaw, 2000. "Teenagers Accused of Killing for a Free Meal." *New York Times*, September 7, p. 1; Reeves, Jay, 2000. "Woman Given 13-Year Prison Term in 'Road Rage' Slaying." *Boston Globe*, December 5, p. A6.

2. Bach, Elizabeth, 2003. "Police Say 'Road Rage' Driver Struck Officer with Car." *Boston Globe*, June 25, p. B1.

3. Trausch, Susan, 1990. "The Generous Greed Machine." *Boston Globe*, March 4, p. 14.

4. Polner, Rob, 1992. "A Real Education in the New York City School System." *In These Times*, April 11–17, p. 12.

5. Belluck, Pam, 2006. "A New Reality for First 'Survivor' Winner: Tax Evasion Trial." *New York Times*, January 22, p. 14.

6. Sloan, Allan, 1996. "Jobs—The Hit Men." *Newsweek*, February 26.

7. Kaplan, Don, 2001. "Host: Rich Wouldn't Survive New Cast." *New York Post*, January 11. Retrieved from http://www.foxnews.com/entertainment/ 011101/survivor hatch.sml on January 2006.

8. Sepinwall, Alan, 2001. "Extreme TV: The (Rear) End of Civilization as We Know It." Newhouse News Service, February 2. Retrieved from http:// www.mercurycenter.com/tv/center/extremetv.htm on February 2001.

9. St. John, Warren, 2005. "What Men Want: Neanderthal TV." *New York Times*, December 11, section 9, pp. 1–2.

10. Ibid., p. 2.

11. Cited in ibid., p. 1.

12. Cited in ibid., p. 2.

13. Ibid., p. 2.

14. Ibid.

15. Ibid.

16. Collins, Chuck, and Felice Yeskel, 2000. *Economic Apartheid in America*. New York: New Press.

17. Krugman, Paul, 2003. "The Death of Horatio Alger." *The Nation*, December 23.
18. Derber, Charles, 2000. *Corporation Nation*. New York: St. Martin's Press.
19. "Warning: The Standard of Living Is Slipping." 1987. *Business Week*, April 20, p. 48.
20. Phillips, Kevin, 1990. *Politics of the Rich and Poor*. New York: Random House, p. 10.
21. "Warning," pp. 46, 52; "The Face of the Recession." 1990. *Boston Globe*, August 14, pp. 24–25.
22. Collins and Yeskel. *Economic Apartheid in America*, p. 17.
23. "Warning," pp. 46, 52.
24. Kanter, Donald, and Philip Mirvis, 1989. *The Cynical Americans*. San Francisco: Jossey-Bass, pp. 10, 291.
25. Fiske, Edward B., 1990. "Fabric of Campus Life Is in Tatters, a Study Says." *New York Times*, April 30, p. A15.
26. Knox, Richard A., 1994. "Binge Drinking Linked to Campus Difficulties." *Boston Globe*, December 7, pp. 1, 15.
27. Walsh, Pamela, 1995. "Second Harvard Student Pleads Guilty to Stealing." *Boston Globe*, February 24, p. 8; "Florida Law Student Held in a Murder Plot." 1995. *New York Times*, February 24, p. A16; Johnston, David, 2001. "Second Killing in a Year." *New York Times*, February 5, p. A11.
28. Fiske. "Fabric of Campus Life," p. A15.
29. Butterfield, Fox, 1991. "Scandal over Cheating at M.I.T. Stirs Debate on Limits of Teamwork." *New York Times*, May 22, p. 12.
30. "College Admission Offices Targeting Fraudulent Essays." 2000. *Boston Globe*, November 27, pp. 1, B4.
31. Flint, Anthony, 1992. "Student Markets Primer on the Art of Cheating." *Boston Globe*, February 3, pp. 1, 13.
32. Celis, William, III, 1991. "Blame to Share in Overcharging of U.S. for Research." *New York Times*, May 12, p. 1.
33. Kowalczyk, Liz, 2001. "New Steps Urged on University Research Bias." *Boston Globe*, February 20, pp. A1, D6.
34. I want to express appreciation to Colleen Nugent, who provided me with many of the sources that I relied on to write this section on video games, and also helped me think through the importance of the games to the wilding phenomenon.
35. *Wikipedia*. "Video Game Controversy," Retrieved from http://en.wikipedia.org/wiki/Video-game-controversy on March 13, 2006.
36. Ibid.
37. See Fainaru-Wada, Mark, and Lance Williams, 2006. *Game of Shadows: Barry Bonds, BALCO, and the Steroids Scandal that Rocked Professional Sports*. New York: Gotham Books.

38. Schor, Susan B., 2005. "Violent Video Games Too Accessible to Kids, Say Watchdogs." *Technewsworld.com*, November 18. Retrieved from http://www.linuxinsider.com/story/38455.html on January 2006.

39. *Wikipedia*. "Video Game Controversy." March 13, 2006 . See the description of *Custer's Revenge* on ClassicGaming by Fragment, posted on http://www.classicgaming.com/rotw/custer.shtml.

40. Anderson, C. A., and K. E. Dill, "Video Games and Aggressive Thoughts, Feelings, and Behavior in the Laboratory and in Life." *Journal of Personality and Social Psychology* 78: 772–791; Schor, Susan B. "Violent Video Games Too Accessible."

41. Walsh, David, Douglas Gentile, Jeremy Gleske, Monica Walsh, and Emily Chasco, 2004. "Ninth Annual Media Wise Video Game Report Card." National Institute on Media and the Family, November 23. Retrieved from http://www.mediafamily.org/research/report-vgrc-2004.shtml on January 2006.

42. Both Gee quotes cited in Carlson, Scott, 2003. "Can Grand Theft Auto Inspire Professors?" *Information Technology* and *The Chronicle of Higher Education*, August 15. Retrieved from chronicle.com/free/v49/i49/49a03101.htm on January 2006.

43. Gee, ibid.

44. Bakan, Joel, 2005. *The Corporation*. New York: Free Press.

45. Bourgois, Philippe, 1989. "Just Another Night on Crack Street." *New York Times Magazine*, November 12, pp. 53*ff*.

46. Ibid., p. 62.

47. Ibid., p. 64.

48. Ibid., p. 62.

49. Ibid., p. 65.

50. Ibid., p. 94.

51. Ibid.

52. Adler, William, 1995. *Land of Opportunity: One Family's Quest for the American Dream in the Age of Crack*. Boston: Atlantic Monthly Press.

53. Ibid. Frankel, Max, 1995. "Drug War, II." *New York Times Magazine*, January 29.

Chapter 4

1. "Made in the USA?" 2001. National Labor Committee, New York, February 12. Retrieved from http://www.nlcnet.org on February 12, 2001.

2. NLC, 2003. "American Samoa Sweatshop Owner Convicted of Human Trafficking." Retrieved from www.nlcnet.org/campaigns/archive/samoa/ on January 2006.

3. Herbert, Bob, 1994. "Terror in Toyland." *New York Times*, December 21, p. A27.

4. Anderson, Sarah, John Cavanaugh, and Thea Lee, 2000. *Field Guide to the Global Economy*. New York: New Press.

5. For a concise, readable interpretation of globalization as a "race to the bottom," see Brecher, Jeremy and Tim Costello, 1998. *Global Village or Global Pillage?* 2d ed. Boston: South End Press.

6. Kernaghan, Charles, 2005. "Press Announcement: More News on Wal-Mart Abuses," e-mail report sent by the NLC, December; full report, called "Wal-Mart Sweatshops in China: New Reports Released by National Labor Committee and China Labor Watch," December 15, 2005. Retrieved from http://www.nlcnet.org/news/trucks.asp on January 31, 2006.

7. Kernaghan, Charles, 2005. "Breaking Report: Another Chinese Factory Exposed," a summary of a report from the National Labor Committee and China Labor Watch and sent by e-mail to the author, December 21. See the full report at nlcnet.org/news, which has archived NLC reports as well as reports by numerous other investigative watchdogs and media outlets.

8. Kernaghan, Charles, 2006. "Ask New Balance to Stop its Sweatshop Abuse in China," e-mail report from Kernaghan and the National Labor Committee, January 8. For the full report, go to the NLC Web site (http://www.nlcnet.org) and specifically http://www.nlcnet.org/news/china/pdfs/05_01_06/Full_Report.

9. Reidy, Chris, 2006. "Labor Groups Hit New Balance." January 7. Retrieved from http://www.boston.com/business/globe/articles/2006/01/07/labor_groups_hit_new_balance?mode=PF on January 31, 2006.

10. Barnet, Richard, and John Cavanaugh, 1994. *Global Dreams*. New York: Simon & Schuster, pp. 321*ff.* Fuentes, Annette, and Barbara Ehrenreich, 1992. *Women in the Global Factory*. Boston: South End Press, pp. 10*ff.*

11. La Botz, Dan, 1992. *Mask of Democracy: Labor Suppression in Mexico Today*. Boston: South End Press, p. 162.

12. Kernaghan, Charles, 2005. "Alcoa Workers on *Lou Dobbs*/CNN Tonight," July 22, e-mail report from the National Labor Committee; see the full reports at the nlcnet.org.

13. Kernaghan, Charles. "Wal-Mart Whistle Blower Speaks Out," e-mail report from Kernaghan and the National Labor Committee, July 5. Greenhouse, Steven, 2005. "Fired Officer Is Suing Wal-Mart." *New York Times*, July 21. The article is posted in its entirety at http://www.sweatshopwatch.org/index.php?s=49&n=39.

14. Greenhouse, ibid.

15. Berner, Robert, 2005. "Can Wal-Mart Wear a White Hat?" *Business Week*, September 22. Retrieved from http://www.businessweek.com/bwdaily/dnflash/sep2005/nf20050922_6448_db016.htm on January 31, 2006.

16. Dillon, Sam, 2001. "Profits Raise Pressure on Border Factories." *New York Times*, February 15, pp. A1, A9.

17. La Botz, *Mask of Democracy*, p. 164.
18. Ibid., pp. 164–68.
19. Thompson, Ginger, 2001. "Chasing Mexico's Dream into Squalor." *New York Times*, February 11, pp. A1, A8.
20. Ibid.
21. See Derber, Charles, 2003. *People before Profit*. New York: Picador—for a discussion of the new movements and their vision of a just global economy.
22. Barnet and Cavanaugh, *Global Dreams*. Phillips, Kevin, 1994. *Arrogant Capital*. Boston: Little, Brown, chap. 1.
23. Brecher and Costello, *Global Village or Global Pillage?*
24. Derber, Charles, 2000. *Corporation Nation*. New York: St. Martin's Press, chap. 14; Brecher, Jeremy, Tim Costello, and Brendan Smith, 2000. *Globalization from Below*. Boston: South End Press.
25. Brecher and Costello, Global Village or Global Pillage?
26. Derber, *Corporation Nation*.
27. United Students Against Sweatshops has created a Web site detailing the problems with the FLA. See http:www.flawatch.org.
28. Ibid.

Chapter 5

1. Behr, Peter, and April Witt, 2002. "Visionary's Dream Led to Risky Business." *Washington Post*, July 28, p. A1.
2. Raghavan, Anita, Kathryn Kranhold, and Alexei Barrionuevo, 2002. "How Enron Bosses Created a Culture of Pushing Limits." *Wall Street Journal*, August 26.
3. Nocera, Joseph, Jeremy Kahn, David Rynecki, Clifton Leaf, et al., 2002. "System Failure." *Fortune*, June 24.
4. Cbsnews.com. "Recent High Profile Corporate Scandals." September 30, 2005. Retrieved from http://www.cbsnews.com'stories/2005/03/15/national/main680230. shtml on January 31, 2006; Kristen Hayes, "Witness: Skilling Ordered Earnings Changes," Associated Press, Feb. 21, 2006. Retrieved from http://www.nctimes.com/articles/2006/02/22/business/news/19_16_032_21_06.tx on January 31, 2006.
5. Associated Press, 2002. "Andersen Auditor Cuts Plea Deal." *CBS News.com*, April 9.
6. Tran, Mark, 2002. "Arthur Andersen Appeals for Sympathy." *The Guardian*, January 29.
7. McLean, Bethany, 2004. "Was Andersen Really an Innocent Bystander?" *Fortune*, December 13. Retrieved from http://www.pubs.org/wsw/news/fortunearticle_20050601_html on January 31, 2006.
8. Goldstein, Matthew, 2003. "Four Merrill Bankers Charged in Enron Scandal." *The Street.com*, March 17.

9. Eichenwald, Kurt, with Riva D. Atlas, 2003. "Two Banks Settle Accusations They Aided in Enron Fraud." *New York Times*, July 29, p. 1; Goldstein, Matthew, 2003. "Merrill's Latest Fine Is Tip of the Iceberg." *The Street.com*, February 21.

10. Teather, David, 2002. "The Whores of Wall Street." *The Guardian*, October 2.

11. Goldstein, Matthew, 2003. "Enron Examiner Plans 1,500-Page Valentine." *The Street.com*, January 17.

12. Iwata, Edward, 2002. "Merrill Lynch Probe Widens." *USA Today*, July 31, p. B2.

13. PBS Online and WGBH/*Frontline*, 2002. "Who Dropped the Ball?" *Frontline*. Retrieved from http://www.pbsonline.com on January 2006; PBS Online and WGBH/*Frontline*, 2002. "Dot Con." *Frontline*. Retrieved from http://www.pbsonline.com on January 31, 2006.

14. Morgensen, Gretchen, 2002. "Analyst Coached WorldCom Chief on His Script." *New York Times*, February 27, p. A1.

15. Labaton, Stephen, 2003. "Wall Street Settlement: The Overview; 10 Wall St. Firms Reach Settlement in Analyst Inquiry." *New York Times*, April 29, p. A1.

16. Nocera, Joseph, et al. "System Failure."

17. Derber, Charles, 2003. *People before Profit*. New York: St. Martin's Press; Derber, Charles, 2000. *Corporation Nation*. New York: St. Martin's Press.

18. Center for Responsive Politics, 2002. "Enron's Contributions to Federal Candidates and Parties, 1989–2001," Retrieved from http://www.opensecrets.org/laterts/u6/enron-totals.asp on January 31, 2006.

19. Heller, Doug, 2001. "Commentary; Enron Gets Zapped by Its Own Greed." *Los Angeles Times*, November 30, p. B15.

20. Nocera, Joseph, et al. "System Failure."

Chapter 6

1. CNN.com. 2004. "Sex Abuse Priest Killed in Prison." *CNN.com*, February 23. Retrieved from http://www.cnn.com/2003/US/08/24/geoghan/index.html on January 31, 2006.

2. I want to thank my colleague, Michael Malec, for sharing some of his own very valuable insights about the issues addressed in this chapter. Virtually all the documentation I rely on in this chapter comes from the remarkable reporting by the *Boston Globe* Spotlight team. The journalists have compiled their reporting into a book, *Betrayal: The Crisis in the Catholic Church* (Boston: Little, Brown, 2002). I have referenced this chapter from specific articles largely reported in the *Boston Globe*. For the Geoghan story, see Rezendes, Michael, et al. 2002. "Church Allowed Abuse by Priest for Years." *Boston Globe*, January 6. Retrieved from http://www.boston.com/globe/spotlight/abuse/stories/010602_geoghan.htm on January 31, 2006.

3. Rezendes et al., "Church Allowed Abuse," p. 3.

4. Andersen, Ken. N.D. "Paul Shanley." *Ken Anderson—A Texas Paramedic in Maine: Overview of Bible History.* Retrieved from http://www. kenanderson.net/bible/paul_shanley.html on January 31, 2006.

5. Rezendes, Michael, and Matt Carroll, 2002. "Boston Diocese Gave Letter of Assurance about Shanley." *Boston Globe*, April 8. Retrieved from http://www.boston.com/globe/spotlight/abuse/stories/040802_shanley. htm on April 8, 2002, January 31, 2006.

6. Farragher, Thomas, 2002. "Admission of Awareness Damning for Law." *Boston Globe*, December 14, p. A15. Retrieved from http://www.boston. com/globe/spotlight/abuse/stories3/121402_admission.htm on January 31, 2006.

7. Robinson, Walter, and Matt Carroll, 2002. "Documents Show Church Long Supported Geoghan." *Boston Globe*, January 24, pp. 3–4. Retrieved from http://www.boston.com/globe/spotlight/abuse/stories/012402_ documents.htm on January 31, 2006.

8. Ibid.

9. Rezendes and Carroll. "Boston Diocese Gave Letter," pp. 1–2.

10. Robinson, Walter V., 2002. "Judge Finds Records, Law at Odds." *Boston Globe*, November 26, p. A1. Retrieved from http://www.boston.com/ globe/spotlight/abuse/stories3/112602_records.htm on January 31, 2006; Robinson, Walter V., and Michael Rezendes, 2003. "Abuse Scandal Far Deeper Than Disclosed." *Boston Globe*, July 24, p. 1.

11. Belkin, Douglas, 2003. "Priest Castigates Springfield Diocese for Abuse Dealings." *Boston Globe*, February 17, p. B1.

12. Ibid., p. B1.

13. Ibid., p. B7.

14. Ibid.

15. Ibid.

16. Learn about Voice of the Faithful by going to its Web site at http://www.votf.org.

17. Voice of the Faithful, 2002. "Structural Change Working Group Report as of 9/26/02." Retrieved from http://www.votf.org/Structural_ Change/structural.html on January 31, 2006, pp. 1–3.

18. For information on ARCC, e-mail arccangel@charter.net. I want to thank Michael Malec for informing me of ARCC and providing me with some of its documents.

19. Association for the Rights of Catholics in the Church (ARCC). N.D. "Charter of the Rights of Catholics in the Church, Fifth Edition," Retrieved from http://arcc-catholic-rights.org/charter.htm on January 31, 2006.

20. ARCC, N.D.

21. ARCC, N.D. See Appendix 1: Relevant Canons from the Revised Code of Canon Law, pp. 1–2.

Chapter 7

1. "Boy Accused of Needle Attack." 2001. *New York Times*, February 2, p. A2.
2. Wolf, Craig, 1989. "Ten Teen-Age Girls Held in Upper Broadway Pinprick Attacks." *New York Times*, November 4, p. 27.
3. CNN.com. 2004. "Lionel Tate Released." *CNN.com*, January 27. Retrieved from http://www.cnn.com/2004/LAW/01/26/wrestling.death/ on January 31, 2006.
4. Stepp, Laura, 2000. "U.S. Survey Focuses on At-Risk Teens." *Boston Globe*, November 30, p. A4.
5. "First Grader Shot Dead at School." February 29, 2000. Retrieved from http://abcnews.go.com/sections/us/DailyNews/shooting000229.html on January 2006.
6. "Violence in U.S. Schools." 2000. Retrieved from http://abcnews.go.com/sections/us/DailyNews/schoolshootings990420.html on January 2006.
7. "Fears Rise of a City Consumed by Violence." 1990. *Boston Globe*, March 15, p. 12.
8. Ibid. Jacobs, Sally, 1990. "As Streets Turn Deadly, Youths Revise Their Survival Code." *Boston Globe*, February 24, p. 1.
9. Vaishnav, Anand, 2001. "Perception and Reality in Boston's Safe Schools." *Boston Globe*, February 18, p. D3; Tippit, Sarah, 2001. "Poll Says Violence Is Common in Schools." *Boston Globe*, April 2, p. A-8.
10. Ashbrook, Tom, 1989. "A View from the East," *Boston Globe Sunday Magazine*, February 19, p. 71.
11. Ibid., pp. 71–72.
12. Ibid., p. 76.
13. Mitchell, Philip, 1990. "Saving State Roads." *Boston Globe*, March, p. 11; "Aging Roads, Bridges, Get Scant Notice." 1990. *Boston Globe*, April 11, p. 20.
14. Albert, Michael, 1990. "At the Breaking Point." *Z Magazine*, May, p. 17.
15. Johnson, Kathleen, 2005. "Staff at New Orleans Hospital Debated Euthanizing Patients." *CNN.com*, October 13. Retrieved from www.cnn.com/2005/US/10/12/katrina.hospital/ on January 2006.
16. Henderson, Diedtra, 2005. "Firm Agrees to Discuss Licensing Bird Flu Drug." *Boston Globe*, October 21, p. A3.
17. For a litany of the steps taken by the Bush administration to unravel environmental protection, see the Sierra Club, 2004. "The Bush Record: More Than 300 Crimes against Nature," *Sierra*, September/October. Retrieved from www.sierraclub.org/sierra/200409/bush_record_print.asp on January 2006.
18. Albert. "At the Breaking Point?" p. 17; DeMarco, Susan, and Jim Hightower, 1988. "You've Got to Spread It Around." *Mother Jones*, May,

p. 36; Sege, Irene, 1990. "Poverty, Disease, Poor Education Imperil Nation's Youth, Panel Says." *Boston Globe*, April 27, p. 6.

19. No Child Left Behind. "Get Educated: No Child Left Behind." Retrieved from www.novoteleftbehind.net/getedu_archive/nochild.php on January 2006.

20. Kozol, Jonathan, 2005. *The Shame of the Nation: The Restoration of Apartheid Schooling in America*. New York: Crown.

21. Honan, William, 1995. "14 Million Pupils in Unsuitable or Unsafe Schools, Report Says." *New York Times*, February 1, p. A21.

22. "Consensus Fuels Ascent of Europe." 1990. *Boston Globe*, May 13, p. 19.

23. Derber, Charles, 1993. "Bush's Other War." *Tikkun*, summary.

24. Mitchell, Alison, 2001. "Moderate Republicans Oppose Bush Tax Plan as Democrats Offer Their Own." *New York Times*, February 16, p. A13.

25. "Bush Tax Plan Sent to Congress." 2001. *New York Times*, February 9, pp. A1, A14.

26. Johnston, David Cay, 2001. "Dozens of Rich Americans Join in Fight to Retain the Estate Tax." *New York Times*, February 14, pp. A1, A18.

27. "A Bad Break." 2001. *Boston Globe*, editorial, February 16.

28. Weisman, Jonathan, 2005. "Erosion of Estate Tax is a Lesson in Politics," April 13. Retrieved from www.washingtonpost.com/wp-dyn/articles/A48025-2005Apr12.html on January 2006.

29. Ross, Jeffery Ian, ed., 2000. *Controlling State Crime*. New Brunswick, NJ: Transaction Press.

30. Barsamian, David, 2001. "Angela Davis." *The Progressive*, February, pp. 33–38.

31. Ibid.

32. Mauer, Marc, and Tracy Huling, 1995. "Young Black Americans and the Criminal Justice System: Five Years Later." Retrieved from www.sentencingproject.org on January 2006.

33. Barsamian, "Angela Davis."

34. Jackson, Derrick, 2001. "Superfly Scores in Harlem." *Boston Globe*, February 16, p. A19.

35. Ibid.

36. GAO, 2005. "Elections: Federal Efforts to Improve Security and Reliability of Electronic Voting Systems Are Under Way, but Key Activities Need to Be Completed." September. Retrieved from http://64.233.161.104/search?q=cache:KoqXAm72WqYJ:www.gao.gov/new.items/d05956.pdf+GAO+report+Ohio+voter+fraud&hl=en&client=safari on January 2006.

37. Baker, Joe, 2005. "GAO Report Upholds Ohio Vote Fraud Claims." *Rock River Times*, November 2–8. Retrieved from www.rockrivertimes.com'index.p?cmd=viewstory&cat=2&id=11529 on January 2006.

38. Bugliosi, Vincent, 2001. "None Dare Call It Treason." *The Nation*, February 5, pp. 11–19.

39. For the links between Reed and Abramoff that have been of interest to federal investigators, see "Unraveling Abramoff: Key Players in the Investigation of Lobbyist Jack Abramoff," January 3, 2005. Retrieved from www.washingtonpost.com/wpdyn/content/custom/2005/12/23/CU2005122300939.html on January 2006; *Wikipedia*. "Ralph E. Reed, Jr." Retrieved from http://en.wikipedia.org/wiki/Ralph_E._Reed,_Jr on January 2006.

40. For one of many journalistic descriptions, see Blumenthal, Sidney. 2005. "Republican Tremors." *openDemocracy.net*, October 10. Retrieved from www. opendemocracy.net/globalization-institutions_government/republican_2899.jsp on January 2006.

41. Bernstein, Jake, 2005. "TRMPAC in Its Own Words." *Texas Observer*, April 1. Retrieved from www.texasobserver.org/showArticle.asp?ArticleID=1911 on January 2006.

42. Blumenthal, "Republican Tremors."

43. Ibid.

44. "Poll Finds Anti-incumbent Mood." *CNN.com*, January 10, 2006. Retrieved from http://www.cnn.com/2006/POLITICS/01/09/corruption.poll/index.html on January 2006; Schmidt, Susan, and James Gmaldi, 2006. "Abramoff Pleads Guilty to 3 Counts." *Washington Post*, January 4, p. A01. Retrieved from www.washingtonpost.com/wp-dyn/content/article/2006/01/03/AR2006010300474.html on January 2006.

Chapter 8

1. Wallerstein, Immanuel, 2000. *The Essential Wallerstein*. New York: New Press.

2. Arrighi, Giovanni, 1994. *The Long Twentieth Century*. London: Verso.

3. MacFarquhar, Neil, 2002. "Humiliation and Rage Stalk the Arab World." *New York Times*, April 13, section 4, p. 1.

4. Sachs, Susan, 2003. "Egyptian Intellectual Speaks of the Arab World's Despair." *New York Times*, April 8, pp. B1–2.

5. Shadid, Anthony, 2003. "Hospitals Overwhelmed by Living and the Dead." *Washington Post*, April 8, p. A29; Thanassis, Cambanis, 2003. "Iraqis in Basra Weigh Freedom's Cost." *Boston Globe*, April 8, p. B1.

6. Galston, William. Perils of Preemptive War." *The American Prospect*, 13, no. 17 (Sept. 23, 2002). Available online at http://www.prospect.org/print/V13/17/galston-w.html (accessed March 22, 2006).

7. Falk, Richard, 2002. "The New Bush Doctrine." *The Nation*, July 15. Retrieved from www.thenation.com/doc.mhtml?i520020715&s5falk on January 2006.

8. *Los Angeles Times*, 2003. "Weapons of Mass Destruction May Not Be Found, Bush Says." *Boston Globe*, April 25, p. A17.

9. CNN.com. 2004. "Report: No WMD Stockpiles in Iraq." *CNN.com*, October 7. Retrieved from www.cnn.com/2004/WORLD/meast/10/06/iraq.wmd.report/ on January 2006. The Duelfer final report is posted on www.cia.gov/cia/reports/iraq_wmd_2004/.

10. Dean, John, 2003. "Is Lying about the Reason for a War an Impeachable Offense?" *CNN.com*, June 6. Retrieved from www.cnn.com/2003/LAW/06/06/findlaw.analysis.dean.wmd/index.html on January 2006.

11. Kristof, Nicholas D., 2003. "White House in Denial." *New York Times*, June 13, p. A33.

12. "Iraq: Prime Minister's Meeting, 23 July." 2005. *Sunday Times*, May 1, p. 1.

13. Ibid.

14. CNN.com. 2005. "Cheney's Top Aide Quits after Indictment." *CNN.com*, October 28. Retrieved from http://www.cnn.com/2005/politics/10/28/leak.probe/index.html on January 2006.

15. Lemann, Nicholas, 2002. "The Next World Order." *New Yorker*, April 1; Bacevich, Andrew J., 2002. *American Empire: The Realities and Consequences of U.S. Diplomacy*. Cambridge, MA: Harvard University Press, pp. 44–45.

16. See Lemann, "The Next World Order"; Project for the New American Century, 2000. *Rebuilding America's Defense*. Author: Washington, D.C.

17. Henriques, Diana B., 2003. "Who Will Put Iraq Back Together?" *New York Times*, March 23, Section 3, p. 1.

18. Bumiller, Elisabeth and Alison Mitchell, 2002. "Bush Aides See Political Pluses in Security Plan." *New York Times*, June 15, p. A1.

19. Kifner, John, 2003. "Britain Tried First, Iraq Was No Picnic." *New York Times*, July 20.

20. Whitney, Mike, 2004. "Firebombing Fallujah." December 1. Retrieved from www.zmag.org/content/showarticle.cfm?SectionID=15&ItemID=6772 on January 2006; Escobar, Pepe, 2004. "From Guernica to Fallujah." *Asia Times Online*, December 2. Retrieved from www.atimes.com/atimes/Middle_East/FL02Ak02.html on January 2006

21. BBC News, 2005. "US Used White Phosphorus in Iraq," November 16. Retrieved from www.news.bbc.co.uk/2/hi/middle_east/4440664.stm on January 2006.

22. Cited in Escobar, "From Guernica to Fallujah." For another citation of the "two bullets in every body" quote, see *aljazeera.net*, 2004. "News Arab World: Fallujah Troops Told to Shoot on Sight." December 9. Retrieved from www.english.aljazeera.net/NR/exeres/75E3CA31-83B046FD-A762-0C1157C408F9.htm on January 2006.

23. Escobar, ibid.

24. Kyriakou, Niko, 2005. "In Iraq, Living Conditions 'Tragic.' " Inter Press Service, May 16. Retrieved from www.globalpolicy.org/security/issues/ iraq/attack/cosequences/2005/0516tragic.htm on January 2006.

25. Madhani, Aamer, 2005. "Iraq Health Care So Bad That Doctors Want Out." *Chicago Tribune*, October 5. Retrieved from www.globalpolicy.org/ security/issues/iraq/attack/cosequences/2005/heathcare.htm on January 2006; International Regional Information Networks, 2005. "Iraq: Focus on Boys Trapped in Commercial Sex Trade." August 8. Retrieved from www.globalpolicy.org/security/issues/iraq/attack/cosequences/ 2005/o808trapped.htm on January 2006; Arieff, Irwin, 2005. "39,000 Iraqis Killed in Fighting since March '03—New Study." Reuters, July 12. Retrieved from www.globalpolicy.org/security/issues/iraq/attack/ cosequences/2005/0712study.htm on January 2006.

26. For many of the interviews in "Torture in Question," go to www. pbs.org/wgbh/pages/frontline/torture/themes/blame.html.

27. The Sanchez memo is published online at www.aclu.org/Safeand Free/SafeandFree.cfm?ID=17849&c=206.

28. *Alternet*, 2005. "Treat Them Like Dogs," Karpinski interviewed by Amy Goodman, October 6. Retrieved from www.alternet.org/rights/27402/ on January 2006.

29. See "Torture in Question" documentary interviews at www.pbs.org/ wgbh/pages/frontline/torture/themes/blame.html.

30. For a recent mainstream discussion of the economic foundations of U.S. military interventions, see Bacevich, *American Empire*. For a more radical view emphasizing many of the same themes, see Chomsky, Noam, 1993. *What Uncle Sam Really Wants*. Tucson, AZ: Odonian Press.

31. Baldor, Lolita C., 2005. "21 Detainees Killed in US Custody, ACLU Says." *Boston Globe*, October 25, p. A19.

32. The exchange between Gonzales and Kennedy at the hearings is posted at Center for Cooperative Research, "Profile: Edward Kennedy," in a subsection entitled "January 6, 2005, Torture in Iraq, Afghanistan and Elsewhere." Retrieved from www.cooperativeresearch.org/entity.jsp?id= 1521846767-2387 on January 2006.

33. Steele, Jonathan Steele, 2005. "New War on Terror." *The Guardian*, January 15. Retrieved from www.zmag.org/content/showarticle.cfm? SectionID=40&ItemID=7029 on January 2006.

34. Priest, Dana, 2005. "CIA Holds Terror Suspects in Secret Prisons." *Washington Post*, November 2, p. A01. Retrieved from www.washing-tonpost.com/wpdyn/content/article/2005/11/01/AR2005110101644_ pf.htmls on January 2006.

35. Graham, Bradley, 2005. "US Seeks to Soften Reaction to Report of Burned Taliban." *Boston Globe*, October 21, p. A9; "Legalized Torture, Reloaded." 2005. *New York Times*, editorial, October 26, p. A26.

36. Huq, Aziz, 2006. "Constitutional License." *TomPaine.com*, January 24. Retrieved from www.tompaine.com/articles/20060124/constitutional_license.php on January 2006.

37. CNN.com. 2005. "Powell Aide: Torture 'Guidance' from VP." *CNN.com*, November 20. Retrieved from www.cnn.com/2005/US/11/20/torture/ on January 31, 2006. See also CNN.com. 2005. "Ex-CIA Chief: Cheney 'VP for Torture." *CNN.com*, November 18. Retrieved from http://www.cnn.com/2005/WORLD/11/18/turnery.cheney/ on January 31, 2006.

38. Lewis, Anthony, 2005. "License to Torture," *New York Times*, October 15, p. 14.

39. Cole, David, 2005. "On Bush's Bench?" *salon.com*. July 28. Retrieved from www.salon.com/opinion/feature/2005/07/28/roberts_hamdan/ on January 2006; Gorman, Siobhan, 2005. "Roberts Could Swing Higher Court toward Greater Executive Power." *Baltimore Sun*, August 1. Retrieved from www.baltimoresun.com/news/balte.roberts01aug01,0,5302612.story?coll=bal-home-headlines on January 2006.

40. Gorman, ibid.

41. Ibid.

42. DeFazio's comments, and a general discussion of the FBI new surveillance, can be heard on a PBS program, *On Point with Tom Ashbrook*, WBUR, Boston, September 10, 2005.

43. Brecher, Jeremy, and Brendan Smith, 2006. "The Limits of Power: Questions for Alito." *Nation.com*, January 6. Retrieved from www.thenation.com/doc/20060123/questions_for_alito on January 2006.

44. Lichtblau, Erich, and James Risen, 2005. "Spy Agency Mined Vast Data Trove, Officials Report." *New York Times*, December 24, p. 1. Retrieved from www.truthout.org/docs_2005/122405A.shtml on January 2006.

45. Bajaj, Vikas, 2006. "Gore Is Sharply Critical of Bush Policy on Surveillance." *New York Times*, January 16. Retrieved from www.nytimes.com/2006/01/16/politics/16cnd-gore.html on January 2006.

46. Baker, Peter, and Charles Babington, 2005. "Bush Addresses Uproar over Spying," *Washington Post*, December 20. Retrieved from www.washingtonpost.com/wp-dyn/content/article/2005/12/19/AR2005121900211.html on January 2006.

47. Jones, Susan, 2005. "Has Bush Committed an Impeachable Offense?" *CNSnews.com*, December 20. Retrieved from www.cnsnews.com/ViewPolitics.asp?Page=%5CPolitics%5Carchive%5C200512%5CPOL20051220a.html on January 2006.

48. For details on the findings of the Zogby poll, see "Zogby Poll: Americans Support Impeaching Bush for Wiretapping," January 13, 2006. Retrieved from www.democrats.com/bush-impeachment-poll-2 on January 2006; ImpeachBush.org, 2006. "People's Impeachment Lobby Is a Huge Success: Impeachment Is in the Air: New Polls Show Majority Favor Impeachment," January 17, e-mail letter from ImpeachBush.org.

Chapter 9

1. CNN.com. 2005. "New Orleans Police Face Looting Probe." *CNN.com*, September 29. Retrieved from www.cnn.com/2005/US/09/29/nopd.looting/ndex.html on January 2006.
2. Ibid.
3. Nossiter, Adam, 2005. "New Orleans Police under Investigation in Looting Probe." *Boston Globe*, September 30, p. A5.
4. CBS News, 2006. "New Orleans Fights to Stop Looting." August 31. Retrieved from www.cbsnews.com/stories/2005/08/31/katrina/printable 808193 on January 2006.
5. Perry, Ryan. "Brits' Hell Inside the Terror Dome." *Mirror.co.uk*, September 2, 2005. Retrieved from www.mirror.co.uk/printable_version.cfm?objectid+1592236&siteid=94762 on January 2006.
6. Lauer, Nancy Cook, 2005. "Efforts to Track Rape Emerge between Hurricanes." September 23. Retrieved from www.womensenews.org/article.cfm/dyn/aid/2460 on January 2006.
7. Associated Press, 2005. "Man Charged with Firing Gun at Rescue Helicopter Arrested." October 9. Retrieved from www.wwltv.com/topstories/stories/WWL100905rescue.d9c6b807.html on January 2006.
8. New Orleans Independent Media Center, 2005. "Dogs Left by Evacuees Brutally Shot in St. Bernard Parish." September 30. Retrieved from www.neworleans.indymedia.org/news/2005/09/5723.php on January 2006.
9. Brett, Jennifer, 2005. "Thieves Lift Hurricane Donations." *Atlanta Journal-Constitution*, September 23, p. 1.
10. Sussman, Tina, 2005. "Hired to Haul Aid, Arrest in Looting." *US Politics and World News*, September 15, p. A38.
11. U.S. Department of Justice, 2005. "Two Charged with impersonating Red Cross Officials to 'Collect' Donations for Victims of Hurricane Katrina," September 17. Retrieved from www.usdoj.gov/usao/cac/pr2005/132html on January 2006.
12. Retrieved from www.cbsnews.com/stories/2005/09/12/earlyshow/main835066.shtml on January 2006.
13. Roberts, Paul F., 2005. "Cyber-Looters Capitalize on Katrina." *US Politics and World News*, September 12, p. 11.

14. US Newswire, 2005. "Florida Man Charged with Hurricane Katrina Internet Scam." October 3. Retrieved from releases.snewswire.com/GetRelease.asp?id=54458 on January 2006.

15. AP wire report, MSNBC, September 27, 2005. Retrieved from www.msnbc.msn.com/ id/9501181/ on January 2006.

16. Kelley, Rob, 2005. "Thousands of Gouging Complaints Filed." CNN/*Money*, September 7. Retrieved from http://money.cnn.com/2005/09/07/news/gouging_reactions/index.htm on January 31, 2006.

17. Retrieved from www.cbsnews.com/stories/2005/09/12/earlyshow/main835066.shtml on January 2006.

18. Ball, Jeffery, John Fialka and Russell Gold, 2005. "Backlash Spreads as Oil Companies' Profits Surge." *Wall Street Journal* and post-gazette.com, October 28. Retrieved from www.post-gazette.com/pg/05301/596812.stm on January 2006; Isodore, Chris, 2005. "Oil Executives in Hot Seat," November 8. Retrieved from www.money.cnn.com/2005/11/07/news/economy/oil_hearing/?cnn=yes on January 2006.

19. Goodman, Amy. "Democracy Now." September 22. Retrieved from www.democracynow.org/article.pl?sid=05/09/22/1334217 on January 2006.

20. Lipton, Eric, and Ron Nixon. "Many Contracts for Storm Work Raise Questions." *New York Times*, September 26, pp. A1, A12.

21. Witte, Griff, Renae Merle, and Derek Willis, 2005. "Gulf Firms Losing Cleanup Contracts." *Washington Post*, October 4. Retrieved from www.msnbc.msn.com/id/9586284 on January 2006; Hernandez, Raymond, and Eric Lipton, 2005. "In Shift, FEMA Will Seek Bids for Gulf Work." *New York Times*, October 7, p. 1.

22. Barge, Matthew, 2005. "Is Bush to Blame for New Orleans Flooding?" *Fact Check*, September 2. Retrieved from www.factcheck.org/article 344.html on January 2006.

23. *Times-Picayune*, June 18, 2004; Chatterjee, Pratap, 2005. "Big, Easy Iraqi-style Contracts Flood New Orleans." *CorpWatch*, September 20. Retrieved from http://corpwatch.org/print-article.php?id=12647 on January 2006.

24. Figures for both 2004 and 2005 cited in Barge, "Is Bush to Blame?"

25. Warrick, Joby, and Michael Grimwald, 2005. "Investigators Posit Levee Design Flaws." *Boston Globe*, October 26, p. A3.

26. Davis, Mike, 2005. "The Mystery of New Orleans." *The Nation*, October 1. Retrieved from www.the nation.com/doc/10051017/davis-30k-Oct 1, 2005 on January 2006. On the budget priorities of the administration, as developed in a Republican study committee recommending paying for corporate reconstruction subsidies by cutting domestic spending, see Democracy Now. 2005. "Disaster Profiteering: Purging the Poor in New Orleans." Amy Goodman interviews Naomi Klein, September 23.

Retrieved from www.democracynow.org/article.pl?sid=05/09/23/1338233 on January 2006.

27. CNN.com. 2005. "The Big Disconnect on New Orleans." *CNN.com*, September 2. Retrieved from www.sent.cnn.com/2005/US/09/02/katrina. response/ on January 2006.

28. Ibid.

29. Ibid.

30. Democracy Now, 2005. "FEMA Head Fabricated Parts of Resume." September 9. Retrieved from www.democracynow.org/article.pl?sid=05/09/091411222&mode=threat&tid=25 on January 2006.

31. Klein, Naomi, 2005. "The Rise of Disaster Capitalism." *The Nation*, May 2. Retrieved from www.thenation.com/doc/20050502/klein on January 2006; Klein, Naomi, 2005. "Purging the Poor." The Nation, October 10. Retrieved from www.thenation.com/doc/20051010/klein on January 2006; Featherstone, Lisa, 2005. "The Other Side of the Big Easy." *Grist*, September 12. Retrieved from www.alternet.org/story/25278 on January 2006.

32. Klein. "The Rise of Disaster Capitalism."

33. Klein. "Purging the Poor."

34. Klein, Rick, 2005. "Rebuilding Plan Paving Way for Conservative Goals." *Boston Globe*, September 25, p. 22.

35. Klein. "Rebuilding Plan," p. 22.

36. Klein. "Purging the Poor."

37. Filosa, Gwen, 2005. "A War Zone." *Times-Picayune*, December 2. Retrieved from www.nola.com/news/t-p/frontpage/index.ssf?/base/news-4/1133506902162130.xml on January 2006.

38. Klein. "Purging the Poor."

39. Chen, Michelle, 2005. "New Orleans' Displaced Struggle for Housing, Jobs, Neighborhood," Part 3. *New Standard*, October 21. Retrieved from www.newstandardnews.net/content/index.cfm/items/2514 on January 2006.

40. Ibid.

41. Burdeau, Cain, 2006. "Rebuilding Plan Angers Some New Orleanians." *Yahoo!News*, January 12. Retrieved from www.news.yahoo.com/s/ap/20060112/ap_on_re_us/katrina_rebuilding_new_orleans_13;_ylt=Al74pghKMbtm4kETrhU7h8EbLisB;_ylu=X3oDMTBiMW04NW9mBHNlYwMlJVRPUCUl on January 2006; Barrett, Jennifer, 2006. "A Right to Rebuild." *Newsweek*, January 13. Retrieved from www.msnbc.msn.com/id/10841718/site/newsweek/ on January 2006.

42. Barrett, "A Right to Rebuild."

43. Alter, Jonathan, 2005. "The Other America." *Newsweek*, September 19.

44. Derber, Charles, 2005. *Hidden Power*. San Francisco: Berrett-Koehler, chaps 1–2.

45. Ibid., chap. 2.

46. Alter, "The Other America."

47. Biguenet, John, 2005. "Turkey with a Dash of Bitterness." *New York Times*, November 23, p. A29.

48. AP, 2005. "Officials: Rape, Murder Reports at Katrina Sites Probably Exaggerated." September 27. Retrieved from www.news.bostonherald. com/national/view.bg?articleid=104513 on January 2006.

49. "Reports of Mass Murder, 'Thugs' in New Orleans Shown to Be False." 2005. September 26. Retrieved from www.neworleans.indymedia.org/ print.php?+)5685 on January 2006.

50. Will, George F., 2005. "A Poverty of Thought." *Washington Post*, September 13. Retrieved from washingtonpost.com//wp-dyn/content/article/ 2005/09/12/AR2005091201260.html on January 2006.

51. Michaels, Cash, 2005. "Conservatives Attack Katrina Victims." *Wilmington Journal*, September 3, p. 1.

52. CBS News, 2005. "The Bridge to Gretna." December 15. Retrieved from www.cbsnews.com/stories/2005/12/15/60minutes/main1129400.shmtl on January 2006.

53. Blanco cited in "In Quotes: Chaos in New Orleans," *ABC News Online*, September 2, 2005. Retrieved from www.abc.net.au/news/newsitems/ 200509/s1452244.htm on January 2006; Michaels, Cash. "Conservatives Attack Katrina Victims."

54. Witte, Griff, 2005. "Private Security Contractors Head to the Gulf." *Washington Post*, September 8. Retrieved from www.washingtonpost. com/wpdyn/content/article/2005/09/07/AR20050907 on January 2006; "Gulf War 3: Why Is Blackwater USA Patrolling New Orleans with M-16s?" *Philadelphia Daily News*. September 9, 2005. Retrieved from www.pnionline.com/dnblog/attytood/archives/002349.html on January 2006.

55. To listen to a story online about Bush's policy, see Siegal, Robert. 2005. "Gauging Bush's Use of Domestic Military." *All Things Considered*, September 16. Retrieved from www.npr.org/templates/story/story.php? storyId=4851777 on January 2006.

Chapter 10

1. Tocqueville, Alexis de, [1840] 1985. *Democracy in America*. Vol. II. New York: Knopf, pp. 119–20, 121, 123.

2. Ibid., p. 128.

3. Ibid., p. 129.

4. Bradshow, Larry, and Lorrie Beth Slonsky, 2005. "The Real Heroes and Sheroes of New Orleans." September 9. Retrieved from www.socialist worker.org/2005-2/556/556_04_RealHeroes.shtml on January 2006.

5. Preer, Robert, 1991. "Volunteers Plug Cash Gap in the Suburbs." *Boston Globe*, June 9, pp. 1, 8.
6. Hodgkinson, Virginia Ann, and Murray S. Weitzman, 1989. *Dimensions of the Independent Sector*. Washington, D.C.: Independent Sector, pp. 7–9.
7. Combs, James, 1984. *Polpop: Politics and Popular Culture in America*. Bowling Green, OH: Bowling Green University Popular Press, p. 29.
8. Ibid., p. 34.
9. Phillips, Kevin, 1990. *Politics of Rich and Poor*. New York: Random House, chap. 1.
10. "Consensus Fuels Ascent of Europe." 1990. *Boston Globe*, May 13, p. 19.
11. Bruyn, Severyn, 1991. *A Future for the American Economy*. Stanford, CA: Stanford University Press; Bruyn, Severyn, 1987. *The Field of Social Investment*. Cambridge: Cambridge University Press; Bruyn, Severyn, and James Meehan, 1985. *Beyond the Market and the State*. Philadelphia: Temple University Press; Lowry, Ritchie, 1991. *Good Money*. New York: Norton.
12. Bruyn, *A Future for the American Economy*.
13. Louis Henkin, cited in Savoy, Paul. "Time for a Second Bill of Rights." *The Nation*, 252, no. 23 (June 17, 1991), p. 797.
14. Savoy, Paul, 1991. "Time for a Second Bill of Rights." *The Nation*, June 17, pp. 815–16.
15. Ibid.
16. Reich, Robert, 1992. *Work of Nations*. New York: Vintage.
17. Tye, Larry, 1991. "Local Heroes on Planetary Matters." *Boston Globe*, June 22, p. 3.
18. Loth, Renee, 1991. "Small Cities, Big Problems." *Boston Globe*, June 23, pp. A25, A28.
19. Tocqueville, *Democracy in America*.
20. Marx, Gary T., 1994. "Fragmentation and Cohesion in American Society." In R. Dynes and K. Tierney, *Disasters, Collective Behavior, and Social Organization*. Newark: University of Delaware Press.

Index